Practical Cookery

Vegetarian

Vegetarian

p

This is a Parragon Book
First printed in 2000

Parragon
Queen Street House
4 Queen Street
Bath BA1 1HE, UK

Copyright © Parragon 2000

ISBN: 0-75254-094-7

Printed in Indonesia

NOTE

Cup measurements in this book are for American cups.
Tablespoons are assumed to be 15ml. Unless otherwise stated,
milk is assumed to be full fat, eggs are medium
and pepper is freshly ground black pepper.

Recipes using uncooked eggs should be
avoided by infants, the elderly, pregnant women and anyone
suffering from an illness.

Contents

Light Meals (continued)

Pasta, Grains & Pulses

Stir-Fries & Sautés

Casseroles & Bakes

Salads

Introduction

Vegetarian food need not be boring, as this inspirational cookbook will demonstrate! Packed full of delicious recipes that are nutritious and substantial, even the most diserning palate is sure to be satisfied.

Variety, of course, is the keynote to healthy eating, whatever the diet. As long as the day's meals contain a good mixture of different food types – carboydrates, proteins and fats – a balanced diet and adequate supplies of essential vitamins and proteins are almost guarenteed. Typical dishes that are based on fresh vegetables, pulses, pasta or rice, for example, also have the advantages of being low in fats, particularly saturated fats, and high in complex carbohydrates and fibre, resulting in a diet that is in tune with modern nutritional thinking.

Vegetables are an important source of vitamins, especially vitamin C. Green vegetables and pulses contain many B-group vitamins. Both carrots and dark green vegetables contain high levels of carotene, which is used by the body to manufacture vitamin A. Carrots also contain useful quantities of vitamins B3, C and E. Vegetable oils contain vitamin E and most are also high in polyunsaturated fats. Vegetables are also a particularly good source of many essential minerals, especially calcium, iron, magnesium and potassium.

There is a long and honourable tradition of the specific, healthgiving properties of different vegetables, which dates back at least as far as the Middle Ages. These qualities, once dismissed as old wives' tales, are now being recognized and valued again. Onions and garlic, for example, contain cycloallin, an anticoagulant that helps protect against heart disease. Garlic also contains a stong antibiotic, is thought to protect the body against some major diseases and also increases the absorption of many vitamins.

There is no question that a sensible vegetarian diet is at least as healthy as a sensible meat-eating diet and some nutritionalists maintain that it is better. However there are one or two particular points that are worth noting. Proteins are made up of 'building blocks' called amino acids and, while all those essential to the human body are easily obtained from most animal products, they are not always present in many vegetarian foods. A good mixed diet will prevent this from being a problem. For example, pulses are an excellent source of protein, but they do lack one essential amino acid called methionine. Grains, on the other hand, contain this amino acid, although they lack two others, trptophan and lysine. A dish that contains both rice and peas, a plate of hummus and pitta bread, or bowl of bean soup and slice of wholemeal toast, for example, will ensure that all the necessary first-class proteins are available to the body.

Dairy products are also a valuable source of protein, but they are high in fat. It is very easy for busy people to fall into the habit of basing rather a lot of meals around cheese, for example, resulting in an unhealthily high intake of cholesterol. Eaten in

Introduction

moderation, however, cheese is a very useful and versatile ingredient in the vegetarian diet. If you do use dairy products a lot, it may be worth considering buying low-fat types, such as skimmed or semi-skimmed milk, fromage frais and soft cheeses.

It is important to be aware that the body cannot absorb iron from vegetable sources unless vitamin C is ingested at the same meal. Although many vegetables also contain vitamin C, this is easily destroyed through cooking. Some raw fruit, a glass of fruit juice or a side salad are simple and tasty solutions.

Vegans, who do not eat any dairy products, must be a little more scrupulous than straightforward vegetarians about ensuring that they obtain all the necessary nutrients. A lack of calcium, in particular, can be a problem, but this can be countered with a mineral supplement or by using calcium-enriched soya milk. A vegan diet can be just as healthy as a vegetarian or meat-eating one.

No foods can really be said to be bad for you, although some are best eaten in

moderation. It is sensible to keep an eye on the quantities of butter, cream, high-fat cheese, dried fruits, oils and unsalted nuts that you eat each day. Other popular vegetarian ingredients, such as grains, vegetables, pulses (legumes), fruit, bread, pasta and noodles can be eaten more freely. All diets should include raw vegetables and fruit and these should comprise as much as 40 per cent of a vegetarian diet.

Finally, a hidden advantage to changing to a vegetarian diet is that, usually, it initially entails thinking in a more detailed way about all the thing that you eat. This may extend across the whole spectrum of nutrition, including such things as your intake of salt, sugar and refined foods. As a result, many long-term vegetarians have developed eating patterns that are among the healthiest in the world.

Vegetables

Vegetables are, of course, at the heart of a vegetarian diet, offering an almost endless choice of flavours and textures. Preparing and cooking them with care ensures that they may be enjoyed at their best and that they retain their full nutritional value.

Buying

The fresher vegetables are, the better. Nevertherless, some, such as root vegetables, can be stored for relatively long periods in a cool, dark place, and most will keep for two or three days in the salad drawer of the refrigerator. While supermarkets are very convenient and carry a wide range of good-quality vegetables, time spent finding a really high-quality supplier – possibly of organically-grown vegetables – will be repaid many times over in terms of flavour and nutritional value.

Whatever type you are buying, always look for unblemished and undamaged vegetables with no discolouration. Greens should have good colour, with no wilting leaves, root vegetables should be firm and crisp, vegetable fruits, such as tomatoes and (bell) peppers, should not have soggy patches or wrinkled skin. No vegetables should ever look or smell stale.

Preparing

Use vegetables as soon as possible after buying them, but try not to prepare them much in advance of cooking. If they are left exposed to air or soaking in water, many vitamins and other valuable nutrients are leached out or destroyed.

The highest concentration of nutrients is in the layer directly under the skin, so if possible. avoid peeling them altogether. If they must be peeled, try to do it very thinly. A swivel vegetable peeler is a worthwhile investment.

Also consider cooking potatoes, for example, in their skins – first scrubbing off any soil or dirt – and peeling them afterwards. The skin comes off in a much thinner layer than when they are peeled raw.

How thickly or thinly vegetables are sliced, or how large or small they are chopped will depend, to some extent, on the method of cooking and the individual recipe instructions. However, remember that the smaller and finer the pieces, the greater the surface area from which nutrients can leach.

Basic Recipes

Fresh Vegetable Stock

225 g/8 oz shallots

1 large carrot, diced

1 celery stalk, chopped

½ fennel bulb

1 garlic clove

1 bay leaf

a few fresh parsley and tarragon sprigs

2 litres/3½ pints/8¾ cups water

pepper

1 Put all of the ingredients in a large saucepan and bring to the boil. Skim off the surface scum with a flat spoon and reduce to a gentle simmer. Partially cover and cook for 45 minutes. Leave to cool.

2 Line a sieve (strainer) with clean muslin (cheesecloth) and put over a jug or bowl. Pour the stock through the sieve (strainer). Discard the herbs and vegetables. Cover and store in small quantities in the refridgerator for up to 3 days.

Tahini Cream

3 tbsp tahini (sesame paste)

6 tbsp water

2 tsp lemon juice

1 garlic clove, crushed

salt and pepper

1 Blend together the tahini (sesame seed paste) and water.

2 Stir in the lemon juice and garlic. Season with salt and pepper to taste. The tahini cream is now ready to serve.

Sesame Dressing

2 tbsp tahini (sesame seed paste)

2 tbsp cider vinegar

2 tbsp medium sherry

2 tbsp sesame oil

1 tbsp soy sauce

1 garlic clove, crushed

1 Put the tahini (sesame seed paste) in a bowl and gradually mix in the vinegar and sherry until smooth. Add the sesame oil, soy sauce and garlic and mix together thoroughly.

Béchamel Sauce

600 m/1 pint/2½ cups of milk

4 cloves

1 bay leaf

pinch of freshly grated nutmeg

25 g/1 oz/2 tbsp butter or margarine

25 g/1 oz/2 tbsp (all-purpose) flour

salt and pepper

1 Put the milk in a saucepan and add the cloves, bay leaf and nutmeg. Gradually bring to the boil. Remove from the heat and leave for 15 minutes.

2 Melt the butter or margarine in another saucepan and stir in the flour to make a roux. Cook, stirring, for 1 minute. Remove the pan from the heat.

3 Strain the milk and gradually blend into the roux. Return the pan to the heat and bring to the boil, stirring, until the sauce thickens. Season with salt and pepper to taste and add any flavourings.

Green Herb Dressing

15 g/½ oz/¼ cup parsley

15 g/½ oz/¼ cup mint

15 g/½ oz/¼ cup chives

150 ml/¼ pint/⅔ cup natural yogurt

salt and pepper

1 Remove the stalks from the parsley and mint and put the leaves in a blender or food processor.

2 Add the chives, garlic and yogurt and salt and pepper to taste. Blend until smooth, then store in the refridgerator until needed.

Cucumber Dressing

200 g/7 oz/scant 1 cup natural yogurt

5 cm/2 inch piece of cucumber, peeled

1 tbsp chopped fresh mint leaves

½ tsp grated lemon rind

pinch of caster (superfine) sugar

salt and pepper

1 Put the yogurt, cucumber, mint, lemon rind, sugar and salt and pepper to taste in a blender or food processor and work until smooth. Alternatively, finely chop the cucumber and combine with the other ingredients. Serve chilled.

Warm Walnut Dressing

6 tbsp walnut oil

3 tbsp white wine vinegar

1 tbsp clear honey

1 tsp wholegrain mustard

1 garlic clove, sliced

salt and pepper

1 Put the oil, vinegar, honey, mustard and salt and pepper to taste in a saucepan and whisk together.

2 Add the garlic and heat very gently for 3 minutes. Remove the garlic slices with a perforated spoon and discard. Pour the dressing over the salad and serve immediately.

Apple & Cider Vinegar Dressing

2 tbsp sunflower oil

2 tbsp concentrated apple juice

2 tbsp cider vinegar

1 tbsp Meaux mustard

1 garlic clove, crushed

salt and pepper

1 Put the oil, apple juice, cider vinegar, mustard, garlic and salt and pepper to taste in a screw-top jar and shake vigorously until well-mixed.

Tomato Dressing

125 ml/4 fl oz/½ cup tomato juice

1 garlic clove, crushed

2 tbsp lemon juice

1 tbsp soy sauce

1 tsp clear honey

2 tbsp chopped chives

salt and pepper

1 Put the tomato juice, garlic, lemon juice, soy sauce, honey, chives and salt and pepper to taste in a screw-top jar and shake vigorously until well-mixed.

How to Use This Book

Each recipe contains a wealth of useful information, including a breakdown of nutritional quantities, preparation and cooking times, and level of difficulty. All of this information is explained in detail below.

The nutritional information provided for each recipe is per serving or per portion. Optional ingredients, variations or serving suggestions have not been included in the calculations.

The number of chef's hats represents the difficulty of each recipe, ranging from easy (1 chef's hat) to difficult (5 chef's hats).

This amount of time represents the preparation of ingredients, including cooling, chilling and soaking times.

This represents the cooking time.

The ingredients for each recipe are listed in the order that they are used.

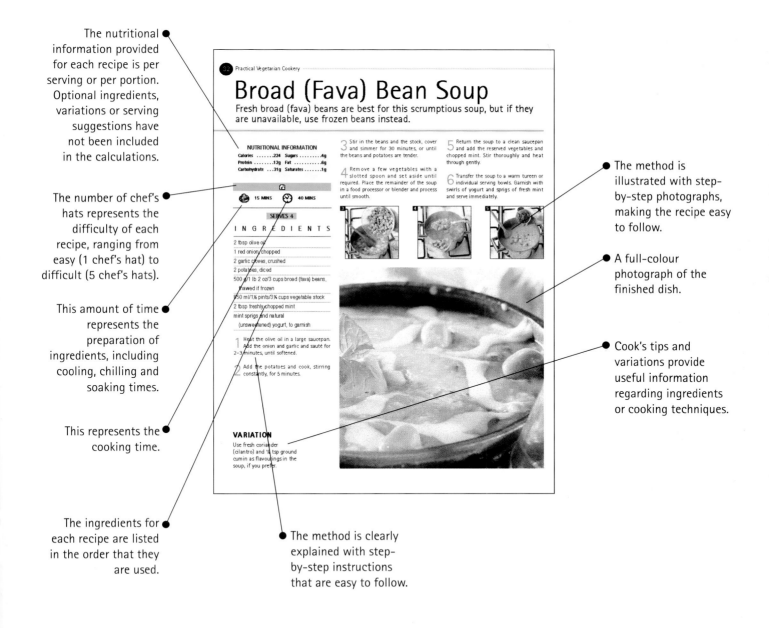

Practical Vegetarian Cookery

Broad (Fava) Bean Soup

Fresh broad (fava) beans are best for this scrumptious soup, but if they are unavailable, use frozen beans instead.

NUTRITIONAL INFORMATION

Calories ....224 Sugars 4g
Protein ....12g Fat 6g
Carbohydrate ...31g Saturates 1g

15 MINS   40 MINS

SERVES 4

INGREDIENTS

2 tbsp olive oil

1 red onion, chopped

2 garlic cloves, crushed

2 potatoes, diced

500 g/1 lb 2 oz/3 cups broad (fava) beans, thawed if frozen

850 ml/1½ pints/3¾ cups vegetable stock

2 tbsp freshly chopped mint

mint sprigs and natural
(unsweetened) yogurt, to garnish

1 Heat the olive oil in a large saucepan. Add the onion and garlic and sauté for 2–3 minutes, until softened.

2 Add the potatoes and cook, stirring constantly, for 5 minutes.

3 Stir in the beans and the stock, cover and simmer for 30 minutes, or until the beans and potatoes are tender.

4 Remove a few vegetables with a slotted spoon and set aside until required. Place the remainder of the soup in a food processor or blender and process until smooth.

5 Return the soup to a clean saucepan and add the reserved vegetables and chopped mint. Stir thoroughly and heat through gently.

6 Transfer the soup to a warm tureen or individual serving bowls. Garnish with swirls of yogurt and sprigs of fresh mint and serve immediately.

VARIATION

Use fresh coriander (cilantro) and ¼ tsp ground cumin as flavourings in the soup, if you prefer.

The method is illustrated with step-by-step photographs, making the recipe easy to follow.

A full-colour photograph of the finished dish.

Cook's tips and variations provide useful information regarding ingredients or cooking techniques.

The method is clearly explained with step-by-step instructions that are easy to follow.

Soups

Soup is easy to make but always produces delicious results. There is an enormous variety of soups which you can make with vegetables. They can be rich and creamy, thick and chunky, light and delicate, and hot or chilled. The vegetables are often puréed to give a smooth consistency and thicken the soup, but you can also purée just some of

the mixture to give the soup more texture and interest. A wide range of ingredients can be used in addition to vegetables – pulses (legumes), grains, noodles, cheese and yogurt all work

well. You can also experiment with different substitutions if you don't have certain ingredients to hand. Whatever your preference, you're sure to enjoy the variety of tasty soups contained in this chapter. Serve with fresh, crusty bread for a truly delicious meal.

Winter Soup

A thick vegetable soup which is a delicious meal in itself. Serve the soup with thin shavings of Parmesan and warm ciabatta bread.

NUTRITIONAL INFORMATION

Calories	285	Sugars	........11g
Protein	........16g	Fat	..........12g
Carbohydrate	...29g	Saturates	.......3g

10 MINS   20 MINS

SERVES 4

I N G R E D I E N T S

2 tbsp olive oil

2 leeks, thinly sliced

2 courgettes (zucchini), chopped

2 garlic cloves, crushed

2 x 400 g/14 oz cans chopped tomatoes

1 tbsp tomato purée (paste)

1 bay leaf

900 ml/1½ pints/3¾ cups vegetable stock

400 g/14 oz can chickpeas (garbanzo
   beans), drained

225 g/8 oz spinach

25 g/1 oz Parmesan cheese,
   thinly shaved

salt and pepper

crusty bread, to serve

1 Heat the oil in a heavy-based saucepan. Add the sliced leeks and courgettes (zucchini) and cook over a medium heat, stirring constantly, for 5 minutes.

2 Add the garlic, chopped tomatoes, tomato purée (paste), bay leaf, vegetable stock and chickpeas (garbanzo beans). Bring to the boil, lower the heat and simmer, stirring occasionally, for 5 minutes.

3 Shred the spinach finely, add to the soup and boil for 2 minutes. Season to taste with salt and pepper.

4 Remove the bay leaf. Pour into a soup tureen and sprinkle over the Parmesan. Serve with crusty bread.

Plum Tomato Soup

Homemade tomato soup is easy to make and always tastes better than bought varieties. Try this version with its Mediterranean influences.

NUTRITIONAL INFORMATION

Calories ....402 Sugars 14g
Protein ....7g Fat 32g
Carbohydrate ...16g Saturates 3g

 20 MINS   30–35 MINS

SERVES 4

INGREDIENTS

2 tbsp olive oil

2 red onions, chopped

2 celery sticks, chopped

1 carrot, chopped

500 g/1 lb 2 oz plum tomatoes, halved

750 ml/1¼ pints/3 cups vegetable stock

1 tbsp chopped oregano

1 tbsp chopped basil

150 ml/¼ pint/⅔ cup dry white wine

2 tsp caster (superfine) sugar

125 g/4½ oz/1 cup hazelnuts, toasted

125 g/4½ oz/1 cup black or green olives

handful of basil leaves

1 tbsp olive oil

1 loaf ciabatta bread (Italian-style loaf)

salt and pepper

basil sprigs to garnish

1 Heat the oil in a large saucepan. Add the onions, celery and carrot and fry over a low heat, stirring frequently, until softened, but not coloured.

2 Add the tomatoes, stock, chopped herbs, wine and sugar. Bring to the boil, cover and simmer for 20 minutes.

3 Place the toasted hazelnuts in a blender or food processor, together with the olives and basil leaves and process until thoroughly combined, but not too smooth. Alternatively, finely chop the nuts, olives and basil leaves and pound them together in a mortar with a pestle, then turn into a small bowl. Add the olive oil and process or beat thoroughly for a few seconds. Turn the mixture into a serving bowl.

4 Warm the ciabatta bread in a preheated oven, 190°C/375°F/ Gas Mark 5, for 3–4 minutes.

5 Process the soup in a blender or a food processor, or press through a strainer, until smooth, Check the seasoning. Ladle into warmed soup bowls and garnish with sprigs of basil. Slice the warm bread and spread with the olive and hazelnut paste. Serve with the soup.

Gazpacho

This Spanish soup is full of chopped and grated vegetables with a puréed tomato base. It requires chilling, so prepare well in advance.

NUTRITIONAL INFORMATION

Calories 140   Sugars 12g
Protein ....3g   Fat 9g
Carbohydrate ...13g   Saturates 1g

6½ HOURS   0 MINS

SERVES 4

INGREDIENTS

½ small cucumber

½ small green (bell) pepper, seeded and
    very finely chopped

500 g/1 lb 2 oz ripe tomatoes, peeled or
    400 g/14 oz can chopped tomatoes

½ onion, coarsely chopped

2–3 garlic cloves, crushed

3 tbsp olive oil

2 tbsp white wine vinegar

1–2 tbsp lemon or lime juice

2 tbsp tomato purée (paste)

450 ml/16 fl oz/scant 2 cups tomato juice

salt and pepper

TO SERVE

chopped green (bell) pepper

thinly sliced onion rings

garlic croûtons

1 Coarsely grate the cucumber into a large bowl and add the chopped green (bell) pepper.

2 Process the tomatoes, onion and garlic in a food processor or blender, then add the oil, vinegar, lemon or lime juice and tomato purée (paste) and process until smooth. Alternatively, finely chop the tomatoes and finely grate the onion, then mix both with the garlic, oil, vinegar, lemon or lime juice and tomato purée (paste).

3 Add the tomato mixture to the bowl and mix well, then add the tomato juice and mix again.

4 Season to taste, cover the bowl with clear film (plastic wrap) and chill thoroughly – for at least 6 hours and preferably longer so that the flavours have time to meld together.

5 Prepare the side dishes of green (bell) pepper, onion rings and garlic croûtons, and arrange in individual serving bowls.

6 Ladle the soup into bowls, preferably from a soup tureen set on the table with the side dishes placed around it. Hand the dishes around to allow the guests to help themselves.

Gardener's Broth

This hearty soup uses a variety of green vegetables with a flavouring of ground coriander. A finishing touch of thinly sliced leeks adds texture.

NUTRITIONAL INFORMATION

Calories ....169 Sugars 5g
Protein ....4g Fat 13g
Carbohydrate ....8g Saturates 5g

 10 MINS   45 MINS

SERVES 6

I N G R E D I E N T S

40 g/1½ oz/3 tbsp butter

1 onion, chopped

1–2 garlic cloves, crushed

1 large leek

225 g/8 oz Brussels sprouts

125 g/4½ oz French (green) or runner
   (string) beans

1.2 litres/2 pints/5 cups vegetable stock

125 g/4½ oz/1 cup frozen peas

1 tbsp lemon juice

½ tsp ground coriander

4 tbsp double (heavy) cream

salt and pepper

M E L B A   T O A S T

4–6 slices white bread

1 Melt the butter in a saucepan. Add the onion and garlic and fry over a low heat, stirring occasionally, until they begin to soften, but not colour.

2 Slice the white part of the leek very thinly and reserve; slice the remaining leek. Slice the Brussels sprouts and thinly slice the beans.

3 Add the green part of the leeks, the Brussels sprouts and beans to the saucepan. Add the stock and bring to the boil. Simmer for 10 minutes.

4 Add the frozen peas, seasoning, lemon juice and coriander and continue to simmer for 10–15 minutes, until the vegetables are tender.

5 Cool the soup a little, then press through a strainer or process in a food processor or blender until smooth. Pour into a clean pan.

6 Add the reserved slices of leek to the soup, bring back to the boil and simmer for about 5 minutes, until the leek is tender. Adjust the seasoning, stir in the cream and reheat gently.

7 To make the melba toast, toast the bread on both sides under a preheated grill (broiler). Cut horizontally through the slices, then toast the uncooked sides until they curl up. Serve immediately with the soup.

Speedy Beetroot (Beet) Soup

Quick and easy to prepare in a microwave oven, this deep red soup of puréed beetroot (beets) and potatoes makes a stunning first course.

NUTRITIONAL INFORMATION

Calories ....120 Sugars 11g
Protein ....4g Fat 2g
Carbohydrate ...22g Saturates 1g

 20 MINS   30 MINS

SERVES 6

I N G R E D I E N T S

1 onion, chopped

350 g/12 oz potatoes, diced

1 small cooking apple, peeled,
    cored and grated

3 tbsp water

1 tsp cumin seeds

500 g/1 lb 2 oz cooked beetroot (beets),
    peeled and diced

1 bay leaf

pinch of dried thyme

1 tsp lemon juice

600 ml/1 pint/2½ cups hot vegetable stock

4 tbsp soured cream

salt and pepper

few dill sprigs, to garnish

1 Place the onion, potatoes, apple and water in a large bowl. Cover and cook on HIGH power for 10 minutes.

2 Stir in the cumin seeds and cook on HIGH power for 1 minute.

3 Stir in the beetroot (beets), bay leaf, thyme, lemon juice and hot vegetable stock. Cover and cook on HIGH power for 12 minutes, stirring halfway through the cooking time.

4 Leave to stand, uncovered, for 5 minutes. Remove and discard the bay leaf. Strain the vegetables and reserve the liquid. Process the vegetables with a little of the reserved liquid in a food processor or blender until they are smooth and creamy. Alternatively, either mash the vegetables with a potato masher or press them through a strainer with the back of a wooden spoon.

5 Pour the vegetable purée into a clean bowl with the reserved liquid and mix well. Season to taste. Cover and cook on HIGH power for 4–5 minutes, until the soup is piping hot.

6 Serve the soup in warmed bowls. Swirl 1 tablespoon of soured cream into each serving and garnish with a few sprigs of fresh dill.

Pumpkin Soup

This is an American classic that has now become popular worldwide.
When pumpkin is out of season use butternut squash in its place.

NUTRITIONAL INFORMATION

Calories 112   Sugars 7g
Protein . . . . .4g   Fat 7g
Carbohydrate . . . .8g   Saturates 2g

10 MINS   30 MINS

SERVES 6

INGREDIENTS

about 1 kg/2 lb 4 oz pumpkin

40 g/1½ oz/3 tbsp butter or margarine

1 onion, sliced thinly

1 garlic clove, crushed

900 ml/1½ pints/3½ cups vegetable stock

½ tsp ground ginger

1 tbsp lemon juice

3–4 thinly pared strips of orange
    rind (optional)

1–2 bay leaves or 1 bouquet garni

300 ml/½ pint/1¼ cups milk

salt and pepper

TO GARNISH

4–6 tablespoons single (light) or double
    (heavy) cream, natural yogurt
    or fromage frais

snipped chives

1 Peel the pumpkin, remove the seeds and then cut the flesh into 2.5 cm/ 1 inch cubes.

2 Melt the butter or margarine in a large, heavy-based saucepan. Add the onion and garlic and fry over a low heat until soft but not coloured.

3 Add the pumpkin and toss with the onion for 2–3 minutes.

4 Add the stock and bring to the boil over a medium heat. Season to taste with salt and pepper and add the ginger, lemon juice, strips of orange rind, if using, and bay leaves or bouquet garni. Cover and simmer over a low heat for about 20 minutes, until the pumpkin is tender.

5 Discard the orange rind, if using, and the bay leaves or bouquet garni. Cool the soup slightly, then press through a strainer or process in a food processor until smooth. Pour into a clean saucepan.

6 Add the milk and reheat gently. Adjust the seasoning. Garnish with a swirl of cream, natural yogurt or fromage frais and snipped chives, and serve.

(Bell) Pepper & Chilli Soup

This soup has a real Mediterranean flavour, using sweet red (bell) peppers, tomato, chilli and basil. It is great served with an olive bread.

NUTRITIONAL INFORMATION

Calories	55	Sugars	........10g
Protein	.........2g	Fat	..........0.5g
Carbohydrate	....11g	Saturates	.....0.1g

 10 MINS   25 MINS

SERVES 4

INGREDIENTS

225 g/8 oz red (bell) peppers,
   seeded and sliced

1 onion, sliced

2 garlic cloves, crushed

1 green chilli, chopped

300 ml/½ pint/1¼ cups passata
   (sieved tomatoes)

600 ml/1 pint/2½ cups vegetable stock

2 tbsp chopped basil

basil sprigs, to garnish

1 Put the (bell) peppers in a large saucepan with the onion, garlic and chilli. Add the passata (sieved tomatoes) and vegetable stock and bring to the boil, stirring well.

VARIATION

This soup is also delicious served cold with 150 ml/¼ pint/⅔ cup of natural (unsweetened) yogurt swirled into it.

2 Reduce the heat to a simmer and cook for 20 minutes, or until the (bell) peppers have softened. Drain, reserving the liquid and vegetables separately.

3 Press the vegetables through a strainer with the back of a spoon. Alternatively, process in a food processor until smooth.

4 Return the vegetable purée to a clean saucepan with the reserved cooking liquid. Add the basil and heat through until hot. Garnish the soup with fresh basil sprigs and serve immediately.

Avocado & Mint Soup

A rich and creamy pale green soup made with avocados and enhanced by a touch of chopped mint. Serve chilled in summer or hot in winter.

NUTRITIONAL INFORMATION

Calories	199	Sugars	........3g
Protein	.........3g	Fat	..........18g
Carbohydrate	....7g	Saturates	.......6g

15 MINS   35 MINS

SERVES 6

INGREDIENTS

40 g/1½ oz/3 tbsp butter or margarine

6 spring onions (scallions), sliced

1 garlic clove, crushed

25 g/1 oz/¼ cup plain (all-purpose) flour

600 ml/1 pint/2½ cups vegetable stock

2 ripe avocados

2–3 tsp lemon juice

pinch of grated lemon rind

150 ml/¼ pint/⅔ cup milk

150 ml/¼ pint/⅔ cup single (light) cream

1–1½ tbsp chopped mint

salt and pepper

mint sprigs, to garnish

MINTED GARLIC BREAD

125 g/4½ oz/½ cup butter

1–2 tbsp chopped mint

1–2 garlic cloves, crushed

1 wholemeal (whole wheat) or
   white French bread stick

1 Melt the butter or margarine in a large, heavy-based saucepan. Add the spring onions (scallions) and garlic clove and fry over a low heat, stirring occasionally, for about 3 minutes, until soft and translucent.

2 Stir in the flour and cook, stirring, for 1–2 minutes. Gradually stir in the stock, then bring to the boil. Simmer gently while preparing the avocados.

3 Peel the avocados, discard the stones (pits) and chop coarsely. Add to the soup with the lemon juice and rind and seasoning. Cover and simmer for about 10 minutes, until tender.

4 Cool the soup slightly, then press through a strainer with the back of a spoon or process in a food processor or blender until a smooth purée forms. Pour into a bowl.

5 Stir in the milk and cream, adjust the seasoning, then stir in the mint. Cover and chill thoroughly.

6 To make the minted garlic bread, soften the butter and beat in the mint and garlic. Cut the loaf into slanting slices but leave a hinge on the bottom crust. Spread each slice with the butter and reassemble the loaf. Wrap in foil and place in a preheated oven, 180°C/350°F/Gas Mark 4, for about 15 minutes.

7 Serve the soup garnished with a sprig of mint and accompanied by the minted garlic bread.

Minted Pea & Yogurt Soup

A deliciously refreshing, summery soup that is full of goodness. It is also extremely tasty served chilled.

NUTRITIONAL INFORMATION

Calories 208   Sugars 9g
Protein . . . . .10g   Fat 7g
Carbohydrate . . .26g   Saturates 2g

 15 MINS   25 MINS

SERVES 6

I N G R E D I E N T S

2 tbsp vegetable ghee or sunflower oil

2 onions, coarsely chopped

225 g/8 oz potato, coarsely chopped

2 garlic cloves, crushed

2.5 cm/1 inch root ginger, chopped

1 tsp ground coriander

1 tsp ground cumin

1 tbsp plain (all-purpose) flour

850 ml/1½ pints/3½ cups vegetable stock

500 g/1 lb 2 oz frozen peas

2-3 tbsp chopped mint

salt and pepper

150 ml/¼ pint/⅔ cup strained
    Greek yogurt, plus extra to serve

½ tsp cornflour (cornstarch)

300 ml/½ pint/1¼ cups milk

mint sprigs, to garnish

1 Heat the vegetable ghee or sunflower oil in a saucepan, add the onions and potato and cook over a low heat, stirring occasionally, for about 3 minutes, until the onion is soft and translucent.

2 Stir in the garlic, ginger, coriander, cumin and flour and cook, stirring constantly, for 1 minute.

3 Add the vegetable stock, peas and the chopped mint and bring to the boil, stirring. Reduce the heat, cover and simmer gently for 15 minutes, or until the vegetables are tender.

4 Process the soup, in batches, in a blender or food processor. Return the mixture to the pan and season with salt and pepper to taste. Blend the yogurt with the cornflour (cornstarch) to a smooth paste and stir into the soup.

5 Add the milk and bring almost to the boil, stirring constantly. Cook very gently for 2 minutes. Serve the soup hot, garnished with the mint sprigs and a swirl of extra yogurt.

Stilton & Walnut Soup

Full of flavour, this rich and creamy soup is very simple to make and utterly delicious to eat.

NUTRITIONAL INFORMATION

Calories	392	Sugars	.........8g
Protein	........15g	Fat	..........30g
Carbohydrate	...15g	Saturates	......16g

10 MINS   30 MINS

SERVES 4

INGREDIENTS

60 g/2 oz/4 tbsp butter

2 shallots, chopped

3 celery sticks, chopped

1 garlic clove, crushed

2 tbsp plain (all-purpose) flour

600 ml/1 pint/2½ cups vegetable stock

300 ml/½ pint/1¼ cups milk

150 g/5½ oz/1½ cups blue Stilton cheese, crumbled, plus extra to garnish

2 tbsp walnut halves, roughly chopped

150 ml/¼ pint/⅔ cup natural (unsweetened) yogurt

salt and pepper

chopped celery leaves, to garnish

1 Melt the butter in a large, heavy-based saucepan and sauté the shallots, celery and garlic, stirring occasionally, for 2–3 minutes, until softened.

2 Lower the heat, add the flour and cook, stirring constantly, for 30 seconds.

3 Gradually stir in the vegetable stock and milk and bring to the boil.

4 Reduce the heat to a gentle simmer and add the crumbled blue Stilton cheese and walnut halves. Cover and simmer for 20 minutes.

5 Stir in the yogurt and heat through for a further 2 minutes without boiling.

6 Season the soup to taste with salt and pepper, then transfer to a warm soup tureen or individual serving bowls, garnish with chopped celery leaves and extra crumbled blue Stilton cheese and serve at once.

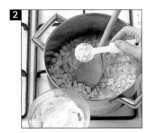

COOK'S TIP

As well as adding protein, vitamins and useful fats to the diet, nuts add important flavour and texture to vegetarian meals.

Thick Onion Soup

A delicious creamy soup with grated carrot and parsley for texture and colour. Serve with crusty cheese scones (biscuits) for a hearty lunch.

NUTRITIONAL INFORMATION

Calories 277   Sugars 12g
Protein ....6g   Fat 20g
Carbohydrate ...19g   Saturates 8g

20 MINS   1HR 10 MINS

SERVES 6

INGREDIENTS

75 g/2¾ oz/5 tbsp butter

500 g/1 lb 2 oz onions, finely chopped

1 garlic clove, crushed

40 g/1½ oz/6 tbsp plain (all-purpose) flour

600 ml/1 pint/2½ cups vegetable stock

600 ml/1 pint/2½ cups milk

2–3 tsp lemon or lime juice

good pinch of ground allspice

1 bay leaf

1 carrot, coarsely grated

4–6 tbsp double (heavy) cream

2 tbsp chopped parsley

salt and pepper

CHEESE SCONES (BISCUITS)

225 g/8 oz/2 cups malted wheat or wholemeal (whole wheat) flour

2 tsp baking powder

60 g/2 oz/¼ cup butter

4 tbsp grated Parmesan cheese

1 egg, beaten

about 75 ml/3 fl oz/⅓ cup milk

1 Melt the butter in a saucepan and fry the onions and garlic over a low heat, stirring frequently, for 10–15 minutes, until soft, but not coloured. Stir in the flour and cook, stirring, for 1 minute, then gradually stir in the stock and bring to the boil, stirring frequently. Add the milk, then bring back to the boil.

2 Season to taste with salt and pepper and add 2 teaspoons of the lemon or lime juice, the allspice and bay leaf. Cover and simmer for about 25 minutes until the vegetables are tender. Discard the bay leaf.

3 Meanwhile, make the scones (biscuits). Combine the flour, baking powder and seasoning and rub in the butter until the mixture resembles fine breadcrumbs. Stir in 3 tablespoons of the cheese, the egg and enough milk to mix to a soft dough.

4 Shape into a bar about 2 cm/¾ inch thick. Place on a floured baking tray (cookie sheet) and mark into slices. Sprinkle with the remaining cheese and bake in a preheated oven, 220°C/425°F/ Gas Mark 7, for about 20 minutes, until risen and golden brown.

5 Stir the carrot into the soup and simmer for 2–3 minutes. Add more lemon or lime juice, if necessary. Stir in the cream and reheat. Garnish and serve with the warm scones (biscuits).

Curried Parsnip Soup

Parsnips make a delicious soup as they have a slightly sweet flavour. In this recipe, spices are added to complement this sweetness.

NUTRITIONAL INFORMATION

Calories	152	Sugars	.........7g
Protein	.........3g	Fat	...........8g
Carbohydrate	...18g	Saturates	.......3g

 10 MINS   35 MINS

SERVES 4

I N G R E D I E N T S

1 tbsp vegetable oil

15 g/½ oz/1 tbsp butter

1 red onion, chopped

3 parsnips, chopped

2 garlic cloves, crushed

2 tsp garam masala

½ tsp chilli powder

1 tbsp plain (all-purpose) flour

850 ml/1½ pints/3¾ cups vegetable stock

grated rind and juice of 1 lemon

salt and pepper

lemon rind, to garnish

1 Heat the oil and butter in a large saucepan until the butter has melted. Add the onion, parsnips and garlic and sauté, stirring frequently, for about 5–7 minutes, until the vegetables have softened, but not coloured.

2 Add the garam masala and chilli powder and cook, stirring constantly, for 30 seconds. Sprinkle in the flour, mixing well and cook, stirring constantly, for a further 30 seconds.

3 Stir in the stock, lemon rind and juice and bring to the boil. Reduce the heat and simmer for 20 minutes.

4 Remove some of the vegetable pieces with a slotted spoon and reserve until required. Process the remaining soup and vegetables in a food processor or blender for about 1 minute, or until a smooth purée. Alternatively, press the vegetables through a strainer with the back of a wooden spoon.

5 Return the soup to a clean saucepan and stir in the reserved vegetables. Heat the soup through for 2 minutes until piping hot.

6 Season to taste with salt and pepper, then transfer to soup bowls, garnish with grated lemon rind and serve.

Broad (Fava) Bean Soup

Fresh broad (fava) beans are best for this scrumptious soup, but if they are unavailable, use frozen beans instead.

NUTRITIONAL INFORMATION

Calories	224	Sugars	. . . . .4g
Protein	. . . . .12g	Fat	. . . . .6g
Carbohydrate	. . .31g	Saturates	. . . . . . .1g

15 MINS   40 MINS

SERVES 4

I N G R E D I E N T S

2 tbsp olive oil

1 red onion, chopped

2 garlic cloves, crushed

2 potatoes, diced

500 g/1 lb 2 oz/3 cups broad (fava) beans, thawed if frozen

850 ml/1½ pints/3¾ cups vegetable stock

2 tbsp freshly chopped mint

mint sprigs and natural (unsweetened) yogurt, to garnish

1 Heat the olive oil in a large saucepan. Add the onion and garlic and sauté for 2–3 minutes, until softened.

2 Add the potatoes and cook, stirring constantly, for 5 minutes.

3 Stir in the beans and the stock, cover and simmer for 30 minutes, or until the beans and potatoes are tender.

4 Remove a few vegetables with a slotted spoon and set aside until required. Place the remainder of the soup in a food processor or blender and process until smooth.

5 Return the soup to a clean saucepan and add the reserved vegetables and chopped mint. Stir thoroughly and heat through gently.

6 Transfer the soup to a warm tureen or individual serving bowls. Garnish with swirls of yogurt and sprigs of fresh mint and serve immediately.

VARIATION

Use fresh coriander (cilantro) and ½ tsp ground cumin as flavourings in the soup, if you prefer.

Spinach & Mascarpone Soup

Spinach is the basis for this delicious soup, which has creamy mascarpone cheese stirred through it to give it a wonderful texture.

NUTRITIONAL INFORMATION

Calories 402	Sugars 2g
Protein 11g	Fat 36g
Carbohydrate ...10g	Saturates 21g

15 MINS   30 MINS

SERVES 4

INGREDIENTS

60 g/2 oz/¼ cup butter

1 bunch spring onions (scallions),
    trimmed and chopped

2 celery sticks, chopped

350 g/12 oz/3 cups spinach or sorrel, or
    3 bunches watercress

850 ml /1½ pints/3½ cups vegetable stock

225 g/8 oz/1 cup mascarpone cheese

1 tbsp olive oil

2 slices thick-cut bread, cut into cubes

½ tsp caraway seeds

salt and pepper

sesame bread sticks, to serve

1 Melt half the butter in a very large saucepan. Add the spring onions (scallions) and celery, and cook over a medium heat, stirring frequently, for about 5 minutes, until softened.

2 Pack the spinach, sorrel or watercress into the saucepan. Add the stock and bring to the boil, then reduce the heat, cover and simmer for 15–20 minutes.

3 Transfer the soup to a blender or food processor and process until smooth. Alternatively, rub it through a strainer. Return to the saucepan.

4 Add the mascarpone to the soup and heat gently, stirring constantly, until smooth and blended. Season to taste with salt and pepper.

5 Heat the remaining butter with the oil in a frying pan (skillet). Add the bread cubes and fry, turning frequently, until golden brown, adding the caraway seeds towards the end of cooking, so that they do not burn.

6 Ladle the soup into warmed bowls. Sprinkle with the croûtons and serve with the sesame bread sticks.

VARIATION

Any leafy vegetable can be used to make this soup to give variations to the flavour. For anyone who grows their own vegetables, it is the perfect recipe for experimenting with a glut of produce. Try young beetroot (beet) leaves or surplus lettuces for a change.

Leek, Potato & Carrot Soup

A quick chunky soup, ideal for a snack or a quick lunch. The leftovers can be puréed to make one portion of creamed soup for the next day.

NUTRITIONAL INFORMATION

Calories ....156 Sugars 7g
Protein ....4g Fat 6g
Carbohydrate ...22g Saturates 0.7g

10 MINS   25 MINS

SERVES 2

INGREDIENTS

1 leek, about 175 g/6 oz

1 tbsp sunflower oil

1 garlic clove, crushed

700 ml/1¼ pints/3 cups vegetable stock

1 bay leaf

¼ tsp ground cumin

175 g/6 oz/1 cup potatoes, diced

125 g/4½ oz/1 cup coarsely grated carrot

salt and pepper

chopped parsley, to garnish

PUREED SOUP

5–6 tbsp milk

1–2 tbsp double (heavy) cream, crème
    fraîche or soured cream

1 Trim off and discard some of the coarse green part of the leek, then slice thinly and rinse thoroughly in cold water. Drain well.

2 Heat the sunflower oil in a heavy-based saucepan. Add the leek and garlic, and fry over a low heat for about 2–3 minutes, until soft, but barely coloured. Add the vegetable stock, bay leaf and cumin and season to taste with salt and pepper. Bring the mixture to the boil, stirring constantly.

3 Add the diced potato to the saucepan, cover and simmer over a low heat for 10–15 minutes until the potato is just tender, but not broken up.

4 Add the grated carrot and simmer for a further 2–3 minutes. Adjust seasoning, discard the bay leaf and serve sprinkled liberally with chopped parsley.

5 To make a puréed soup, first process the leftovers (about half the original soup) in a blender or food processor or press through a strainer until smooth and then return to a clean saucepan with the milk. Bring to the boil and simmer for 2–3 minutes. Adjust the seasoning and stir in the cream or crème fraîche before serving sprinkled with chopped parsley.

Broccoli & Potato Soup

This creamy soup has a delightful pale green colouring and rich flavour from the blend of tender broccoli and blue cheese.

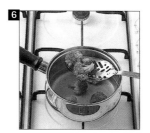

NUTRITIONAL INFORMATION

Calories 452	Sugars 4g	
Protein 14g	Fat 35g	
Carbohydrate ...20g	Saturates 19g	

 5-10 MINS   40 MINS

SERVES 4

I N G R E D I E N T S

2 tbsp olive oil

2 potatoes, diced

1 onion, diced

225 g/8 oz broccoli florets

125 g/4½ oz blue cheese, crumbled

1 litre/1¾ pints/4½ cups vegetable stock

150 ml/¼ pint/⅔ cup double (heavy) cream

pinch of paprika

salt and pepper

1 Heat the oil in a large saucepan. Add the potatoes and onion. Sauté, stirring constantly, for 5 minutes.

2 Reserve a few broccoli florets for the garnish and add the remaining broccoli to the pan. Add the cheese and vegetable stock.

COOK'S TIP

This soup freezes very successfully. Follow the method described here up to step 4, and freeze the soup after it has been puréed. Add the cream and paprika just before serving. Garnish and serve.

3 Bring to the boil, then reduce the heat, cover the pan and simmer for 25 minutes, until the potatoes are tender.

4 Transfer the soup to a food processor or blender in batches and process until the mixture is smooth. Alternatively, press the vegetables through a strainer with the back of a wooden spoon.

5 Return the purée to a clean saucepan and stir in the double (heavy) cream and a pinch of paprika. Season to taste with salt and pepper.

6 Blanch the reserved broccoli florets in a little boiling water for about 2 minutes, then lift them out of the pan with a slotted spoon.

7 Pour the soup into warmed individual bowls and garnish with the broccoli florets and a sprinkling of paprika. Serve immediately.

Potato & Split Pea Soup

Split green peas are sweeter than other varieties of split pea and reduce down to a purée when cooked, which acts as a thickener in soups.

NUTRITIONAL INFORMATION

Calories ....260 Sugars 5g
Protein ....11g Fat 10g
Carbohydrate ...32g Saturates 3g

 5–10 MINS   45 MINS

SERVES 4

INGREDIENTS

2 tbsp vegetable oil

2 unpeeled floury (mealy) potatoes, diced

2 onions, diced

75 g/2¾ oz split green peas

1 litre/1¾ pints/4½ cups vegetable stock

5 tbsp grated Gruyère cheese

salt and pepper

CROUTONS

40 g/1½ oz/3 tbsp butter

1 garlic clove, crushed

1 tbsp chopped parsley

1 thick slice white bread, cubed

1 Heat the vegetable oil in a large saucepan. Add the potatoes and onions and sauté over a low heat, stirring constantly, for about 5 minutes.

VARIATION

For a richly coloured soup, red lentils could be used instead of split green peas. Add a large pinch of brown sugar to t he recipe for extra sweetness if red lentils are used.

2 Add the split green peas to the pan and stir to mix together well.

3 Pour the vegetable stock into the pan and bring to the boil. Reduce the heat to low and simmer for 35 minutes, until the potatoes are tender and the split peas cooked.

4 Meanwhile, make the croûtons. Melt the butter in a frying pan (skillet). Add the garlic, parsley and bread cubes and cook, turning frequently, for about 2 minutes, until the bread cubes are golden brown on all sides.

5 Stir the grated cheese into the soup and season to taste with salt and pepper. Heat gently until the cheese is starting to melt.

6 Pour the soup into warmed individual bowls and sprinkle the croûtons on top. Serve at once.

Indian Potato & Pea Soup

A slightly hot and spicy Indian flavour is given to this soup with the use of garam masala, chilli, cumin and coriander.

NUTRITIONAL INFORMATION

Calories 153	Sugars 6g	
Protein 6g	Fat 6g	
Carbohydrate ...18g	Saturates 1g	

10 MINS   35 MINS

SERVES 4

I N G R E D I E N T S

2 tbsp vegetable oil

225 g/8 oz floury (mealy) potatoes, diced

1 large onion, chopped

2 garlic cloves, crushed

1 tsp garam masala

1 tsp ground coriander

1 tsp ground cumin

850 ml/1½ pints/3¾ cups vegetable stock

1 red chilli, chopped

100 g/3½ oz/scant 1 cup frozen peas

4 tbsp natural (unsweetened) yogurt

salt and pepper

chopped coriander (cilantro),
    to garnish

warm bread, to serve

VARIATION

For slightly less heat, seed the chilli before adding it to the soup. Always wash your hands after handling chillies as they contain volatile oils that can irritate the skin and make your eyes burn if you touch your face.

1 Heat the vegetable oil in a large saucepan. Add the potatoes, onion and garlic and sauté over a low heat, stirring constantly, for about 5 minutes.

2 Add the garam masala, ground coriander and cumin and cook, stirring constantly, for 1 minute.

3 Stir in the vegetable stock and chopped red chilli and bring the mixture to the boil. Reduce the heat, cover the pan and simmer for 20 minutes, until the potatoes begin to break down.

4 Add the peas and cook for a further 5 minutes. Stir in the yogurt and season to taste with salt and pepper.

5 Pour into warmed soup bowls, garnish with chopped fresh coriander (cilantro) and serve hot with warm bread.

Cauliflower & Broccoli Soup

Full of flavour, this creamy cauliflower and broccoli soup is simple to make and absolutely delicious to eat.

NUTRITIONAL INFORMATION

Calories	378	Sugars	........14g
Protein	........18g	Fat	..........26g
Carbohydrate	...20g	Saturates	.......7g

10 MINS   35 MINS

SERVES 4

I N G R E D I E N T S

3 tbsp vegetable oil

1 red onion, chopped

2 garlic cloves, crushed

300 g/10½ oz cauliflower florets

300 g/10½ oz broccoli florets

1 tbsp plain (all-purpose) flour

600 ml/1 pint/2½ cups milk

300 ml/½ pint/1¼ cups vegetable stock

75 g/2¾ oz/¾ cup Gruyère cheese, grated

pinch of paprika

150 ml/¼ pint/⅔ cup single (light) cream

paprika and Gruyère cheese shavings,
   to garnish

COOK'S TIP

The soup must not start to boil after the cream has been added, otherwise it will curdle. Use natural (unsweetened) yogurt instead of the cream if preferred, but again do not allow it to boil.

1 Heat the oil in a large, heavy-based saucepan. Add the onion, garlic, cauliflower florets and broccoli florets and sauté over a low heat, stirring constantly, for 3–4 minutes. Add the flour and cook, stirring constantly for a further 1 minute.

2 Gradually stir in the milk and stock and bring to the boil, stirring constantly. Reduce the heat and simmer for 20 minutes.

3 Remove about a quarter of the vegetables with a slotted spoon and set aside. Put the remaining soup in a food processor or blender and process for about 30 seconds, until smooth. Alternatively, press the vegetables through a strainer with the back of a wooden spoon. Transfer the soup to a clean saucepan.

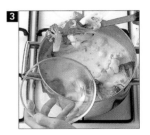

4 Return the reserved vegetable pieces to the soup. Stir in the grated cheese, paprika and single (light) cream and heat through over a low heat, without boiling, for 2–3 minutes, or until the cheese starts to melt.

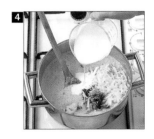

5 Transfer to warmed individual serving bowls, garnish with shavings of Gruyère and dust with paprika and serve immediately.

Asparagus Soup

Fresh asparagus is now available for most of the year, so this soup can be made at any time. It can also be made using canned asparagus.

NUTRITIONAL INFORMATION

Calories	196	Sugars	.........7g
Protein	.........7g	Fat	..........12g
Carbohydrate	...15g	Saturates	.......4g

 5–10 MINS   55 MINS

SERVES 6

I N G R E D I E N T S

1 bunch asparagus, about 350 g/12 oz,
   or 2 packs mini asparagus,
   about 150 g/5½ oz each

700 ml/1¼ pints/3 cups vegetable stock

60 g/2 oz/¼ cup butter or margarine

1 onion, chopped

3 tbsp plain (all-purpose) flour

¼ tsp ground coriander

1 tbsp lemon juice

450 ml/16 fl oz/2 cups milk

4–6 tbsp double (heavy) or single
   (light) cream

salt and pepper

COOK'S TIP

If using canned asparagus, drain off the liquid and use as part of the measured stock. Remove a few small asparagus tips for garnish and chop the remainder. Continue as above.

1 Wash and trim the asparagus, discarding the woody part of the stem. Cut the remainder into short lengths, keeping a few tips for garnish. Mini asparagus does not need to be trimmed.

2 Cook the tips in the minimum of boiling salted water for 5–10 minutes. Drain and set aside.

3 Put the asparagus in a saucepan with the stock, bring to the boil, cover and simmer for about 20 minutes, until soft. Drain and reserve the stock.

4 Melt the butter or margarine in a saucepan. Add the onion and fry over a low heat until soft, but only barely coloured. Stir in the flour and cook for 1 minute, then gradually whisk in the reserved stock and bring to the boil.

5 Simmer for 2–3 minutes, until thickened, then stir in the cooked asparagus, seasoning, coriander and lemon juice. Simmer for 10 minutes, then cool a little and either press through a strainer or process in a blender or food processor until smooth.

6 Pour into a clean pan, add the milk and reserved asparagus tips and bring to the boil. Simmer for 2 minutes. Stir in the cream, reheat gently and serve.

Jerusalem Artichoke Soup

Jerusalem artichokes are native to North America, but are also grown in Europe. They have a nutty flavour which combines well with orange.

NUTRITIONAL INFORMATION

Calories . . . . .211 Sugars 17g
Protein . . . . .7g Fat 8g
Carbohydrate . . .29g Saturates 4g

 10 MINS   30 MINS

SERVES 4

INGREDIENTS

675 g/1½ lb Jerusalem artichokes

5 tbsp orange juice

25 g/1 oz/2 tbsp butter

1 leek, chopped

1 garlic clove, crushed

300 ml/½ pint/1¼ cups vegetable stock

150 ml/¼ pint/⅔ cup milk

2 tbsp chopped coriander (cilantro)

150 ml/¼ pint/⅔ cup natural
    (unsweetened) yogurt

grated orange rind, to garnish

1 Rinse the Jerusalem artichokes and place in a large saucepan with 2 tablespoons of the orange juice and enough water to cover. Bring to the boil, reduce the heat and cook for 20 minutes, or until the artichokes are tender.

2 Drain the artichokes, reserving 425 ml/¾ pint/ 2 cups of the cooking liquid. Leave the artichokes to cool, then peel and place in a large bowl. Mash the flesh with a potato masher.

3 Melt the butter in a large saucepan. Add the leek and garlic and fry over a low heat, stirring frequently, for 2–3 minutes, until the leek soft.

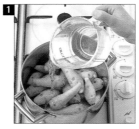

4 Stir in the mashed artichoke, stock, milk, remaining orange juice and reserved cooking water. Bring to the boil, then simmer for 2–3 minutes.

5 Remove a few pieces of leek with a slotted spoon and reserve. Process the remainder in a food processor for 1 minute until smooth. Alternatively, press through a strainer with the back of a spoon.

6 Return the soup to a clean saucepan and stir in the reserved leeks, coriander (cilantro) and yogurt and heat through. Transfer to individual soup bowls, garnish with orange rind and serve.

Avocado & Vegetable Soup

Avocado has a rich flavour and colour which makes a creamy flavoured soup. It is best served chilled, but may be eaten warm as well.

NUTRITIONAL INFORMATION

Calories 167	Sugars 5g
Protein 4g	Fat 13g
Carbohydrate 8g	Saturates 3g

 15 MINS   10 MINS

SERVES 4

INGREDIENTS

1 large, ripe avocado

2 tbsp lemon juice

1 tbsp vegetable oil

50 g/1¾ oz/½ cup canned
    sweetcorn (corn), drained

2 tomatoes, peeled and seeded

1 garlic clove, crushed

1 leek, chopped

1 red chilli, chopped

425 ml/¾ pint/2 cups vegetable stock

150 ml/¼ pint/⅔ cup milk

shredded leek, to garnish

1 Peel the avocado and mash the flesh with a fork, stir in the lemon juice and reserve until required.

2 Heat the oil in a large saucepan. Add the sweetcorn (corn), tomatoes, garlic, leek and chilli and sauté over a low heat for 2–3 minutes, or until the vegetables have softened.

3 Put half the vegetable mixture in a food processor or blender, together with the mashed avocado and process until smooth. Transfer the mixture to a clean saucepan.

4 Add the vegetable stock, milk and reserved vegetables and cook over a low heat for 3–4 minutes, until hot. Transfer to a warmed individual serving bowls, garnish with shredded leek and serve immediately.

COOK'S TIP

If serving chilled, transfer from the food processor to a bowl, stir in the vegetable stock and milk, cover and chill in the refrigerator for at least 4 hours..

Vichyssoise

This is a classic creamy soup made from potatoes and leeks. To achieve the delicate pale colour, be sure to use only the white parts of the leeks.

NUTRITIONAL INFORMATION

Calories ....208 Sugars 5g
Protein ....5g Fat 12g
Carbohydrate ...20g Saturates 6g

10 MINS   40 MINS

SERVES 6

I N G R E D I E N T S

3 large leeks

40 g/1½ oz/3 tbsp butter or margarine

1 onion, thinly sliced

500 g/1 lb 2 oz potatoes, chopped

850 ml/1½ pints/3½ cups vegetable stock

2 tsp lemon juice

pinch of ground nutmeg

¼ tsp ground coriander

1 bay leaf

1 egg yolk

150 ml/¼ pint/⅔ cup single (light) cream

salt and white pepper

T O   G A R N I S H

freshly snipped chives

1 Trim the leeks and remove most of the green part. Slice the white part of the leeks very finely.

2 Melt the butter or margarine in a saucepan. Add the leeks and onion and fry, stirring occasionally, for about 5 minutes without browning.

3 Add the potatoes, vegetable stock, lemon juice, nutmeg, coriander and bay leaf to the pan, season to taste with salt and pepper and bring to the boil. Cover and simmer for about 30 minutes, until all the vegetables are very soft.

4 Cool the soup a little, remove and discard the bay leaf and then press through a strainer or process in a food processor or blender until smooth. Pour into a clean pan.

5 Blend the egg yolk into the cream, add a little of the soup to the mixture and then whisk it all back into the soup and reheat gently, without boiling. Adjust the seasoning to taste. Cool and then chill thoroughly in the refrigerator.

6 Serve the soup sprinkled with freshly snipped chives.

Vegetable & Corn Chowder

This is a really filling soup, which should be served before a light main course. It is easy to prepare and filled with flavour.

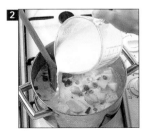

NUTRITIONAL INFORMATION

Calories 378	Sugars 20g	
Protein 16g	Fat 13g	
Carbohydrate ...52g	Saturates 6g	

 15 MINS   30 MINS

SERVES 4

INGREDIENTS

1 tbsp vegetable oil

1 red onion, diced

1 red (bell) pepper, seeded and diced

3 garlic cloves, crushed

1 large potato, diced

2 tbsp plain (all-purpose) flour

600 ml/1 pint/2½ cups milk

300 ml/½ pint/1¼ cups vegetable stock

50 g/1¾ oz broccoli florets

300 g/10½ oz/3 cups canned
   sweetcorn (corn), drained

75 g/2¾ oz/¾ cup Cheddar cheese, grated

salt and pepper

1 tbsp chopped coriander (cilantro),
   to garnish

COOK'S TIP

Vegetarian cheeses are made
with rennets of
non-animal origin, using
microbial or fungal enzymes.

1 Heat the oil in a large saucepan. Add the onion, (bell) pepper, garlic and potato and sauté over a low heat, stirring frequently, for 2–3 minutes.

2 Stir in the flour and cook, stirring for 30 seconds. Gradually stir in the milk and stock.

3 Add the broccoli and sweetcorn (corn). Bring the mixture to the boil, stirring constantly, then reduce the heat and simmer for about 20 minutes, or until all the vegetables are tender.

4 Stir in 50 g/1¾ oz/½ cup of the cheese until it melts.

5 Season and spoon the chowder into a warm soup tureen. Garnish with the remaining cheese and the coriander (cilantro) and serve.

Dhal Soup

Dahl is the name given to a delicious Indian lentil dish. This soup is a variation of the theme – it is made with red lentils and curry powder.

NUTRITIONAL INFORMATION

Calories 284	Sugars 13g
Protein 16g	Fat 9g
Carbohydrate ...38g	Saturates 5g

 5 MINS   40 MINS

SERVES 4

INGREDIENTS

25 g/1 oz/2 tbsp butter

2 garlic cloves, crushed

1 onion, chopped

½ tsp turmeric

1 tsp garam masala

¼ tsp chilli powder

1 tsp ground cumin

1 kg/2 lb 4 oz canned, chopped
	tomatoes, drained

175 g/6 oz/1 cup red lentils

2 tsp lemon juice

600 ml/1 pint/2½ cups vegetable stock

300 ml/½ pint/1¼ cups coconut milk

salt and pepper

chopped coriander (cilantro) and lemon
	slices, to garnish

naan bread, to serve

1 Melt the butter in a large saucepan. Add the garlic and onion and sauté, stirring, for 2–3 minutes. Add the turmeric, garam masala, chilli powder and cumin and cook for a further 30 seconds.

2 Stir in the tomatoes, red lentils, lemon juice, vegetable stock and coconut milk and bring to the boil.

3 Reduce the heat to low and simmer the soup, uncovered, for about 25–30 minutes, until the lentils are tender and cooked.

4 Season to taste with salt and pepper and ladle the soup into a warm tureen. Garnish with chopped coriander (cilantro) and lemon slices and serve immediately with warm naan bread.

COOK'S TIP

You can buy cans of coconut milk from supermarkets and delicatessens. It can also be made by grating creamed coconut, which comes in the form of a solid bar, and then mixing it with water.

Spicy Dhal & Carrot Soup

This nutritious soup uses split red lentils and carrots as the two main ingredients and includes a selection of spices to give it a kick.

NUTRITIONAL INFORMATION

Calories ....173 Sugars 11g
Protein ....9g Fat 5g
Carbohydrate ...24g Saturates 1g

 15 MINS   45 MINS

SERVES 6

INGREDIENTS

125 g/4½ oz split red lentils

1.2 litres/2 pints/5 cups vegetable stock

350 g/12 oz carrots, sliced

2 onions, chopped

225 g/8 oz can chopped tomatoes

2 garlic cloves, chopped

2 tbsp vegetable ghee or oil

1 tsp ground cumin

1 tsp ground coriander

1 fresh green chilli, seeded and chopped,
   or 1 tsp minced chilli

½ tsp ground turmeric

1 tbsp lemon juice

salt

300 ml/½ pint/1¼ cups milk

2 tbsp chopped coriander (cilantro)

natural (unsweetened) yogurt, to serve

1 Place the lentils in a strainer and rinse well under cold running water. Drain and place in a large saucepan, together with 850 ml/1½ pints/3½ cups of the stock, the carrots, onions, tomatoes and garlic. Bring the mixture to the boil, reduce the heat, cover and simmer for 30 minutes or until the vegetables and lentils are tender.

2 Meanwhile, heat the ghee or oil in a small pan. Add the cumin, ground coriander, chilli and turmeric and fry over a low heat for 1 minute. Remove from the heat and stir in the lemon juice. Season with salt to taste.

3 Process the soup in batches in a blender or food processor. Return the soup to the saucepan, add the spice mixture and the remaining 300 ml/ ½ pint/1¼ cups stock and simmer over a low heat for 10 minutes.

4 Add the milk, taste and adjust the seasoning, if necessary. Stir in the chopped coriander (cilantro) and reheat gently. Serve hot with a swirl of yogurt.

Bean Soup

Beans feature widely in Mexican cooking, and here pinto beans are used to give an interesting texture. Pinto beans require soaking overnight.

NUTRITIONAL INFORMATION

Calories ....188 Sugars 9g
Protein ....13g Fat 1g
Carbohydrate ...33g Saturates 0.3g

20 MINS   3 HOURS

SERVES 4

INGREDIENTS

175 g/6 oz pinto beans

1.25 litres/2¼ pints water

175–225 g/6–8 oz carrots, finely chopped

1 large onion, finely chopped

2–3 garlic cloves, crushed

½–1 chilli, seeded and finely chopped

1 litre /1¾ pints vegetable stock

2 tomatoes, peeled and finely chopped

2 celery sticks, very thinly sliced

salt and pepper

1 tbsp chopped coriander
   (cilantro) (optional)

CROUTONS

3 slices white bread, crusts removed

oil, for deep-frying

1–2 garlic cloves, crushed

VARIATION

Pinto beans are widely
available, but if you cannot
find them or you wish to vary
the recipe, you can use cannellini
beans or black-eyed beans (peas) as
an alternative.

1 Soak the beans overnight in cold water; drain and place in a pan with the water. Bring to the boil and boil vigorously for 10 minutes. Lower the heat, cover and simmer for 2 hours, or until the beans are tender.

2 Add the carrots, onion, garlic, chilli and stock and bring back to the boil. Cover and simmer for a further 30 minutes, until very tender.

3 Remove half the beans and vegetables with the cooking juices and press through a strainer or process in a food processor or blender until smooth.

4 Return the bean purée to the saucepan and add the tomatoes and celery. Simmer for 10–15 minutes, or until the celery is just tender, adding a little more stock or water if necessary.

5 Meanwhile, make the croûtons. Dice the bread. Heat the oil with the garlic in a small frying pan (skillet) and fry the croûtons until golden brown. Drain on kitchen paper (paper towels).

6 Season the soup and stir in the chopped coriander (cilantro), if using. Transfer to a warm tureen and serve immediately with the croûtons.

Indian Bean Soup

A thick and hearty soup, nourishing and substantial enough to serve as a main meal with wholemeal (whole wheat) bread.

NUTRITIONAL INFORMATION

Calories 237	Sugars 9g	
Protein 9g	Fat 9g	
Carbohydrate ...33g	Saturates 1g	

20 MINS   50 MINS

SERVES 6

I N G R E D I E N T S

4 tbsp vegetable ghee or vegetable oil

2 onions, peeled and chopped

225 g/8 oz/1½ cups potato, cut
   into chunks

225 g/8 oz/1½ cups parsnip, cut
   into chunks

225 g/8 oz/1½ cups turnip or swede
   (rutabaga), cut into chunks

2 celery sticks, sliced

2 courgettes (zucchini), sliced

1 green (bell) pepper, seeded and cut into
   1 cm/½ inch pieces

2 garlic cloves, crushed

2 tsp ground coriander

1 tbsp paprika

1 tbsp mild curry paste

1.2 litres/2 pints/5 cups vegetable stock

salt

400 g/14 oz can black-eye beans (peas),
   drained and rinsed

chopped coriander (cilantro),
   to garnish (optional)

1 Heat the ghee or oil in a saucepan, add all the prepared vegetables, except the courgettes (zucchini) and green (bell) pepper, and cook over a moderate heat, stirring frequently, for 5 minutes. Add the garlic, ground coriander, paprika and curry paste and cook, stirring constantly, for 1 minute.

2 Stir in the stock and season with salt to taste. Bring to the boil, cover and simmer over a low heat, stirring occasionally, for 25 minutes.

3 Stir in the black-eye beans (peas), sliced courgettes (zucchini) and green (bell) pepper, cover and continue cooking for a further 15 minutes, or until all the vegetables are tender.

4 Process 300 ml/½ pint/1¼ cups of the soup mixture (about 2 ladlefuls) in a food processor or blender. Return the puréed mixture to the soup in the saucepan and reheat until piping hot. Sprinkle with chopped coriander (cilantro), if using and serve hot.

Mixed Bean Soup

This is a really hearty soup, filled with colour, flavour and goodness, which may be adapted to any vegetables that you have at hand.

NUTRITIONAL INFORMATION

Calories	190	Sugars	........9g
Protein	........10g	Fat	..........4g
Carbohydrate	...30g	Saturates	.....0.5g

 10 MINS   40 MINS

SERVES 4

I N G R E D I E N T S

1 tbsp vegetable oil

1 red onion, halved and sliced

100 g/3½ oz/⅔ cup potato, diced

1 carrot, diced

1 leek, sliced

1 green chilli, sliced

3 garlic cloves, crushed

1 tsp ground coriander

1 tsp chilli powder

1 litre/1¾ pints/4 cups vegetable stock

450 g/1 lb mixed canned beans,
    such as red kidney, borlotti, black eye
    or flageolet, drained

salt and pepper

2 tbsp chopped coriander (cilantro),
    to garnish

COOK'S TIP

Serve this soup with slices of warm corn bread or a cheese loaf.

1 Heat the vegetable oil in a large saucepan. Add the onion, potato, carrot and leek and sauté, stirring constantly, for about 2 minutes, until the vegetables are slightly softened.

2 Add the sliced chilli and crushed garlic and cook for a further 1 minute.

3 Stir in the ground coriander, chilli powder and the vegetable stock.

4 Bring the soup to the boil, reduce the heat and cook for 20 minutes, or until the vegetables are tender.

5 Stir in the beans, season well with salt and pepper and cook, stirring occasionally, for a further 10 minutes.

6 Transfer the soup to a warm tureen or individual bowls, garnish with chopped coriander (cilantro) and serve.

Cream Cheese & Herb Soup

Make the most of home-grown herbs to create this wonderfully creamy soup with its marvellous garden-fresh fragrance.

NUTRITIONAL INFORMATION

Calories 275	Sugars 5g
Protein 7g	Fat 22g
Carbohydrate ...14g	Saturates 11g

 15 MINS   35 MINS

SERVES 4

I N G R E D I E N T S

25 g/1 oz/2 tbsp butter or margarine

2 onions, chopped

850 ml/1½ pints/3½ cups vegetable stock

25 g/1 oz coarsely chopped mixed
   herbs, such as parsley, chives, thyme,
   basil and oregano

200 g/7 oz/1 cup full-fat soft cheese

1 tbsp cornflour (cornstarch)

1 tbsp milk

chopped chives, to garnish

1 Melt the butter or margarine in a large, heavy-based saucepan. Add the onions and fry over a medium heat for 2 minutes, then cover and turn the heat to low. Continue to cook the onions for 5 minutes, then remove the lid.

2 Add the vegetable stock and herbs to the saucepan. Bring to the boil over a moderate heat. Lower the heat, cover and simmer gently for 20 minutes.

3 Remove the saucepan from the heat. Transfer the soup to a food processor or blender and process for about 15 seconds, until smooth. Alternatively, press it through a strainer with the back of a wooden spoon. Return the soup to the saucepan.

4 Reserve a little of the cheese for garnish. Spoon the remaining cheese into the soup and whisk until it has melted and is incorporated.

5 Mix the cornflour (cornstarch) with the milk to a paste, then stir the mixture into the soup. Heat, stirring constantly, until thickened and smooth.

6 Pour the soup into warmed individual bowls. Spoon some of the reserved cheese into each bowl and garnish with chives. Serve at once.

Starters

With so many fresh ingredients readily available, it is very easy to create some deliciously different starters to make the perfect introduction to a vegetarian meal. The ideas in this chapter are an inspiration to cook and a treat to eat, and they give an edge to the appetite that makes the main course even more enjoyable. When choosing a starter,

make sure that you provide a good balance of flavours, colours and textures that offer variety and contrast. Balance the nature of the recipes too – a rich main course is best preceded by a light starter, which is just enough to interest the palate and stimulate the tastebuds.

Heavenly Garlic Dip

Anyone who loves garlic will adore this dip – it is very potent! Serve it at a barbecue and dip raw vegetables or chunks of French bread into it.

NUTRITIONAL INFORMATION

Calories 344   Sugars 2g
Protein ....6g   Fat 34g
Carbohydrate ....3g   Saturates 5g

 15 MINS   20 MINS

SERVES 4

I N G R E D I E N T S

2 bulbs garlic

6 tbsp olive oil

1 small onion, finely chopped

2 tbsp lemon juice

3 tbsp tahini (sesame seed paste)

2 tbsp chopped parsley

salt and pepper

TO SERVE

fresh vegetable crudités

French bread or warmed pitta
   (pocket) breads

1 Separate the bulbs of garlic into individual cloves. Place them on a baking tray (cookie sheet) and roast in a preheated oven, 200°C/400°F/Gas Mark 6, for 8–10 minutes. Set aside to cool for a few minutes.

VARIATION

If you come across smoked garlic, use it in this recipe – it tastes wonderful. There is no need to roast the smoked garlic, so omit the first step. This dip can also be used to baste kebabs (kabobs) and vegetarian burgers.

2 When they are cool enough to handle, peel the garlic cloves and then chop them finely.

3 Heat the olive oil in a saucepan or frying pan (skillet) and add the garlic and onion. Fry over a low heat, stirring occasionally, for 8–10 minutes, until softened. Remove the pan from the heat.

4 Mix in the lemon juice, tahini (sesame seed paste) and parsley. Season to taste with salt and pepper. Transfer to a small heatproof bowl and keep warm at one side of the barbecue.

5 Serve with fresh vegetable crudités, chunks of French bread or warm pitta (pocket) breads.

Mint & Cannellini Bean Dip

This dip is ideal for pre-dinner drinks or for handing around at a party. The cannellini beans require soaking overnight, so prepare in advance.

NUTRITIONAL INFORMATION

Calories ....208 Sugars 1g
Protein ....10g Fat 12g
Carbohydrate ...16g Saturates 2g

 40 MINS   30 MINS

SERVES 6

INGREDIENTS

175 g/6 oz/1 cup dried cannellini beans

1 small garlic clove, crushed

1 bunch spring onions (scallions),
   roughly chopped

handful of mint leaves

2 tbsp tahini (sesame seed paste)

2 tbsp olive oil

1 tsp ground cumin

1 tsp ground coriander

lemon juice

salt and pepper

sprigs of mint, to garnish

TO SERVE

fresh vegetable crudités, such as
   cauliflower florets, carrots, cucumber,
   radishes and (bell) peppers

1 Soak the cannellini beans overnight in plenty of cold water.

2 Rinse and drain the beans, put them into a large saucepan and cover them with cold water. Bring to the boil and boil rapidly for 10 minutes. Reduce the heat, cover and simmer until tender.

3 Drain the beans and transfer them to a bowl or food processor. Add the garlic, spring onions (scallions), mint, tahini (sesame seed paste) and olive oil.

4 Process the mixture for about 15 seconds or mash well by hand, until smooth.

5 Transfer the mixture to a bowl, stir in the cumin, coriander and lemon juice and season to taste with salt and pepper. Mix thoroughly, cover and leave in a cool place for 30 minutes to allow the flavours to develop fully.

6 Spoon the dip into serving bowls, garnish with sprigs of fresh mint and surround with vegetable crudités. Serve at room temperature.

Buttered Nut & Lentil Dip

This tasty dip is very easy to make. It is perfect to have at barbecues, as it gives your guests something to nibble while they are waiting.

NUTRITIONAL INFORMATION

Calories	395	Sugars	.........4g
Protein	........12g	Fat	..........31g
Carbohydrate	...18g	Saturates	......10g

 5–10 MINS 40 MINS

SERVES 4

INGREDIENTS

60 g/2 oz/¼ cup butter

1 small onion, chopped

90 g/3 oz/⅓ cup red lentils

300 ml/½ pint/1¼ cups vegetable stock

60 g/2 oz/½ cup blanched almonds

60 g/2 oz/½ cup pine nuts

½ tsp ground coriander

½ tsp ground cumin

½ tsp grated root ginger

1 tsp chopped fresh coriander (cilantro)

salt and pepper

sprigs of fresh coriander
  (cilantro) to garnish

TO SERVE

fresh vegetable crudités

bread sticks

VARIATION

Green or brown lentils can be used, but they will take longer to cook than red lentils. If you wish, substitute peanuts for the almonds. Ground ginger can be used instead of fresh – substitute ½ teaspoon and add it with the other spices.

1 Melt half the butter in a saucepan and fry the onion over a medium heat, stirring frequently, until golden brown.

2 Add the lentils and vegetable stock. Bring to the boil, then reduce the heat and simmer gently, uncovered, for about 25–30 minutes, until the lentils are tender. Drain well.

3 Melt the remaining butter in a small frying pan (skillet). Add the almonds and pine nuts and fry them over a low heat, stirring frequently, until golden brown. Remove from the heat.

4 Put the lentils, almonds and pine nuts, with any remaining butter, into a food processor blender. Add the ground coriander, cumin, ginger and fresh coriander (cilantro). Process for about 15–20 seconds, until the mixture is smooth. Alternatively, press the lentils through a strainer to purée them and then mix with the finely chopped nuts, spices and herbs.

5 Season the dip with salt and pepper and garnish with sprigs of fresh coriander (cilantro). Serve with fresh vegetable crudités and bread sticks.

Cheese, Garlic & Herb Pâté

This wonderful soft cheese pâté is fragrant with the aroma of fresh herbs and garlic. Serve with triangles of Melba toast for a perfect starter.

NUTRITIONAL INFORMATION

Calories	392	Sugars	.........1g
Protein	........17g	Fat	..........28g
Carbohydrate	...18g	Saturates	......18g

20 MINS   10 MINS

SERVES 4

I N G R E D I E N T S

15 g/½ oz/1 tbsp butter

1 garlic clove, crushed

3 spring onions (scallions), finely chopped

125 g/4½ oz/½ cup full-fat soft cheese

2 tbsp chopped mixed herbs,
      such as parsley, chives, marjoram,
      oregano and basil

175 g/6 oz/1½ cups finely grated mature
      (sharp) Cheddar cheese

pepper

4–6 slices of white bread from a
      medium-cut sliced loaf

mixed salad leaves (greens) and cherry
tomatoes, to serve

T O   G A R N I S H

ground paprika

herb sprigs

1 Melt the butter in a small frying pan (skillet) and gently fry the garlic and spring onions (scallions) together for 3–4 minutes, until softened. Allow to cool.

2 Beat the soft cheese in a large mixing bowl until smooth, then add the garlic and spring onions (scallions). Stir in the herbs, mixing well.

3 Add the Cheddar and work the mixture together to form a stiff paste. Cover and chill until ready to serve.

4 To make the Melba toast, toast the slices of bread on both sides, and then cut off the crusts. Using a sharp bread knife, cut through the slices horizontally to make very thin slices. Cut into triangles and then lightly grill (broil) the untoasted sides until golden.

5 Arrange the mixed salad leaves (greens) on 4 serving plates with the cherry tomatoes. Pile the cheese pâté on top and sprinkle with a little paprika. Garnish with sprigs of fresh herbs and serve with the Melba toast.

Walnut, Egg & Cheese Pâté

This unusual pâté, flavoured with parsley and dill, can be served with crackers, crusty bread or toast. The pâté requires chilling until set.

NUTRITIONAL INFORMATION

Calories ....438 Sugars 2g
Protein ....21g Fat 38g
Carbohydrate ....2g Saturates 18g

 20 MINS   2 MINS

SERVES 2

INGREDIENTS

1 celery stick

1–2 spring onions (scallions), trimmed

25 g/1 oz/¼ cup shelled walnuts

1 tbsp chopped fresh parsley

1 tsp chopped fresh dill or ½ tsp dried dill

1 garlic clove, crushed

dash of vegetarian Worcestershire sauce

125 g/4½ oz/½ cup cottage cheese

60 g/2 oz/½ cup blue cheese, such as
    Stilton or Danish Blue

1 hard-boiled (hard-cooked) egg

25 g/1 oz/2 tbsp butter

salt and pepper

herbs, to garnish

crackers, toast or crusty bread and
    crudités, to serve

COOK'S TIP

You can also use this as a stuffing for vegetables. Cut the tops off extra-large tomatoes, scoop out the seeds and fill with the pâté, piling it well up, or spoon into the hollows of celery sticks cut into 5 cm/2 inch pieces.

1 Finely chop the celery, slice the spring onions (scallions) very finely and chop the walnuts evenly. Place in a bowl.

2 Add the chopped herbs and garlic and Worcestershire sauce to taste and mix well, then stir the cottage cheese evenly through the mixture.

3 Grate the blue cheese and hard-boiled (hard-cooked) egg finely into the pâté mixture, and season with salt and pepper.

4 Melt the butter and stir through the pâté, then spoon into one serving dish or two individual dishes, but do not press down firmly. Chill until set.

5 Garnish with fresh herbs and serve with crackers, toast or fresh, crusty bread and a few crudités, if liked.

Lentil Pâté

Red lentils are used in this spicy recipe for speed as they do not require pre-soaking. You can substitute other types of lentils, if preferred.

NUTRITIONAL INFORMATION

Calories 267   Sugars 12g
Protein . . . . .14g   Fat 8g
Carbohydrate . . .37g   Saturates 1g

30 MINS   1¼ HOURS

SERVES 4

I N G R E D I E N T S

1 tbsp vegetable oil, plus extra for greasing

1 onion, chopped

2 garlic cloves, crushed

1 tsp garam masala

½ tsp ground coriander

850 ml/1½ pints/3¾ cups vegetable stock

175 g/6 oz/¾ cup red lentils

1 small egg

2 tbsp milk

2 tbsp mango chutney

2 tbsp chopped parsley

fresh parsley sprigs, to garnish

salad leaves (greens) and toast, to serve

1 Heat the oil in a large saucepan and sauté the onion and garlic, stirring constantly, for 2–3 minutes. Add the spices and cook for a further 30 seconds.

2 Stir in the stock and lentils and bring the mixture to the boil. Reduce the heat and simmer for 20 minutes, until the lentils are cooked and softened. Remove the pan from the heat and drain off any excess moisture.

3 Put the mixture in a food processor and add the egg, milk, mango chutney and parsley. Process until smooth.

4 Grease and line the base of a 450 g/ 1 lb loaf tin (pan) and spoon in the mixture, levelling the surface. Cover and cook in a preheated oven, 200°C/400°F/ Gas Mark 6, for 40–45 minutes, or until firm to the touch.

5 Cool in the tin (pan) for 20 minutes, then transfer to the refrigerator.

6 Turn out the pâté on to a serving plate, slice and garnish with fresh parsley. Serve with salad leaves (greens) and toast.

COOK'S TIP

It is always better to make your own stock, if you have time, rather than use stock cubes, as the flavour of homemade stock is far superior.

Mixed Bean Pâté

This is a really quick starter to prepare if canned beans are used. Choose a wide variety of beans for colour and flavour.

NUTRITIONAL INFORMATION

Calories	126	Sugars	.........3g
Protein	.........5g	Fat	...........6g
Carbohydrate	...13g	Saturates	.......1g

  45 MINS   0 MINS

SERVES 4

I N G R E D I E N T S

400 g/14 oz can mixed beans, drained

2 tbsp olive oil

juice of 1 lemon

2 garlic cloves, crushed

1 tbsp chopped coriander (cilantro)

2 spring onions (scallions), chopped

salt and pepper

shredded spring onions (scallions),
   to garnish

1 Rinse the beans thoroughly under cold running water and drain well.

2 Transfer the beans to a food processor or blender and process until smooth. Alternatively, place the beans in a bowl and mash thoroughly with a fork or potato masher.

3 Add the olive oil, lemon juice, garlic, coriander (cilantro) and spring onions (scallions) and blend until fairly smooth. Season with salt and pepper to taste.

4 Transfer the pâté to a serving bowl and chill in the refrigerator for at least 30 minutes.

5 Garnish with shredded spring onions (scallions) and serve.

Avocado Cream Terrine

The smooth, rich taste of ripe avocados combines well with thick, creamy yogurt and single (light) cream to make this impressive terrine.

NUTRITIONAL INFORMATION

Calories 327   Sugars 3g
Protein ....6g   Fat 32g
Carbohydrate ....4g   Saturates 8g

2¼ HOURS   0 MINS

SERVES 6

I N G R E D I E N T S

2 ripe avocados

4 tbsp cold water

2 tsp vegetarian gelatine (gelozone)

1 tbsp lemon juice

4 tbsp mayonnaise

150 ml/¼ pint/⅔ cup thick natural
   (unsweetened) yogurt

150 ml/¼ pint/⅔ cup single (light) cream

salt and pepper

mixed salad leaves (greens), to serve

T O   G A R N I S H

cucumber slices

nasturtium flowers

1 Peel the avocados and remove and discard the stones (pits). Put the flesh in a blender or food processor or a large bowl, together with the water, vegetarian gelatine (gelozone), lemon juice, mayonnaise, yogurt and cream. Season to taste with salt and pepper.

2 Process for about 10–15 seconds, or beat by hand, using a fork or whisk, until smooth.

3 Transfer the mixture to a small saucepan and heat gently, stirring constantly, until just boiling.

4 Pour the mixture into a 900 ml/ 1½ pint/3½ cup plastic food storage box or terrine and smooth the top. Allow the mixture to cool and set, and then leave to chill in the refrigerator for about 1½–2 hours.

5 Turn the mixture out of its container and cut into neat slices. Arrange a bed of salad leaves (greens) on 6 serving plates. Place a slice of avocado terrine on top and garnish with cucumber slices and nasturtium flowers.

Toasted Nibbles

These tiny cheese balls are rolled in fresh herbs, toasted nuts or paprika to make tasty nibbles for parties, buffets, or pre-dinner drinks.

NUTRITIONAL INFORMATION

Calories . . . . .310 Sugars 1g
Protein . . . . .15g Fat 27g
Carbohydrate . . . .1g Saturates 12g

40 MINS   5 MINS

SERVES 4

I N G R E D I E N T S

125 g/4½ oz/½ cup ricotta cheese

125 g/4½ oz/1 cup finely grated Double
   Gloucester (brick) cheese

2 tsp chopped parsley

60 g/2 oz/½ cup chopped mixed nuts

3 tbsp chopped herbs, such as parsley,
   chives, marjoram, lovage and chervil

2 tbsp mild paprika

pepper

herb sprigs, to garnish

1 Mix together the ricotta and Double Gloucester (brick) cheeses. Add the parsley and pepper and work together until thoroughly combined.

2 Form the mixture into small balls and place on a plate. Cover and chill in the refrigerator for about 20 minutes, until they are firm.

3 Scatter the chopped nuts on to a baking tray (cookie sheet) and place them under a preheated grill (broiler) until lightly browned. Take care as they can easily burn. Leave them to cool.

4 Sprinkle the nuts, herbs and paprika into 3 separate small bowls. Remove the cheese balls from the refrigerator and

divide into 3 equal piles. Roll 1 quantity of the cheese balls in the nuts, 1 quantity in the herbs and 1 quantity in the paprika until they are all well coated.

5 Arrange the coated cheese balls alternately on a large serving platter. Chill in the refrigerator until ready to serve and then garnish with sprigs of fresh herbs.

Spinach Filo Baskets

If you use frozen spinach, it only needs to be thawed and drained before being mixed with the cheeses and seasonings.

NUTRITIONAL INFORMATION

Calories	533	Sugars	........3g
Protein	........24g	Fat	..........38g
Carbohydrate	...26g	Saturates	......22g

55 MINS   30 MINS

MAKES 2

INGREDIENTS

125 g/4½ oz/3 cups fresh leaf spinach,
   washed and chopped roughly, or
   90 g/3 oz/½ cup thawed frozen spinach

2–4 spring onions (scallions), trimmed and
   chopped, or 1 tbsp finely chopped onion

1 garlic clove, crushed

2 tbsp grated Parmesan cheese

90 g/3 oz/¾ cup grated mature (sharp)
   Cheddar cheese

pinch of ground allspice

1 egg yolk

4 sheets filo pastry

25 g/1 oz/2 tbsp butter, melted

salt and pepper

2 spring onions (scallions), to garnish

1 If using fresh spinach, cook it in the minimum of boiling salted water for 3–4 minutes, until tender. Drain very thoroughly, using a potato masher to remove excess liquid, then chop and put into a bowl. If using frozen spinach, simply drain and chop.

2 Add the spring onions (scallions) or onion, garlic, cheeses, allspice, egg yolk and seasoning, and mix well.

3 Grease 2 individual Yorkshire pudding tins (muffin pans), or ovenproof dishes or tins (pans) about 12 cm/5 inches in diameter, and 4 cm/1½ inches deep. Cut the filo pastry sheets in half to make 8 pieces and brush each lightly with melted butter.

4 Place one piece of filo pastry in a tin (pan) or dish and then cover with a second piece at right angles to the first. Add two more pieces at right angles, so that all the corners are in different places. Line the other tin (pan) in the same way.

5 Spoon the spinach mixture into the 'baskets' and cook in a preheated oven, 180°C/350°F/Gas Mark 4, for about 20 minutes, or until the pastry is golden brown. Garnish with a spring onion (scallion) tassel and serve hot or cold.

6 Make spring onion (scallion) tassels about 30 minutes before required. Trim off the root end and cut to a length of 5–7 cm/2–3 inches. Make a series of cuts from the green end to within 2 cm/¾ inch of the other end. Place in a bowl of iced water to open out. Drain well before use.

Feta Cheese Tartlets

These crisp-baked bread cases, filled with sliced tomatoes, feta cheese, black olives and quail's eggs, are quick to make and taste delicious.

NUTRITIONAL INFORMATION

Calories 570   Sugars 3g
Protein . . . . .14g   Fat 42g
Carbohydrate . . .36g   Saturates 23g

30 MINS   10 MINS

SERVES 4

I N G R E D I E N T S

8 slices bread from a medium-cut large loaf

125 g/4½ oz/ ½ cup butter, melted

125 g/4½ oz feta cheese,
   cut into small cubes

4 cherry tomatoes, cut into wedges

8 pitted black or green olives, halved

8 quail's eggs, hard-boiled (hard-cooked)

2 tbsp olive oil

1 tbsp wine vinegar

1 tsp wholegrain mustard

pinch of caster (superfine) sugar

salt and pepper

parsley sprigs, to garnish

1 Remove the crusts from the bread. Trim the bread into squares and flatten each piece with a rolling pin.

2 Brush the bread with melted butter, and then arrange them in bun or muffin tins (pans). Press a piece of crumpled foil into each bread case to secure in place. Bake in a preheated oven, 190°C/375°F/Gas Mark 5, for about 10 minutes, or until crisp and browned.

3 Meanwhile, mix together the feta cheese, tomatoes and olives. Shell the eggs and quarter them. Mix together the

olive oil, vinegar, mustard and sugar. Season to taste with salt and pepper.

4 Remove the bread cases from the oven and discard the foil. Leave to cool.

5 Just before serving, fill the bread cases with the cheese and tomato mixture. Arrange the eggs on top and spoon over the dressing. Garnish with parsley sprigs.

Tzatziki & Black Olive Dip

Tzatziki is a Greek dish, made with yogurt, mint and cucumber.
It tastes superb with warm pitta (pocket) bread.

NUTRITIONAL INFORMATION

Calories	381	Sugars	. . . . .8g
Protein	. . . . .11g	Fat	. . . . .15g
Carbohydrate	. . .52g	Saturates	. . . . . . .2g

 1 HOUR   3 MINS

SERVES 4

I N G R E D I E N T S

½ cucumber

225 g/8 oz/1 cup thick natural
(unsweetened) yogurt

1 tbsp chopped mint

salt and pepper

4 pitta (pocket) breads

D I P

2 garlic cloves, crushed

125 g/4½ oz/1 cup pitted black olives

4 tbsp olive oil

2 tbsp lemon juice

1 tbsp chopped parsley

T O   G A R N I S H

mint sprigs

parsley sprigs

COOK'S TIP

Sprinkling the cucumber
with salt draws out some of its
moisture, making it crisper. If
you are in a hurry, you can omit
this procedure. Use green olives
instead of black ones if you prefer.

1 To make the tzatziki, peel the cucumber and chop roughly. Sprinkle it with salt and leave to stand for 15–20 minutes. Rinse with cold water and drain well.

2 Mix the cucumber, yogurt and mint together. Season to taste with salt and pepper and transfer to a serving bowl. Cover and chill for 20–30 minutes.

3 To make the black olive dip, put the crushed garlic and olives into a blender or food processor and process for 15–20 seconds. Alternatively, chop them very finely.

4 Add the olive oil, lemon juice and parsley to the blender or food processor and process for a few more seconds. Alternatively, mix with the chopped garlic and olives and mash together. Season with salt and pepper.

5 Wrap the pitta (pocket) breads in foil and place over a barbecue for 2–3 minutes, turning once to warm through. Alternatively, heat in the oven or under the grill (broiler). Cut into pieces and serve with the tzatziki and black olive dip, garnished with sprigs of fresh mint and parsley.

Hummus & Garlic Toasts

Hummus is a real favourite spread on these flavoursome garlic toasts for a delicious starter or snack.

NUTRITIONAL INFORMATION

Calories . . . . .731 Sugars 2g
Protein . . . . .22g Fat 55g
Carbohydrate . . .39g Saturates 8g

 20 MINS 3 MINS

SERVES 4

INGREDIENTS

HUMMUS

400 g/14 oz can chickpeas
   (garbanzo beans)

juice of 1 large lemon

6 tbsp tahini (sesame seed paste)

2 tbsp olive oil

2 garlic cloves, crushed

salt and pepper

chopped coriander (cilantro) and
   black olives, to garnish

TOASTS

1 ciabatta loaf (Italian bread), sliced

2 garlic cloves, crushed

1 tbsp chopped coriander (cilantro)

4 tbsp olive oil

COOK'S TIP

Make the hummus 1 day in advance, and chill, covered, in the refrigerator until required. Garnish and serve.

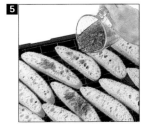

1 To make the hummus, firstly drain the chickpeas (garbanzo beans), reserving a little of the liquid. Put the chickpeas (garbanzo beans) and liquid in a food processor and process, gradually adding the reserved liquid and lemon juice. Blend well after each addition until smooth.

2 Stir in the tahini (sesame seed paste) and all but 1 teaspoon of the olive oil. Add the garlic, season to taste and blend again until smooth.

3 Spoon the hummus into a serving dish and smooth the top. Drizzle the remaining olive oil over the top, garnish with chopped coriander (cilantro) and olives. Set aside in the refrigerator to chill while you are preparing the toasts.

4 Place the slices of ciabatta (Italian bread) on a grill (broiler) rack in a single layer.

5 Mix the garlic, coriander (cilantro) and olive oil together and drizzle over the bread slices. Cook under a hot grill (broiler), turning once, for about 2–3 minutes, until golden brown. Serve the toasts immediately with the hummus.

Onions à la Grecque

This is a well-known method of cooking vegetables
and is perfect with shallots or onions, served with a crisp salad.

NUTRITIONAL INFORMATION

Calories	200	Sugars	........26g
Protein	.........2g	Fat	...........9g
Carbohydrate	...28g	Saturates	.......1g

  10 MINS   15 MINS

SERVES 4

I N G R E D I E N T S

450 g/1 lb shallots

3 tbsp olive oil

3 tbsp clear honey

2 tbsp garlic wine vinegar

3 tbsp dry white wine

1 tbsp tomato purée (paste)

2 celery stalks, sliced

2 tomatoes, seeded and chopped

salt and pepper

chopped celery leaves, to garnish

1 Peel the shallots. Heat the oil in a large saucepan, add the shallots and cook, stirring, for 3–5 minutes, or until they begin to brown.

2 Add the honey and cook over a high heat for a further 30 seconds, then add the garlic wine vinegar and dry white wine, stirring well.

3 Stir in the tomato purée (paste), celery and tomatoes and bring the mixture to the boil. Cook over a high heat for 5–6 minutes. Season to taste and leave to cool slightly.

4 Garnish with chopped celery leaves and serve warm. Alternatively chill in the refrigerator before serving.

Spanish Tortilla

This classic Spanish dish is often served as part of a tapas (appetizer) selection. A variety of cooked vegetables can be added to this recipe.

NUTRITIONAL INFORMATION

Calories 430   Sugars 6g
Protein ....16g   Fat 20g
Carbohydrate ...50g   Saturates 4g

10 MINS   35 MINS

SERVES 4

I N G R E D I E N T S

1 kg/2 lb 4 oz waxy potatoes, thinly sliced

4 tbsp vegetable oil

1 onion, sliced

2 garlic cloves, crushed

1 green (bell) pepper, seeded and diced

2 tomatoes, seeded and chopped

25 g/1 oz canned sweetcorn (corn), drained

6 large eggs, beaten

2 tbsp chopped parsley

salt and pepper

1 Parboil the potatoes in a saucepan of lightly salted boiling water for 5 minutes. Drain well.

2 Heat the oil in a large frying pan (skillet), add the potato and onions and sauté over a low heat, stirring

constantly, for 5 minutes, until the potatoes have browned.

3 Add the garlic, diced (bell) pepper, chopped tomatoes and sweetcorn (corn), mixing well.

4 Pour in the eggs and add the chopped parsley. Season well with salt and pepper. Cook for 10-12 minutes, until the underside is cooked through.

5 Remove the frying pan (skillet) from the heat and continue to cook the tortilla under a preheated medium grill (broiler) for 5-7 minutes, or until the tortilla is set and the top is golden brown.

6 Cut the tortilla into wedges or cubes, depending on your preference, and transfer to serving dishes. Serve with salad. In Spain tortillas are served hot, cold or warm.

COOK'S TIP

Ensure that the handle of your pan is heatproof before placing it under the grill (broiler) and be sure to use an oven glove when removing it as it will be very hot.

Fiery Salsa

Make this Mexican-style salsa to perk up jaded palates. Its lively flavours really get the tastebuds going. Serve with hot tortilla chips.

NUTRITIONAL INFORMATION

Calories 328   Sugars 2g
Protein . . . . .4g   Fat 26g
Carbohydrate . . .21g   Saturates 5g

🍲 30 MINS   ⏲ 0 MINS

SERVES 4

INGREDIENTS

2 small fresh red chillies

1 tbsp lime or lemon juice

2 large ripe avocados

5 cm/2 inch piece of cucumber

2 tomatoes, peeled

1 small garlic clove, crushed

few drops of Tabasco sauce

salt and pepper

lime or lemon slices, to garnish

tortilla chips, to serve

1 Remove and discard the stem and seeds from 1 fresh red chilli. Chop the flesh very finely and place in a large mixing bowl.

2 To make a chilli 'flower' for garnish, using a small, sharp knife, slice the remaining chilli from the stem to the tip several times without removing the stem. Place in a bowl of iced water, so that the 'petals' open out.

3 Add the lime or lemon juice to the mixing bowl. Halve, stone (pit) and peel the avocados. Add the flesh to the mixing bowl and mash thoroughly with a fork. The salsa should be slightly chunky. (The lime or lemon juice prevents the avocado from turning brown.)

4 Chop the cucumber and tomatoes finely and add to the avocado mixture with the crushed garlic.

5 Stir in the Tabasco sauce and season with salt and pepper. Transfer the dip to a serving bowl. Garnish with slices of lime or lemon and the chilli flower.

6 Put the bowl on a large plate, surround with tortilla chips and serve. Do not keep this dip standing for long or it will discolour.

Spring Rolls

Thin slices of vegetables are wrapped in pastry and deep-fried until crisp. Spring roll wrappers are available fresh or frozen.

NUTRITIONAL INFORMATION

Calories	186	Sugars	.........2g
Protein	.........4g	Fat	...........11g
Carbohydrate	...18g	Saturates	.......1g

🔔 45 MINS   🕐 25–30 MINS

MAKES 12

I N G R E D I E N T S

5 Chinese dried mushrooms (if unavailable,
   use open-cup mushrooms)

1 large carrot

60 g/2 oz/1 cup canned bamboo shoots

2 spring onions (scallions)

60 g/2 oz Chinese leaves (cabbage)

2 tbsp vegetable oil

225 g/8 oz/4 cups beansprouts

1 tbsp soy sauce

12 spring roll wrappers

1 egg, beaten

vegetable oil, for deep-frying

salt

1 Place the dried mushrooms in a small bowl and cover with warm water. Leave to soak for 20–25 minutes.

COOK'S TIP

If spring roll wrappers are unavailable, use sheets of filo pastry instead.

2 Drain the mushrooms and squeeze out the excess water. Remove the tough centres and slice the mushroom caps thinly. Cut the carrot and bamboo shoots into very thin julienne strips. Chop the spring onions (scallions) and shred the Chinese leaves (cabbage).

3 Heat the 2 tablespoons of oil in a wok. Add the mushrooms, carrot and bamboo shoots and stir-fry for 2 minutes. Add the spring onions (scallions), Chinese leaves (cabbage), beansprouts and soy sauce. Season with salt and stir-fry for 2 minutes. Leave to cool.

4 Divide the mixture into 12 equal portions and place one portion on the edge of each spring roll wrapper. Fold in the sides and roll each one up, brushing the join with a little beaten egg to seal.

5 Deep-fry the spring rolls in batches in hot oil in a wok or large saucepan for 4–5 minutes, or until golden and crispy. Take care that the oil is not too hot or the spring rolls will brown on the outside before cooking on the inside. Remove and drain on kitchen paper (paper towels). Keep each batch warm while the others are being cooked. Serve at once.

Tofu (Bean Curd) Tempura

Crispy coated vegetables and tofu (bean curd) accompanied by a sweet, spicy dip give a real taste of the Orient in this Japanese-style dish.

NUTRITIONAL INFORMATION

Calories	582	Sugars	........10g
Protein	........16g	Fat	..........27g
Carbohydrate	...65g	Saturates	.......4g

 15 MINS   20 MINS

SERVES 4

I N G R E D I E N T S

125 g/4½ oz baby courgettes (zucchini)

125 g/4½ oz baby carrots

125 g/4½ oz baby corn cobs

125 g/4½ oz baby leeks

2 baby aubergines (eggplants)

225 g/8 oz tofu (bean curd)

vegetable oil, for deep-frying

julienne strips of carrot, root ginger and
    baby leek to garnish

noodles, to serve

B A T T E R

2 egg yolks

300 ml/½ pint/1¼ cups water

225 g/8 oz/2 cups plain (all-purpose) flour

D I P P I N G   S A U C E

5 tbsp mirin or dry sherry

5 tbsp Japanese soy sauce

2 tsp clear honey

1 garlic clove, crushed

1 tsp grated root ginger

1 Slice the courgettes (zucchini) and carrots in half lengthways. Trim the corn. Trim the leeks at both ends. Quarter the aubergines (eggplants). Cut the tofu (bean curd) into 2.5 cm/1 inch cubes.

2 To make the batter, mix the egg yolks with the water. Sift in 175 g/6 oz/1½ cups of the flour and beat with a balloon whisk to form a thick batter. Don't worry if there are any lumps. Heat the oil for deep-frying to 180°C/350°F or until a cube of bread browns in 30 seconds.

3 Place the remaining flour on a large plate and toss the vegetables and tofu (bean curd) until lightly coated.

4 Dip the tofu (bean curd) in the batter and deep-fry for 2–3 minutes, until lightly golden. Drain on kitchen paper (paper towels) and keep warm.

5 Dip the vegetables in the batter and deep-fry, a few at a time, for 3–4 minutes, until golden. Drain and place on a warmed serving plate.

6 To make the dipping sauce, mix all the ingredients together. Serve with the vegetables and tofu (bean curd), accompanied with noodles and garnished with julienne strips of vegetables.

Mixed Bhajis

These small bhajis are often served as accompaniments to a main meal, but they are delicious as a starter with a small salad and yogurt sauce.

NUTRITIONAL INFORMATION

Calories 414   Sugars 7g
Protein . . . . .9g   Fat 26g
Carbohydrate . . .38g   Saturates 3g

 25 MINS   30 MINS

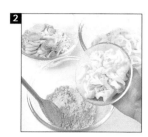

SERVES 4

I N G R E D I E N T S

B H A J I S

175 g/6 oz/1¼ cups gram flour

1 tsp bicarbonate of soda (baking soda)

2 tsp ground coriander

1 tsp garam masala

1½ tsp turmeric

1½ tsp chilli powder

2 tbsp chopped coriander (cilantro)

1 small onion, halved and sliced

1 small leek, sliced

100 g/3½ oz cooked cauliflower

9-12 tbsp cold water

salt and pepper

vegetable oil, for deep-frying

S A U C E

150 ml/¼ pint/⅔ cup natural
   (unsweetened) yogurt

2 tbsp chopped mint

½ tsp turmeric

1 garlic clove, crushed

mint sprigs, to garnish

1 Sift the flour, bicarbonate of soda (baking soda) and salt to taste into a mixing bowl and add the spices and fresh coriander (cilantro). Mix thoroughly.

2 Divide the mixture into 3 and place in separate bowls. Stir the onion into one bowl, the leek into another and the cauliflower into the third bowl. Add 3–4 tbsp of water to each bowl and mix each to form a smooth paste.

3 Heat the oil for deep-frying in a deep fryer to 180°C/350°F or until a cube of bread browns in 30 seconds. Using 2 dessert spoons, form the mixture into rounds and cook each in the oil for 3–4 minutes, until browned. Remove with a slotted spoon and drain well on absorbent kitchen paper (paper towels). Keep the bhajis warm in the oven while cooking the remainder.

4 Mix all of the sauce ingredients together and pour into a small serving bowl. Garnish with mint sprigs and serve with the warm bhajis.

Hyderabad Pickles

This is a very versatile dish that will go with almost anything and can be served warm or cold. It is perfect as a starter for a dinner party.

NUTRITIONAL INFORMATION

Calories ....732 Sugars 6g
Protein ....6g Fat 75g
Carbohydrate ....8g Saturates 10g

30 MINS   30 MINS

SERVES 6

INGREDIENTS

2 tsp ground coriander

2 tsp ground cumin

2 tsp desiccated (shredded) coconut

2 tsp sesame seeds

1 tsp mixed mustard and onion seeds

300 ml/½ pint/1¼ cups vegetable oil

3 medium onions, sliced

1 tsp finely chopped root ginger

1 tsp crushed garlic

½ tsp turmeric

1½ tsp chilli powder

1½ tsp salt

3 medium aubergines (eggplants),
   halved lengthways

1 tbsp tamarind paste

300 ml/½ pint/1¼ cups water

3 hard-boiled (hard-cooked eggs, halved,
   to garnish

BAGHAAR

1 tsp mixed onion and mustard seeds

1 tsp cumin seeds

4 dried red chillies

150 ml/¼ pint/⅔ cup vegetable oil

coriander (cilantro) leaves

1 green chilli, finely chopped

 Dry-fry the ground coriander, cumin, coconut, sesame seeds and mustard and onion seeds in a pan. Grind in a pestle and mortar or food processor and set aside.

2 Heat the oil in a frying pan (skillet) and fry the onions until golden. Reduce the heat and add the ginger, garlic, turmeric, chilli powder and salt, stirring. Leave to cool, then grind this mixture to form a paste.

3 Make 4 cuts across each aubergine (eggplant) half. Blend the spices with the onion paste. Spoon this mixture into the slits in the aubergines (eggplants).

4 In a bowl, mix the tamarind paste and 3 tbsp water to make a fine paste and set aside.

5 For the baghaar, fry the onion and mustard seeds, cumin seeds and chillies in the oil. Reduce the heat, place the aubergines (eggplants) in the baghaar and stir gently. Stir in the tamarind paste and remaining water and cook over a medium heat for 15–20 minutes. Add the coriander (cilantro) and chillies.

6 When cool, transfer to a serving dish and serve garnished with the hard-boiled (hard-cooked) eggs.

Garlicky Mushroom Pakoras

Whole mushrooms are dunked in a spiced garlicky batter and deep-fried until golden. They are at their most delicious served piping hot.

NUTRITIONAL INFORMATION

Calories 297	Sugars 3g
Protein 5g	Fat 21g
Carbohydrate ...24g	Saturates 2g

20 MINS   10-15 MINS

SERVES 6

I N G R E D I E N T S

175 g/6 oz/1½ cups gram flour

½ tsp salt

¼ tsp baking powder

1 tsp cumin seeds

½-1 tsp chilli powder

200 ml/7 fl oz/scant 1cup water

2 garlic cloves, crushed

1 small onion, finely chopped

vegetable oil, for deep-frying

500 g/1 lb 2 oz button mushrooms,
    trimmed and wiped

lemon wedges and coriander (cilantro)
    sprigs, to garnish

COOK'S TIP

Gram flour, also known as besan flour, is a pale yellow flour made from chickpeas. It is now readily available from larger supermarkets, as well as Indian food shops and some ethnic delicatessens. Gram flour is also used to make onion bhajis.

1 Put the gram flour, salt, baking powder, cumin and chilli powder into a bowl and mix well together. Make a well in the centre of the mixture and gradually stir in the water, mixing thoroughly to form a batter.

2 Stir the crushed garlic and the chopped onion into the batter and leave the mixture to infuse for 10 minutes. One-third fill a deep-fat fryer or pan with vegetable oil and heat to 180°C/350°F or until a cube of bread browns in 30 seconds. Lower the basket into the hot oil.

3 Meanwhile, mix the mushrooms into the batter, stirring to coat. Remove a few at a time and place them into the hot oil. Fry for about 2 minutes, or until golden brown.

4 Remove the mushrooms from the pan with a slotted spoon and drain on kitchen paper (paper towels) while you are cooking the remainder in the same way.

5 Serve hot, sprinkled with coarse salt and garnished with lemon wedges and coriander (cilantro) sprigs.

Dumplings in Yogurt Sauce

Adding a baghaar (seasoned oil dressing) just before serving makes this a mouth-watering accompaniment to any meal.

NUTRITIONAL INFORMATION

Calories 719   Sugars 9g
Protein . . . . .9g   Fat 60g
Carbohydrate . . .38g   Saturates 7g

 35 MINS   35 MINS

SERVES 4

I N G R E D I E N T S

D U M P L I N G S

100 g/3½ oz/¾ cup gram flour

1 tsp chilli powder

½ tsp bicarbonate of soda (baking soda)

1 medium onion, finely chopped

2 green chillies

coriander (cilantro) leaves

150 ml/¼ pint/⅔ cup water

300 ml/½ pint/1¼ cups vegetable oil

salt

Y O G U R T   S A U C E

300 ml/½ pint/1¼ cups natural
   (unsweetened) yogurt

3 tbsp gram flour

150 ml/¼ pint/⅔ cup water

1 tsp chopped root ginger

1 tsp crushed garlic

1½ tsp chilli powder

½ tsp turmeric

1 tsp ground coriander

1 tsp ground cumin

S E A S O N E D   D R E S S I N G

150 ml/¼ pint/⅔ cup vegetable oil

1 tsp white cumin seeds

6 dried red chillies

1 To make the dumplings, sift the gram flour into a large bowl. Add the chilli powder, ½ teaspoon salt, bicarbonate of soda (baking soda), onion, green chillies and coriander (cilantro) and mix. Add the water and mix to form a thick paste. Heat the oil in a frying pan (skillet). Place teaspoonfuls of the paste in the oil and fry over a medium heat, turning once, until a crisp golden brown. Set aside.

2 To make the sauce, place the yogurt in a bowl and whisk with the gram flour and the water. Add all of the spices and 1½ teaspoons salt and mix well.

3 Press this mixture through a large strainer into a saucepan. Bring to a boil over a low heat, stirring constantly. If the yogurt sauce becomes too thick, add a little extra water.

4 Pour the sauce into a deep serving dish and arrange all the dumplings on top. Set aside and keep warm.

5 To make the dressing, heat the oil in a frying pan (skillet). Add the white cumin seeds and the dried red chillies and fry until darker in colour and giving off their aroma. Pour the dressing over the dumplings and serve hot.

Samosas

Samosas, which are a sort of Indian Cornish pasty, make excellent snacks. In India, they are popular snacks at roadside stalls.

NUTRITIONAL INFORMATION

Calories	.261	Sugars	.0.4g
Protein	.2g	Fat	.23g
Carbohydrate	.13g	Saturates	.4g

  40 MINS 40 MINS

MAKES 12

INGREDIENTS

PASTRY

100 g/3½ oz/¾ cup self-raising (self-rising) flour

½ tsp salt

40 g/1½ oz/3 tbsp butter, cut into small pieces

4 tbsp water

FILLING

3 medium potatoes, boiled

1 tsp finely chopped ginger root

1 tsp crushed garlic

½ tsp white cumin seeds

½ tsp mixed onion and mustard seeds

1 tsp salt

½ tsp crushed red chillies

2 tbsp lemon juice

2 small green chillies, finely chopped

ghee or oil, for deep-frying

1 Sift the flour and salt into a bowl. Add the butter and rub into the flour until the mixture resembles fine breadcrumbs.

2 Pour in the water and mix with a fork to form a dough. Pat it into a ball and knead for 5 minutes, or until smooth. Cover and leave to rise.

3 To make the filling, mash the boiled potatoes gently and mix with the ginger, garlic, white cumin seeds, onion and mustard seeds, salt, crushed red chillies, lemon juice and green chillies.

4 Break small balls off the dough and roll each out very thinly to form a round. Cut in half, dampen the edges and shape into cones. Fill the cones with a little of the filling, dampen the top and bottom edges of the cones and pinch together to seal. Set aside.

5 Fill a deep pan one-third full with oil and heat to 180°C/350°F or until a small cube of bread browns in 30 seconds. Carefully lower the samosas into the oil, a few at a time, and fry for 2-3 minutes, or until golden brown. Remove from the oil and drain thoroughly on kitchen paper (paper towels). Serve hot or cold.

Vegetable Timbales

This is a great way to serve pasta as a starter, wrapped in an aubergine (eggplant) mould (mold). It looks really impressive, yet it is very easy.

NUTRITIONAL INFORMATION

Calories 291	Sugars 11g	
Protein 8g	Fat 18g	
Carbohydrate . . .25g	Saturates 4g	

30 MINS   45 MINS

SERVES 4

INGREDIENTS

1 large aubergine (eggplant)

50 g/1¾ oz/½ cup macaroni

1 tbsp vegetable oil

1 onion, chopped

2 garlic cloves, crushed

2 tbsp drained canned sweetcorn

2 tbsp frozen peas, thawed

100 g/3½ oz spinach

25 g/1 oz/¼ cup grated Cheddar cheese

1 egg, beaten

225 g/8 oz/3 cups canned,
  chopped tomatoes

1 tbsp chopped basil

salt and pepper

SAUCE

4 tbsp olive oil

2 tbsp white wine vinegar

2 garlic cloves, crushed

3 tbsp chopped basil

1 tbsp caster (superfine) sugar

1 Cut the aubergine (eggplant) lengthways into thin strips, using a potato peeler. Place in a bowl of salted boiling water and leave to stand for 3–4 minutes. Drain well.

2 Lightly grease four 150 ml/¼ pint/⅔ cup individual ramekin dishes and use the aubergine (eggplant) slices to line the dishes, leaving 2.5 cm/1 inch of aubergine (eggplant) overlapping.

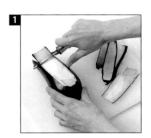

3 Cook the pasta in a pan of boiling water for 8–10 minutes until al dente. Drain. Heat the oil in a pan and sauté the onion and garlic for 2–3 minutes. Stir in the sweetcorn and peas and remove from the heat.

4 Blanch the spinach, drain well, chop and reserve. Add the pasta to the onion mixture with the cheese, egg, tomatoes and basil. Season and mix.

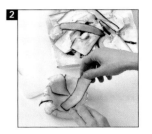

5 Half-fill each ramekin with some of the pasta. Place the spinach on top and then the remaining pasta mixture. Fold the aubergine (eggplant) over the pasta filling to cover. Put the ramekins in a roasting tin (pan) half-filled with boiling water, cover and cook in a preheated oven, 180°C/350°F/Gas Mark 4, for 20–25 minutes, or until set. Meanwhile, heat the sauce ingredients in a pan. Turn out the ramekins and serve immediately with the sauce.

Vegetable Fritters

These mixed vegetable fritters are coated in a light batter and deep-fried until golden. They are ideal with the sweet and sour dipping sauce.

NUTRITIONAL INFORMATION

Calories	479	Sugars	........18g
Protein	.........8g	Fat	..........32g
Carbohydrate	...42g	Saturates	.......5g

20 MINS   20 MINS

SERVES 4

INGREDIENTS

100 g/3½ oz/¾ cup wholemeal (whole
   wheat) flour

pinch of cayenne pepper

4 tsp olive oil

12 tbsp cold water

100 g/3½ oz broccoli florets

100 g/3½ oz cauliflower florets

50 g/1¾ oz mangetout (snow peas)

1 large carrot, cut into batons

1 red (bell) pepper, seeded and sliced

2 egg whites, beaten

oil, for deep-frying

salt

SAUCE

150 ml/¼ pint/⅔ cup pineapple juice

150 ml/¼ pint/⅔ cup vegetable stock

2 tbsp white wine vinegar

2 tbsp light brown sugar

2 tsp cornflour (cornstarch)

2 spring onions (scallions), chopped

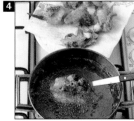

1 Sift the flour and a pinch of salt into a mixing bowl and add the cayenne pepper. Make a well in the centre and gradually beat in the oil and cold water to make a smooth batter.

2 Cook the vegetables in boiling water for 5 minutes and drain well.

3 Whisk the egg whites until they form peaks and gently fold them into the flour batter.

4 Dip the vegetables into the batter, turning to coat well. Drain off any excess batter. Heat the oil for deep-frying in a deep-fryer to 180°C/350°F or until a cube of bread browns in 30 seconds. Fry the coated vegetables, in batches, for 1–2 minutes, until golden. Remove from the oil with a slotted spoon and drain on kitchen paper (paper towels).

5 Place all of the sauce ingredients in a pan and bring to the boil, stirring, until thickened and clear. Serve with the fritters.

Cauliflower Roulade

A light-as-air mixture of eggs and vegetables produces a stylish vegetarian dish that can be enjoyed hot or cold.

NUTRITIONAL INFORMATION

Calories	271	Sugars	.........4g
Protein	........15g	Fat	..........20g
Carbohydrate	....7g	Saturates	......11g

30 MINS   40 MINS

SERVES 6

INGREDIENTS

1 small cauliflower, divided into florets

4 eggs, separated

90 g/3 oz/¾ cup grated Cheddar cheese

60 g/2 oz/¼ cup cottage cheese

pinch of grated nutmeg

½ tsp mustard powder

salt and pepper

FILLING

1 bunch watercress, trimmed

60 g/2 oz/¼ cup butter

25 g/1 oz/¼ cup flour

175 ml/6 fl oz/¾ cup natural
  (unsweetened) yogurt

25 g/1 oz/¼ cup grated Cheddar cheese

60 g/2 oz/¼ cup cottage cheese

1 Line a Swiss roll tin (jelly roll pan) with baking parchment.

2 Steam the cauliflower until just tender, then drain under cold water. Process the cauliflower in a food processor or chop and press through a strainer.

3 Beat the egg yolks, then stir in the cauliflower, 60 g/2 oz/½ cup of the Cheddar and the cottage cheese. Season with nutmeg, mustard, and salt and pepper. Whisk the egg whites until stiff but not dry, then fold them in.

4 Spread the mixture evenly in the tin (pan). Bake in a preheated oven, 190°C/375°F/Gas Mark 5, for about 20-25 minutes, until risen and golden.

5 Chop the watercress, reserving a few sprigs for garnish. Melt the butter in a small pan. Cook the watercress, stirring, for 3 minutes, until wilted. Blend in the flour, then stir in the yogurt and simmer for 2 minutes. Stir in the cheeses.

6 Turn out the roulade on to a damp tea towel (dish cloth) covered with baking parchment. Peel off the paper and leave for a minute to allow the steam to escape. Roll up the roulade, including a new sheet of paper, starting from one narrow end.

7 Unroll the roulade, spread the filling to within 2.5 cm/1 inch of the edges, and roll up. Transfer to a baking tray (cookie sheet), sprinkle with the remaining Cheddar and return to the oven for 5 minutes. Serve immediately if serving hot or allow to cool completely.

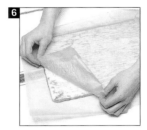

Mini Vegetable Puffs

These are ideal with a more formal meal, as they take a little time to prepare and look really impressive.

NUTRITIONAL INFORMATION

Calories	649	Sugars	........3g
Protein	.........9g	Fat	.........45g
Carbohydrate	...57g	Saturates	......18g

15 MINS | 35 MINS

SERVES 4

INGREDIENTS

450 g/1 lb puff pastry, thawed if frozen

1 egg, beaten

FILLING

225 g/8 oz sweet potato, cubed

100 g/3½ oz baby asparagus spears

25 g/1 oz/2 tbsp butter or margarine

1 leek, sliced

2 small open-cap mushrooms, sliced

1 tsp lime juice

1 tsp chopped thyme

pinch of dried mustard

salt and pepper

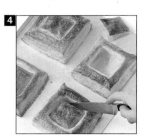

1 Cut the pastry into 4 equal pieces. Roll each piece out on a lightly floured surface to form a 12.5 cm/5 inch square. Place on a dampened baking tray (cookie sheet) and score a smaller 7.5 cm/2.5 inch square inside each one.

2 Brush with beaten egg and cook in a preheated oven, 200°C/400°F/Gas Mark 6, for 20 minutes, or until risen and golden brown.

3 Meanwhile, make the filling, cook the sweet potato in a saucepan of boiling water for 15 minutes, until tender. Drain well and set aside. Meanwhile, blanch the asparagus in a saucepan of boiling water for about 10 minutes, or until tender. Drain and reserve.

4 Remove the pastry squares from the oven, then carefully cut out the central square of pastry with a sharp knife, lift out and reserve.

5 Melt the butter or margarine in a saucepan and sauté the leek and mushrooms for 2–3 minutes. Add the lime juice, thyme and mustard, season well and stir in the sweet potatoes and asparagus. Spoon the mixture into the pastry cases, top with the reserved pastry squares and serve immediately.

Mushroom & Garlic Soufflés

These individual soufflés are very impressive starters, but must be cooked just before serving to prevent them from sinking.

NUTRITIONAL INFORMATION

Calories	179	Sugars	.........3g
Protein	.........6g	Fat	...........14g
Carbohydrate	....8g	Saturates	.......8g

10 MINS   20 MINS

SERVES 4

I N G R E D I E N T S

50 g/1¾ oz/4 tbsp butter

75 g/2¾ oz/1 cup chopped flat mushrooms,

2 tsp lime juice

2 garlic cloves, crushed

2 tbsp chopped marjoram

25 g/1 oz/¼ cup plain (all-purpose) flour

225 ml/8 fl oz/1 cup milk

salt and pepper

2 eggs, separated

1 Lightly grease the inside of four 150 ml/¼ pint/⅔ cup individual soufflé dishes with a little butter.

2 Melt 25 g/1 oz/2 tbsp of the butter in a frying pan (skillet). Add the mushrooms, lime juice and garlic and sauté for 2–3 minutes. Remove the mushroom mixture from the frying pan

COOK'S TIP

Insert a skewer into the centre of the soufflés to test if they are cooked through – it should come out clean. If not, cook for a few minutes longer, but do not overcook otherwise they will become rubbery.

(skillet) with a slotted spoon and transfer to a mixing bowl. Stir in the marjoram.

3 Melt the remaining butter in a pan. Add the flour and cook for 1 minute, then remove from the heat. Stir in the milk and return to the heat. Bring to the boil, stirring until thickened.

4 Mix the sauce into the mushroom mixture and beat in the egg yolks.

5 Whisk the egg whites until they form peaks and fold into the mushroom mixture until fully incorporated.

6 Divide the mixture between the soufflé dishes. Place the dishes on a baking tray (cookie sheet) and cook in a preheated oven, 200°C/400°F/Gas Mark 6, for about 8–10 minutes, or until the soufflés have risen and are cooked through. Serve immediately.

Snacks & Light Meals

The ability to rustle up a simple snack or a quickly-prepared light meal can be very important in our busy lives. Sometimes we may not feel like eating a full-scale

meal but nevertheless want something appetizing and satisfying. Or if lunch or dinner is going to be served very late, then we may want something to tide us over and stave off those hunger pangs! Whether it is for a sustaining snack to break the day, or hearty nibbles to serve with pre-dinner drinks, or an informal lunch or supper party, you'll find a mouthwatering collection of recipes in this chapter.

Roasted Vegetables

Roasted vegetables are delicious and attractive. Served on warm muffins with a herb sauce, they are unbeatable.

NUTRITIONAL INFORMATION

Calories ....509 Sugars 12g
Protein ....15g Fat 28g
Carbohydrate ...50g Saturates 12g

1¼ HOURS   30 MINS

SERVES 4

INGREDIENTS

1 red onion, cut into 8 pieces

1 aubergine (eggplant), halved and sliced

1 yellow (bell) pepper, seeded and sliced

1 courgette (zucchini), sliced

4 tbsp olive oil

1 tbsp garlic vinegar

2 tbsp vermouth

2 garlic cloves, crushed

1 tbsp chopped thyme

2 tsp light brown sugar

4 muffins, halved

salt and pepper

SAUCE

2 tbsp butter

1 tbsp flour

150 ml/¼ pint/⅔ cup milk

75 ml/3 fl oz vegetable stock

75 g/2¾ oz/¾ cup grated Cheddar cheese

1 tsp wholegrain mustard

3 tbsp chopped mixed herbs

1 Arrange the vegetables in a shallow ovenproof dish. Mix together the oil, vinegar, vermouth, garlic, thyme and sugar and pour over the vegetables. Set aside to marinate for 1 hour.

2 Transfer the vegetables to a baking tray (cookie sheet). Cook in a preheated oven, 200°C/400°F/Gas Mark 6, for 20–25 minutes, or until the vegetables have softened and become tender.

3 Meanwhile, make the sauce. Melt the butter in a small pan and add the flour. Cook for 1 minute, stirring constantly, and then remove from the heat. Gradually, stir in the milk and stock and return the pan to the heat. Bring to the boil, stirring constantly, until thickened. Stir in the cheese, mustard and mixed herbs and season to taste with salt and pepper.

4 Preheat the grill (broiler) to high. Cut the muffins in half and grill (broil) for 2–3 minutes, until golden brown, then remove and arrange on a serving plate.

5 Spoon the roasted vegetables on to the muffins and pour the sauce over the top. Serve immediately.

Lentils & Mixed Vegetables

The green lentils used in this recipe require soaking but are worth it for the flavour. If time is short, you could use red split peas instead.

NUTRITIONAL INFORMATION

Calories	386	Sugars	........16g
Protein	........12g	Fat	..........23g
Carbohydrate	...35g	Saturates	......12g

 45 MINS 40–45 MINS

SERVES 4

I N G R E D I E N T S

150 g/5½ oz/¾ cups green lentils

60 g/2 oz/4 tbsp butter or margarine

2 garlic cloves, crushed

2 tbsp olive oil

1 tbsp cider vinegar

1 red onion, cut into 8

50 g/1¾ oz baby corn cobs,
   halved lengthways

1 yellow (bell) pepper, seeded and
   cut into strips

1 red (bell) pepper, seeded and
   cut into strips

50 g/1¾ oz French (green) beans, halved

125 ml/4 fl oz/6 tbsp vegetable stock

2 tbsp clear honey

salt and pepper

crusty bread, to serve

VARIATION

This pan-fry is very versatile:
you can use a mixture of your
favourite vegetables, if you prefer.
Try courgettes (zucchini), carrots or
mangetout (snow peas).

1 Soak the lentils in a large saucepan of cold water for 25 minutes. Bring to the boil, reduce the heat and simmer for 20 minutes. Drain thoroughly.

2 Add 1 tablespoon of the butter or margarine, 1 garlic clove, 1 tablespoon of oil and the vinegar to the lentils and mix well.

3 Melt the remaining butter, garlic and oil in a frying pan (skillet) and stir-fry the onion, corn cobs, (bell) peppers and beans for 3–4 minutes.

4 Add the vegetable stock and bring to the boil. Boil for about 10 minutes, or until the liquid has evaporated.

5 Add the honey and season with salt and pepper to taste. Stir in the lentil mixture and cook for 1 minute to heat through. Spoon on to warmed serving plates and serve with crusty bread.

Vegetable Enchiladas

This Mexican dish uses prepared tortillas which are readily available in supermarkets, which are then filled with a spicy vegetable mixture.

NUTRITIONAL INFORMATION

Calories 309	Sugars 14g	
Protein 12g	Fat 19g	
Carbohydrate ...23g	Saturates 8g	

20 MINS   55 MINS

SERVES 4

INGREDIENTS

4 flour tortillas

75 g/2¾ oz/¾ cup grated

  Cheddar cheese

FILLING

75 g/2¾ oz spinach

2 tbsp olive oil

8 baby corn cobs, sliced

25 g/1 oz/1 tbsp frozen peas, thawed

1 red (bell) pepper, seeded and diced

1 carrot, diced

1 leek, sliced

2 garlic cloves, crushed

1 red chilli, chopped

salt and pepper

SAUCE

300 ml/½ pint/1¼ cups passata

  (sieved tomatoes)

2 shallots, chopped

1 garlic clove, crushed

300 ml/½ pint/1¼ cups vegetable stock

1 tsp caster (superfine) sugar

1 tsp chilli powder

1 To make the filling, blanch the spinach in a pan of boiling water for 2 minutes. Drain well, pressing out as much excess moisture as possible, and chop.

2 Heat the oil in a frying pan (skillet) over a medium heat. Add the baby corn cobs, peas, (bell) pepper, carrot, leek, garlic and chilli and sauté, stirring briskly, for 3–4 minutes. Stir in the spinach and season well with salt and pepper to taste.

3 Put all the sauce ingredients in a heavy-based saucepan and bring to the boil, stirring constantly. Cook over a high heat, stirring constantly, for 20 minutes, until thickened and reduced by a third.

4 Spoon a quarter of the filling along the centre of each tortilla. Roll the tortillas around the filling and place, seam side down, in a single layer in an ovenproof dish.

5 Pour the sauce over the tortillas and sprinkle the cheese on top. Cook in a preheated oven, 180°C/350°F/Gas Mark 4, for 20 minutes, or until the cheese has melted and browned. Serve immediately.

Vegetable Crêpes

Crêpes or pancakes are ideal for filling with your favourite ingredients. In this recipe they are packed with a spicy vegetable filling.

NUTRITIONAL INFORMATION

Calories	509	Sugars	........10g
Protein	........17g	Fat	.........34g
Carbohydrate	...36g	Saturates	.......9g

 15 MINS   45 MINS

SERVES 4

INGREDIENTS

CREPES

100 g/3½ oz/¾ cup plain (all-purpose) flour

pinch of salt

1 egg, beaten

300 ml/½ pint/1¼ cups milk

vegetable oil, for frying

FILLING

2 tbsp vegetable oil

1 leek, shredded

½ tsp chilli powder

½ tsp ground cumin

50 g/1¾ oz mangetout (snow peas)

100 g/3½ oz button mushrooms,

1 red (bell) pepper, sliced

25 g/1 oz/¼ cup cashew nuts, chopped

SAUCE

25 g/1 oz/2 tbsp margarine

25 g/1 oz/3 tbsp plain (all-purpose) flour

150 ml/¼ pint/⅔ cup vegetable stock

150 ml/¼ pint/⅔ cup milk

1 tsp Dijon mustard

75 g/2¾ oz/¾ cup grated Cheddar cheese

2 tbsp chopped coriander (cilantro)

1 For the crêpes, sift the flour and salt into a bowl. Beat in the egg and milk to make a batter.

2 For the filling, heat the oil and sauté the leek for 2–3 minutes. Add the remaining ingredients and cook, stirring, for 5 minutes.

3 For the sauce, melt the margarine in a pan and add the flour. Cook, stirring, for 1 minute. Remove from the heat, stir in the stock and milk and return to the heat. Bring to the boil, stirring until thick.

Add the mustard, half the cheese and the coriander (cilantro); cook for 1 minute.

4 Heat 1 tbsp of oil in a small frying pan (skillet). Pour off the oil and add an eighth of the batter. Tilt to cover the base. Cook for 2 minutes, turn and cook the other side for 1 minute. Repeat with the remaining batter. Spoon a little of the filling along the centre of each crêpe and roll up. Place in a flameproof dish and pour the sauce on top. Top with cheese and heat under a hot grill (broiler) for 3–5 minutes or until the cheese melts.

Vegetable Jambalaya

This dish traditionally contains spicy sausage, but it is equally delicious filled with vegetables in this spicy vegetarian version.

NUTRITIONAL INFORMATION

Calories 181	Sugars 8g	
Protein 6g	Fat 7g	
Carbohydrate . . .25g	Saturates 1g	

10 MINS   55 MINS

SERVES 4

INGREDIENTS

75 g/2¾ oz/½ cup brown rice

2 tbsp olive oil

2 garlic cloves, crushed

1 red onion, cut into eight

1 aubergine (eggplant), diced

1 green (bell) pepper, diced

50 g/1¾ oz baby corn cobs,
    halved lengthways

50 g/1¾ oz/½ cup frozen peas

100 g/3½ oz small broccoli florets

150 ml/¼ pint/⅔ cup vegetable stock

225 g/8 oz can chopped tomatoes

1 tbsp tomato purée (paste)

1 tsp creole seasoning

½ tsp chilli flakes

salt and pepper

COOK'S TIP

Use a mixture of different kinds of rice, such as wild or red rice, for colour and texture. Cook the rice in advance for a speedier recipe.

1 Cook the rice in a large saucepan of salted boiling water for 20 minutes, or until cooked through. Drain, rinse with boiling water, drain again and set aside.

2 Heat the oil in a heavy-based frying pan (skillet) and cook the garlic and onion, stirring constantly, for 2–3 minutes.

3 Add the aubergine (eggplant), (bell) pepper, corn, peas and broccoli to the pan and cook, stirring occasionally, for 2–3 minutes.

4 Stir in the vegetable stock and canned tomatoes, tomato purée (paste), creole seasoning and chilli flakes.

5 Season to taste and cook over a low heat for 15–20 minutes, or until the vegetables are tender.

6 Stir the brown rice into the vegetable mixture and cook, mixing well, for 3–4 minutes, or until hot. Transfer the vegetable jambalaya to a warm serving dish and serve immediately.

Vegetable Burgers & Chips

These spicy vegetable burgers are delicious, especially when
served with the light oven chips (fries) and in a warm bun or roll.

NUTRITIONAL INFORMATION

Calories 461	Sugars 4g
Protein 18g	Fat 17g
Carbohydrate . . .64g	Saturates 2g

  45 MINS   1 HOUR

SERVES 4

I N G R E D I E N T S

VEGETABLE BURGERS

100 g/3½ oz spinach

1 tbsp olive oil

1 leek, chopped

2 garlic cloves, crushed

100 g/3½ oz/1½ cups chopped mushrooms

300 g/10½ oz firm tofu (bean
   curd), chopped

1 tsp chilli powder

1 tsp curry powder

1 tbsp chopped coriander (cilantro)

75 g/2¾ oz/1½ cups fresh wholemeal
   (whole wheat) breadcrumbs

1 tbsp olive oil

burger bap or roll and salad, to serve

CHIPS (FRIES)

2 large potatoes

2 tbsp flour

1 tsp chilli powder

2 tbsp olive oil

1 To make the burgers, cook the spinach in a little boiling water for 2 minutes. Drain thoroughly and pat dry with kitchen paper (paper towels).

2 Heat the oil in a frying pan (skillet) and sauté the leek and garlic for 2–3 minutes. Add the remaining ingredients, except the breadcrumbs, and cook for 5–7 minutes, until the vegetables have softened. Toss in the spinach and cook for 1 minute.

3 Transfer the mixture to a food processor and process for 30 seconds, until almost smooth. Transfer to a bowl, stir in the breadcrumbs, mixing well, and leave until cool enough to handle. Using floured hands, form the mixture into four equal-size burgers. Leave to chill for 30 minutes.

4 To make the chips (fries), cut the potatoes into thin wedges and cook in a pan of boiling water for 10 minutes. Drain and toss in the flour and chilli powder. Lay the chips on a baking tray (cookie sheet) and sprinkle with the oil. Cook in a preheated oven, 200°C/400°F/ Gas Mark 6, for 30 minutes, or until golden.

5 Meanwhile, heat 1 tbsp oil in a frying pan (skillet) and cook the burgers for 8–10 minutes, turning once. Serve with salad in a bap with the chips (fries).

Falafel

These are a very tasty, well-known Middle Eastern dish of small chickpea (garbanzo bean) based balls, spiced and deep-fried.

NUTRITIONAL INFORMATION

Calories	.491	Sugars	.3g
Protein	.15g	Fat	.30g
Carbohydrate	.43g	Saturates	.3g

🍲 25 MINS 🕐 10–15 MINS

SERVES 4

INGREDIENTS

675 g/1½ lb/6 cups canned chickpeas
   (garbanzo beans), drained

1 red onion, chopped

3 garlic cloves, crushed

100 g/3½ oz wholemeal (whole
   wheat) bread

2 small fresh red chillies

1 tsp ground cumin

1 tsp ground coriander

½ tsp turmeric

1 tbsp chopped coriander (cilantro), plus
   extra to garnish

1 egg, beaten

100 g/3½ oz/1 cup wholemeal (whole
   wheat) breadcrumbs

vegetable oil, for
   deep-frying

salt and pepper

tomato and cucumber salad
   and lemon wedges, to serve

1 Put the chickpeas (garbanzo beans), onion, garlic, bread, chillies, spices and coriander (cilantro) in a food processor and process for 30 seconds. Stir and season to taste with salt and pepper.

2 Remove the mixture from the food processor and shape into walnut-sized balls.

3 Place the beaten egg in a shallow bowl and place the wholemeal (whole wheat) breadcrumbs on a plate. Dip the balls first into the egg to coat and then roll them in the breadcrumbs, shaking off any excess.

4 Heat the oil for deep-frying to 180°C/350°F or until a cube of bread browns in 30 seconds. Fry the falafel, in batches if necessary, for 2–3 minutes, until crisp and browned. Remove from the oil with a slotted spoon and dry on absorbent kitchen paper (paper towels). Garnish with coriander (cilantro) and serve with a tomato and cucumber salad and lemon wedges.

Potato Fritters with Relish

These are incredibly simple to make and sure to be popular served as a tempting snack or as an accompaniment to almost any Indian meal.

NUTRITIONAL INFORMATION

Calories 294	Sugars 4g	
Protein 4g	Fat 24g	
Carbohydrate ...18g	Saturates 3g	

40 MINS   15 MINS

SERVES 8

I N G R E D I E N T S

60 g/2 oz/½ cup plain wholemeal (whole wheat) flour

½ tsp ground coriander

½ tsp cumin seeds

¼ tsp chilli powder

½ tsp ground turmeric

¼ tsp salt

1 egg

3 tbsp milk

350 g/12 oz potatoes, peeled

1-2 garlic cloves, crushed

4 spring onions (scallions), chopped

60 g/2 oz corn kernels

vegetable oil, for shallow frying

O N I O N   &   T O M A T O
R E L I S H

1 onion, peeled

225 g/8 oz tomatoes

2 tbsp chopped coriander (cilantro)

2 tbsp chopped mint

2 tbsp lemon juice

½ tsp roasted cumin seeds

¼ tsp salt

pinch of cayenne pepper

1 First make the relish. Cut the onion and tomatoes into small dice and place in a bowl with the remaining ingredients. Mix together well and leave to stand for at least 15 minutes before serving to allow time for the flavours to blend.

2 Place the flour in a bowl, stir in the spices and salt and make a well in the centre. Add the egg and milk and mix to form a fairly thick batter.

3 Coarsely grate the potatoes, place in a sieve and rinse well under cold running water. Drain and squeeze dry, then stir into the batter with the garlic, spring onions (scallions) and corn.

4 Heat about 5 mm/¼ inches vegetable oil in a large frying pan and add a few tablespoonfuls of the mixture at a time, flattening each one to form a thin cake. Fry over a low heat, turning frequently, for 2-3 minutes, or until golden brown and cooked through.

5 Drain on kitchen paper (paper towels) and keep hot while frying the remaining mixture in the same way. Serve hot with onion and tomato relish.

Potato & Mushroom Bake

Use any mixture of mushrooms to hand for this creamy layered bake. It can be served straight from the dish in which it is cooked.

NUTRITIONAL INFORMATION

Calories	...304	Sugars	...2g
Protein	...4g	Fat	...24g
Carbohydrate	...20g	Saturates	...15g

15 MINS   1 HOUR

SERVES 4

INGREDIENTS

25 g/1 oz/2 tbsp butter

500 g/1 lb 2 oz waxy potatoes, thinly sliced

150 g/5½ oz/2 cups sliced
   mixed mushrooms

1 tbsp chopped rosemary

4 tbsp chopped chives

2 garlic cloves, crushed

150 ml/¼ pint/⅔cup double (heavy) cream

salt and pepper

snipped chives, to garnish

1 Grease a shallow round ovenproof dish with butter.

2 Parboil the sliced potatoes in a saucepan of boiling water for 10 minutes. Drain well. Layer a quarter of the potatoes in the base of the dish.

3 Arrange one-quarter of the mushrooms on top of the potatoes and sprinkle with one-quarter of the rosemary, chives and garlic. Continue making layers in the same order, finishing with a layer of potatoes on top.

4 Pour the cream over the top of the potatoes. Season to taste with salt and pepper.

5 Cook in a preheated oven, 190°C/375°F/Gas Mark 5, for about 45 minutes, or until the bake is golden brown and piping hot.

6 Garnish with snipped chives and serve at once straight from the dish.

COOK'S TIP

For a special occasion, the bake may be made in a lined cake tin (pan) and then turned out to serve.

Grilled (Broiled) Potatoes

This dish is ideal with grilled (broiled) or barbecued foods, as the potatoes themselves may be cooked by either method.

NUTRITIONAL INFORMATION

Calories . . . . .417 Sugars 1g
Protein . . . . .3g Fat 37g
Carbohydrate . . .20g Saturates 10g

 15 MINS   20 MINS

SERVES 4

I N G R E D I E N T S

450 g/1 lb potatoes, unpeeled and scrubbed

40 g/1½ oz/3 tbsp butter, melted

2 tbsp chopped thyme

paprika, for dusting

L I M E M A Y O N N A I S E

150 ml/¼ pint/⅔ cup mayonnaise

2 tsp lime juice

finely grated rind of 1 lime

1 garlic clove, crushed

pinch of paprika

salt and pepper

1 Cut the potatoes into 1 cm/½ inch thick slices.

2 Cook the potatoes in a saucepan of boiling water for 5–7 minutes – they should still be quite firm. Remove the potatoes with a slotted spoon and drain thoroughly.

3 Line a grill (broiler) pan with kitchen foil. Place the potato slices on top of the foil.

4 Brush the potatoes with the melted butter and sprinkle the chopped thyme on top. Season to taste with salt and pepper.

5 Cook the potatoes under a preheated grill (broiler) at medium heat for 10 minutes, turning once.

6 Meanwhile, make the lime mayonnaise. Thoroughly combine the mayonnaise, lime juice, lime rind, garlic, paprika and salt and pepper to taste in a small bowl.

7 Dust the hot potato slices with a little paprika and serve immediately with the lime mayonnaise.

COOK'S TIP
The lime mayonnaise may be spooned over the grilled (broiled) potatoes to coat them just before serving, if you prefer.

Paprika Crisps (Chips)

These wafer-thin potato crisps are great cooked over a barbecue and served with spicy vegetable kebabs (kabobs).

NUTRITIONAL INFORMATION

Calories ....149 Sugars 0.6g
Protein ....2g Fat 8g
Carbohydrate ...17g Saturates 1g

 5 MINS   7 MINS

SERVES 4

I N G R E D I E N T S

2 large potatoes

3 tbsp olive oil

½ tsp paprika

salt

1 Using a sharp knife, slice the potatoes very thinly so that they are almost transparent. Drain the potato slices thoroughly and pat dry with kitchen paper (paper towels).

2 Heat the oil in a large frying pan (skillet) and add the paprika, stirring constantly to ensure that the paprika doesn't catch and burn.

3 Add the potato slices to the frying pan (skillet) and cook them in a single layer for about 5 minutes or until the potato slices just begin to curl slightly at the edges.

VARIATION

You could use curry powder or any other spice to flavour the crisps (chips) instead of the paprika, if you prefer.

4 Remove the potato slices from the pan using a slotted spoon and transfer them to kitchen paper (paper towels) to drain thoroughly.

5 Thread the potato slices on to several wooden kebab (kabob) skewers.

6 Sprinkle the potato slices with a little salt and cook over a medium hot barbecue or under a medium grill (broiler), turning frequently, for 10 minutes, until the potato slices begin to crispen. Sprinkle with a little more salt, if preferred, and serve immediately.

Mixed Bean Pan-Fry

Fresh green beans have a wonderful flavour that is hard to beat.
If you cannot find fresh beans, use thawed, frozen beans instead.

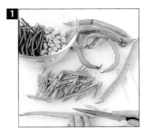
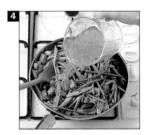

NUTRITIONAL INFORMATION

Calories 179   Sugars 4g
Protein ....10g   Fat 11g
Carbohydrate ...10g   Saturates 1g

 10 MINS   15 MINS

SERVES 4

I N G R E D I E N T S

350 g/12 oz/4 cups mixed
   green beans, such as French (green)
   and broad (fava) beans, podded

2 tbsp vegetable oil

2 garlic cloves, crushed

1 red onion, halved and sliced

225 g/8 oz firm marinated tofu
   (bean curd), diced

1 tbsp lemon juice

½ tsp turmeric

1 tsp ground mixed spice

150 ml/¼ pint/⅔ cup vegetable stock

2 tsp sesame seeds

1 Trim and chop the French (green) beans and set aside until required.

2 Heat the oil in a medium frying pan (skillet). Add the garlic and onion and sauté, stirring frequently, over a low heat for 2 minutes.

3 Add the tofu (bean curd) and cook for 2–3 minutes, until just beginning to turn golden brown.

4 Add the French (green) beans and broad (fava) beans. Stir in the lemon juice, turmeric, ground mixed spice and vegetable stock and bring to the boil over a medium heat.

5 Reduce the heat and simmer for 5–7 minutes, or until the beans are tender. Sprinkle with sesame seeds and serve immediately.

VARIATION

Use smoked tofu (bean curd) instead of marinated tofu (bean curd) for an alternative and quite distinctive flavour.

Stuffed Mushrooms

Use large open-cap mushrooms for this recipe for their flavour and suitability for filling.

NUTRITIONAL INFORMATION

Calories	273	Sugars	.........5g
Protein	........13g	Fat	..........18g
Carbohydrate	...15g	Saturates	.......5g

  15 MINS   25 MINS

SERVES 4

INGREDIENTS

8 open-cap mushrooms

1 tbsp olive oil

1 small leek, chopped

1 celery stick, chopped

100 g/3½ oz firm tofu (bean curd), diced

1 courgette (zucchini), chopped

1 carrot, chopped

100 g/3½ oz/1 cup wholemeal (whole
   wheat) breadcrumbs

2 tbsp chopped basil

1 tbsp tomato purée (paste)

2 tbsp pine nuts

75 g/2¾ oz/¾ cup grated
   Cheddar cheese

150 ml/¼ pint/⅔ cup vegetable stock

salt and pepper

salad, to serve

1 Remove the stalks from the mushrooms and chop finely. Reserve the caps.

2 Heat the olive oil in a large, heavy-based frying pan (skillet) over a medium heat. Add the chopped mushroom stalks, leek, celery, tofu (bean curd), courgette (zucchini) and carrot and cook, stirring constantly, for 3–4 minutes.

3 Stir in the breadcrumbs, chopped basil, tomato purée (paste) and pine nuts. Season with salt and pepper to taste and mix thoroughly.

4 Spoon the mixture into the mushroom caps and top with the grated cheese.

5 Place the mushrooms in a shallow ovenproof dish and pour the vegetable stock around them.

6 Cook in a preheated oven, 220°C/425°F/Gas Mark 7, for 20 minutes, or until cooked through and the cheese has melted. Remove the mushrooms from the dish and serve immediately with a salad.

Stuffed Globe Artichokes

This imaginative and attractive recipe for artichokes stuffed with nuts, tomatoes, olives and mushrooms, has been adapted for the microwave.

NUTRITIONAL INFORMATION

Calories 248   Sugars 8g
Protein ....5g   Fat 19g
Carbohydrate ...16g   Saturates 2g

 30 MINS   25 MINS

SERVES 4

INGREDIENTS

4 globe artichokes

8 tbsp water

4 tbsp lemon juice

1 onion, chopped

1 garlic clove, crushed

2 tbsp olive oil

225 g/8 oz/2 cups button
   mushrooms, chopped

40 g/1½ oz/½ cup pitted black
   olives, sliced

60 g/2 oz/¼ cup sun-dried tomatoes in oil,
   drained and chopped

1 tbsp chopped fresh basil

60 g/2 oz/1 cup fresh
   white breadcrumbs

25 g/1 oz/¼ cup pine nuts, toasted

oil from the jar of sun-dried tomatoes
   for drizzling

salt and pepper

1 Cut the stalks and lower leaves off the artichokes. Snip off the leaf tips with scissors. Place 2 artichokes in a large bowl with half the water and half the lemon juice. Cover and cook on HIGH power for 10 minutes, turning the artichokes over halfway through, until a leaf pulls away easily from the base. Leave to stand, covered, for 3 minutes before draining. Turn the artichokes upside down and leave to cool. Repeat to cook the remaining artichokes.

2 Place the onion, garlic and oil in a bowl. Cover and cook on HIGH power for 2 minutes, stirring once. Add the mushrooms, olives and sun-dried tomatoes. Cover and cook on HIGH power for 2 minutes.

3 Stir in the basil, breadcrumbs and pine nuts. Season to taste with salt and pepper.

4 Turn the artichokes the right way up and carefully pull the leaves apart. Remove the purple-tipped central leaves. Using a teaspoon, scrape out the hairy choke and discard.

5 Divide the stuffing into 4 equal portions and spoon into the centre of each artichoke. Push the leaves back around the stuffing.

6 Arrange in a shallow dish and drizzle over a little oil from the jar of sun-dried tomatoes. Cook on HIGH power for 7–8 minutes to reheat, turning the artichokes around halfway through.

Spinach Pancakes

Serve these pancakes as a light lunch or supper dish, with a tomato and basil salad for a dramatic colour contrast.

NUTRITIONAL INFORMATION

Calories 663   Sugars 9g
Protein ....32g   Fat 48g
Carbohydrate ...28g   Saturates 18g

  25 MINS   1¼ HOURS

SERVES 4

I N G R E D I E N T S

90 g/3 oz/¾ cup wholemeal (whole wheat) flour

1 egg

150 ml/¼ pint/⅔ cup natural (unsweetened) yogurt

3 tbsp water

1 tbsp vegetable oil, plus extra for brushing

200 g/7 oz frozen leaf spinach, thawed and puréed

pinch of grated nutmeg

salt and pepper

T O   G A R N I S H

lemon wedges

fresh coriander (cilantro) sprigs

F I L L I N G

1 tbsp vegetable oil

3 spring onions (scallions), thinly sliced

225 g/8 oz/1 cup ricotta cheese

4 tbsp natural (unsweetened) yogurt

90 g/3 oz/¾ cup grated Gruyère cheese

1 egg, lightly beaten

125 g/4½ oz/1 cup unsalted cashew nuts

2 tbsp chopped parsley

pinch of cayenne pepper

1 Sift the flour and salt into a bowl and tip in any bran in the strainer. Beat together the egg, yogurt, water and oil. Gradually pour it on to the flour, beating constantly. Stir in the spinach and season with pepper and nutmeg.

2 To make the filling, heat the oil in a pan and fry the spring onions (scallions) until translucent. Remove with a slotted spoon and drain on kitchen paper (paper towels). Beat together the ricotta, yogurt and half the Gruyère. Beat in the egg and stir in the cashew nuts and parsley. Season with salt and cayenne.

3 Lightly brush a small, heavy frying pan (skillet) with oil and heat. Pour in 3–4 tablespoons of the pancake batter and tilt the pan so that it covers the base.

Cook for about 3 minutes, until bubbles appear in the centre. Turn and cook the other side for about 2 minutes, until lightly browned. Slide the pancake on to a warmed plate, cover with foil and keep warm while you cook the remainder. The batter should make 8–12 pancakes.

4 Spread a little filling over each pancake and fold in half and then half again, envelope style. Spoon the remaining filling into the opening.

5 Grease a shallow, ovenproof dish and arrange the pancakes in a single layer. Sprinkle on the remaining cheese and cook in a preheated oven. 180°C/350°F/Gas Mark 4, for about 15 minutes. Serve hot, garnished with lemon wedges and coriander (cilantro) sprigs.

Marinated Fennel

Fennel has a wonderful aniseed flavour which is ideal for grilling (broiling) or barbecuing. This marinated recipe is really delicious.

NUTRITIONAL INFORMATION

Calories	117	Sugars	3g
Protein	1g	Fat	11g
Carbohydrate	3g	Saturates	2g

 1¼ HOURS 10 MINS

SERVES 4

INGREDIENTS

2 fennel bulbs

1 red (bell) pepper, seeded and cut into
   large cubes

1 lime, cut into 8 wedges

MARINADE

2 tbsp lime juice

4 tbsp olive oil

2 garlic cloves, crushed

1 tsp wholegrain mustard

1 tbsp chopped thyme

fennel fronds, to garnish

crisp salad, to serve

1 Cut each of the fennel bulbs into 8 pieces and place in a shallow dish. Mix in the (bell) peppers.

2 To make the marinade, combine the lime juice, oil, garlic, mustard and thyme. Pour the marinade over the fennel and (bell) peppers, toss to coat thoroughly and set aside to marinate for 1 hour.

3 Thread the fennel and (bell) peppers on to wooden skewers with the lime wedges. Preheat a grill (broiler) to medium and grill (broil) the kebabs (kabobs), turning and basting frequently with the marinade, for about 10 minutes.

4 Transfer to serving plates, garnish with fennel fronds and serve immediately with a crisp salad.

COOK'S TIP

Soak the skewers in cold water for 20 minutes before using to prevent them from burning during grilling (broiling). You could substitute 2 tablespoons orange juice for the lime juice and add 1 tbsp honey, if you prefer.

Garlic Mushrooms on Toast

This is so simple to prepare and looks great if you use a variety of mushrooms for shape and texture.

NUTRITIONAL INFORMATION

Calories 366	Sugars 2g
Protein 9g	Fat 18g
Carbohydrate ...45g	Saturates 4g

 10 MINS   10 MINS

SERVES 4

INGREDIENTS

75 g/2¾ oz/6 tbsp margarine

2 garlic cloves, crushed

350 g/12 oz/4 cups mixed mushrooms, such as open-cap, button, oyster and shiitake, sliced

8 slices French bread

1 tbsp chopped parsley

salt and pepper

1 Melt the margarine in a frying pan (skillet). Add the crushed garlic and cook, stirring constantly, for 30 seconds.

2 Add the mushrooms and cook, turning occasionally, for 5 minutes.

3 Toast the French bread slices under a preheated medium grill (broiler) for 2–3 minutes, turning once. Transfer the toasts to a serving plate.

COOK'S TIP

Always store mushrooms for a maximum of 24–36 hours in the refrigerator, in paper bags, as they sweat in plastic. Wild mushrooms should be washed but other varieties can simply be wiped with kitchen paper (paper towels).

4 Toss the parsley into the mushrooms, mixing well, and season well with salt and pepper to taste.

5 Spoon the mushroom mixture over the bread and serve immediately.

Creamy Mushroom & Potato

These oven-baked mushrooms are covered with a creamy potato and mushroom filling topped with melted cheese.

NUTRITIONAL INFORMATION

Calories 214   Sugars 1g
Protein . . . . .5g   Fat 17g
Carbohydrate . . . .11g   Saturates 11g

 40 MINS   40 MINS

SERVES 4

INGREDIENTS

25 g/1 oz dried ceps

225 g/8 oz floury (mealy) potatoes, diced

25 g/1 oz/2 tbsp butter, melted

4 tbsp double (heavy) cream

2 tbsp chopped fresh chives

25 g/1 oz/¼ cup grated Emmenthal cheese

8 large open-capped mushrooms

150 ml/¼ pint/⅔cup vegetable stock

salt and pepper

fresh chives, to garnish

1 Place the dried ceps in a small bowl. Add sufficient boiling water to cover and set aside to soak for 20 minutes.

2 Meanwhile, cook the potatoes in a medium saucepan of lightly salted boiling water for 10 minutes, until cooked through and tender. Drain well and mash until smooth.

3 Drain the soaked ceps and then chop them finely. Mix them into the mashed potato.

4 Thoroughly blend the butter, cream and chives together and pour the mixture into the ceps and potato mixture, mixing well. Season to taste with salt and pepper.

5 Remove the stalks from the open-capped mushrooms. Chop the stalks and stir them into the potato mixture. Spoon the mixture into the open-capped mushrooms and sprinkle the cheese over the top.

6 Arrange the filled mushrooms in a shallow ovenproof dish and pour in the vegetable stock.

7 Cover the dish and cook in a preheated oven, 220°C/425°F/Gas Mark 7, for 20 minutes. Remove the lid and cook for 5 minutes until golden.

8 Garnish the mushrooms with fresh chives and serve at once.

VARIATION

Use fresh mushrooms instead of the dried ceps, if preferred, and stir a mixture of chopped nuts into the mushroom stuffing mixture for extra crunch.

Indian-Style Omelette

Omelettes are very versatile: they go with almost anything and you can also serve them at any time of the day.

NUTRITIONAL INFORMATION

Calories 132   Sugars 1g
Protein ....7g   Fat 11g
Carbohydrate ....2g   Saturates 2g

 10 MINS   20 MINS

SERVES 4

INGREDIENTS

1 small onion, very finely chopped

2 green chillies, finely chopped

coriander (cilantro) leaves, finely chopped

4 medium eggs

1 tsp salt

2 tbsp oil

toasted bread or crisp
   green salad, to serve

1 Place the onion, chillies and coriander (cilantro) in a large mixing bowl. Mix together until well combined.

2 Place the eggs in a separate bowl and whisk together.

3 Add the onion mixture to the eggs and mix together.

4 Add the salt to the egg and onion mixture and whisk together well.

5 Heat 1 tbsp of the oil in a large frying pan (skillet). Place a ladleful of the omelette batter into the pan.

6 Fry the omelette, turning once and pressing down with a flat spoon to make sure that the egg is cooked right through, until the omelette is a golden brown colour.

7 Repeat the same process for the remaining batter. Set the omelettes aside and keep warm while you make the remaining batches of omelettes.

8 Serve the omelettes immediately with toasted bread. Alternatively, simply serve the omelettes with a crisp green salad for a light lunch.

COOK'S TIP

Indian cooks use a variety of vegetable oils, and groundnut or sunflower oils make good alternatives for most dishes, although sometimes more specialist ones, such as coconut oil, mustard oil and sesame oil, are called for.

Cabbage & Walnut Stir-Fry

This is a really quick, one-pan dish using white and red cabbage for both colour and flavour.

NUTRITIONAL INFORMATION

Calories 422	Sugars 9g	
Protein 13g	Fat 37g	
Carbohydrate ...10g	Saturates 5g	

 10 MINS   10 MINS

SERVES 4

I N G R E D I E N T S

350 g/12 oz white cabbage

350 g/12 oz red cabbage

4 tbsp peanut oil

1 tbsp walnut oil

2 garlic cloves, crushed

8 spring onions (scallions)

225 g/8 oz firm tofu (bean curd), cubed

2 tbsp lemon juice

100 g/3½ oz walnut halves

2 tsp Dijon mustard

2 tsp poppy seeds

salt and pepper

1 Using a sharp knife, shred the white and red cabbages thinly and set aside until required.

2 Heat the peanut and walnut oils in a preheated wok or heavy-based frying pan (skillet). Add the garlic, cabbage, spring onions (scallions) and tofu (bean curd) and cook, stirring constantly, for 5 minutes.

3 Add the lemon juice, walnuts and Dijon mustard, season to taste with salt and pepper and cook for a further 5 minutes, or until the cabbage is tender.

4 Transfer the stir-fry to a warm serving bowl, sprinkle with poppy seeds and serve immediately.

COOK'S TIP

As well as adding protein, vitamins and useful fats to the diet, nuts and seeds add flavour and texture to vegetarian meals. Keep a good supply of them in your store-cupboard as they can be used in a great variety of dishes – salads, bakes, stir-fries to name but a few.

Cress & Cheese Tartlets

These individual tartlets are great for lunchtime or for picnic food.
Watercress is a good source of folic acid, important in early pregnancy.

NUTRITIONAL INFORMATION

Calories 410	Sugars 4g
Protein 15g	Fat 29g
Carbohydrate . . .24g	Saturates 19g

 20 MINS   25 MINS

SERVES 4

INGREDIENTS

100 g/3½ oz/¾ cup plain (all-purpose) flour

pinch of salt

75 g/2¾ oz /½ cup butter
  or margarine

2–3 tbsp cold water

2 bunches watercress

2 garlic cloves, crushed

1 shallot, chopped

150 g/5½ oz/scant 1½ cups grated
  Cheddar cheese

4 tbsp natural (unsweetened) yogurt

½ tsp paprika

1 Sift the flour into a mixing bowl and add the salt. Rub 50 g/1¾ oz/⅓ cup of the butter or margarine into the flour until the mixture resembles breadcrumbs.

2 Stir in enough of the cold water to make a smooth dough.

3 Roll the dough out on a lightly floured surface and use to line four 10 cm/ 4 inch tartlet tins (pans). Prick the bases with a fork and leave to chill.

4 Heat the remaining butter or margarine in a frying pan (skillet). Discard the stems from the watercress and add to the pan with the garlic and shallot, cooking for 1–2 minutes, until the watercress has wilted.

5 Remove the pan from the heat and stir in the grated cheese, yogurt and paprika.

6 Spoon the mixture into the pastry cases and cook in a preheated oven, 180°C/350°F/Gas Mark 4, for 20 minutes, or until the filling is firm. Turn out the tartlets and serve immediately.

VARIATION

Use spinach instead of the watercress, making sure it is well drained before mixing with the remaining filling ingredients.

Hash Browns

Hash Browns are a popular American recipe of fried potato squares, often served as brunch. This recipe includes extra vegetables.

NUTRITIONAL INFORMATION

Calories 339   Sugars 9g
Protein . . . . .10g   Fat 21g
Carbohydrate . . .29g   Saturates 7g

20 MINS   45 MINS

SERVES 4

INGREDIENTS

500 g/1 lb 2 oz waxy potatoes

1 carrot, diced

1 celery stick, diced

60 g/2 oz button mushrooms, diced

1 onion, diced

2 garlic cloves, crushed

25 g/1 oz/¼ cup frozen
    peas, thawed

60 g/2 oz/⅔ cup grated
    Parmesan cheese

4 tbsp vegetable oil

25 g/1 oz/2 tbsp butter

salt and pepper

SAUCE

300 ml/½ pint/1¼ cups passata (sieved
    tomatoes)

2 tbsp chopped fresh coriander (cilantro)

1 tbsp vegetarian Worcestershire sauce

½ tsp chilli powder

2 tsp brown sugar

2 tsp American mustard

75 ml/3 fl oz/⅓ cup vegetable stock

1 Cook the potatoes in a saucepan of lightly salted boiling water for 10 minutes. Drain and leave to cool. Meanwhile, cook the carrot in lightly salted boiling water for 5 minutes.

2 Set the potato aside to cool. When cool enough to handle, grate it with a coarse grater.

3 Drain the carrot and add it to the grated potato, together with the celery, mushrooms, onion, garlic, peas and cheese. Season to taste with salt and pepper.

4 Put all of the sauce ingredients in a small saucepan and bring to the boil. Reduce the heat to low and simmer for 15 minutes.

5 Divide the potato mixture into 8 portions of equal size and shape into flattened rectangles with your hands.

6 Heat the oil and butter in a frying pan (skillet) and cook the hash browns over a low heat for 4-5 minutes on each side, until crisp and golden brown.

7 Transfer the hash browns to a serving plate and serve immediately with the tomato sauce.

Sweetcorn (Corn) Patties

These are a delicious addition to any party buffet, and very simple to prepare. Serve with a sweet chilli sauce.

NUTRITIONAL INFORMATION

Calories 90   Sugars 3g
Protein . . . . .2g   Fat 5g
Carbohydrate . . . .11g   Saturates 0.6g

 10 MINS   ⏱ 10 MINS

SERVES 6

I N G R E D I E N T S

325 g/11½ oz can sweetcorn (corn), drained

1 onion, finely chopped

1 tsp curry powder

1 garlic clove, crushed

1 tsp ground coriander

2 spring onions (scallions), chopped

3 tbsp plain (all-purpose) flour

½ tsp baking powder

1 large egg

4 tbsp sunflower oil

salt

1 Mash the drained sweetcorn (corn) lightly in a medium-sized bowl. Add the onion, curry powder, garlic, ground coriander, scallions, flour, baking powder and egg, one at a time, stirring after each addition. Season to taste with salt.

2 Heat the sunflower oil in a frying pan (skillet). Drop tablespoonfuls of the mixture carefully on to the hot oil, far enough apart for them not to run into each other as they cook.

3 Cook for about 4–5 minutes, turning each patty once, until they are golden brown and firm to the touch. Take care not to turn them too soon, or they will break up in the pan.

4 Remove the patties from the pan with a slice and drain on kitchen paper (paper towels). Serve immediately while still warm.

COOK'S TIP

To make this dish more attractive, you can serve the patties on large leaves, like those shown in the photograph. Be sure to cut the spring onions (scallions) on the diagonal, as shown, for a more elegant appearance.

Buck Rarebit

This substantial version of cheese on toast – a creamy cheese sauce topped with a poached egg – makes a tasty, filling snack.

NUTRITIONAL INFORMATION

Calories ....478 Sugars 2g
Protein ....29g Fat 34g
Carbohydrate ...14g Saturates 20g

 10 MINS   15-20 MINS

SERVES 4

INGREDIENTS

350 g/12 oz mature (sharp) Cheddar

125 g/4½ oz Gouda (Dutch), Gruyère or
   Emmenthal (Swiss) cheese

1 tsp mustard powder

1 tsp wholegrain mustard

2-4 tbsp brown ale, cider or milk

½ tsp vegetarian Worcestershire sauce

4 thick slices white or brown bread

4 eggs

salt and pepper

TO GARNISH

tomato wedges

watercress sprigs

1 Grate the cheeses and place in a non-stick saucepan.

2 Add the mustards, seasoning, brown ale, cider or milk and vegetarian Worcestershire sauce and mix well.

3 Heat the cheese mixture gently, stirring until it has melted and is completely thick and creamy. Remove from the heat and leave to cool a little.

4 Toast the slices of bread on each side under a preheated grill (broiler) then spread the rarebit mixture evenly over each piece. Put under a moderate grill (broiler) until golden brown and bubbling.

5 Meanwhile, poach the eggs. If using a poacher, grease the cups, heat the

water in the pan and, when just boiling, break the eggs into the cups. Cover and simmer for 4-5 minutes until just set. Alternatively, bring about 4 cm/1½ inches of water to the boil in a frying pan (skillet) or large saucepan and for each egg quickly swirl the water with a knife and drop the egg into the "hole" created. Cook for about 4 minutes until just set.

6 Top the rarebits with a poached egg and serve garnished with tomato wedges and sprigs of watercress.

VARIATION

For a change, you can use part or all Stilton or other blue cheese; the appearance is not so attractive but the flavour is very good.

Carrot & Potato Soufflé

Hot soufflés have a reputation for being difficult to make, but this one is both simple and impressive. Make sure you serve it as soon as it is ready.

NUTRITIONAL INFORMATION

Calories 294	Sugars 6g
Protein 10g	Fat 9g
Carbohydrate ...46g	Saturates 4g

1¼ HOURS   40 MINS

SERVES 4

I N G R E D I E N T S

25 g/1 oz/2 tbsp butter, melted

4 tbsp fresh wholemeal (whole wheat)
  breadcrumbs

675 g/1½ lb floury (mealy) potatoes, baked
  in their skins

2 carrots, grated

2 eggs, separated

2 tbsp orange juice

¼ tsp grated nutmeg

salt and pepper

carrot curls, to garnish

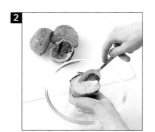

1 Brush the inside of a 900 ml/ 1½ pint/3¾ cup soufflé dish with butter. Sprinkle three-quarters of the breadcrumbs over the base and sides.

2 Cut the baked potatoes in half and scoop the flesh into a mixing bowl.

3 Add the carrot, egg yolks, orange juice and nutmeg to the potato flesh. Season to taste with salt and pepper.

4 In a separate bowl, whisk the egg whites until soft peaks form, then gently fold into the potato mixture with a metal spoon until well incorporated.

5 Gently spoon the potato and carrot mixture into the prepared soufflé dish. Sprinkle the remaining breadcrumbs over the top of the mixture.

6 Cook in a preheated oven, 200°C/ 400°F/Gas Mark 6, for 40 minutes, until risen and golden. Do not open the oven door during the cooking time, otherwise the soufflé will sink. Serve at once, garnished with carrot curls.

COOK'S TIP

To bake the potatoes, prick the skins and cook in a preheated oven, 190°C/375°F/Gas Mark 5, for about 1 hour.

Lentil Croquettes

These croquettes are an ideal light lunch served with a crisp salad and a tahini (sesame seed paste) dip.

NUTRITIONAL INFORMATION

Calories ....409 Sugars 5g
Protein ....19g Fat 17g
Carbohydrate ...48g Saturates 2g

10 MINS   55 MINS

SERVES 4

INGREDIENTS

225 g/8 oz/1¼ cups split red lentils

1 green (bell) pepper, seeded and finely chopped

1 red onion, finely chopped

2 garlic cloves, crushed

1 tsp garam masala

½ tsp chilli powder

1 tsp ground cumin

2 tsp lemon juice

2 tbsp chopped unsalted peanuts

600 ml/1 pint/2½ cups water

1 egg, beaten

3 tbsp plain (all-purpose) flour

1 tsp turmeric

1 tsp chilli powder

4 tbsp vegetable oil

salt and pepper

salad leaves (greens) and herbs, to serve

1 Put the lentils in a large saucepan with the (bell) pepper, onion, garlic, garam masala, chilli powder, ground cumin, lemon juice and peanuts. Add the water and bring to the boil. Reduce the heat and simmer, stirring occasionally, for about 30 minutes, or until the liquid has been absorbed.

2 Remove the mixture from the heat and leave to cool slightly. Beat in the egg and season to taste with salt and pepper. Leave to cool completely.

3 With floured hands, form the mixture into 8 rectangles

4 Mix the flour, turmeric and chilli powder together on a small plate. Roll the croquettes in the spiced flour mixture to coat thoroughly.

5 Heat the oil in a large frying pan (skillet). Add the croquettes, in batches, and fry, turning once, for about 10 minutes, until crisp on both sides. Transfer to warm serving plates and serve the croquettes with crisp salad leaves (greens) and fresh herbs.

Potato Mushroom Cakes

These cakes will be loved by vegetarians and meat-eaters alike. Packed with creamy potato and as wide a variety of mushrooms as possible.

NUTRITIONAL INFORMATION

Calories 298   Sugars 0.8g
Protein ....5g   Fat 22g
Carbohydrate ...22g   Saturates 5g

20 MINS   25 MINS

SERVES 4

I N G R E D I E N T S

500 g/1 lb 2 oz floury (mealy) potatoes,
   diced

25 g/1 oz/2 tbsp butter

175 g/6 oz mixed mushrooms, chopped

2 garlic cloves, crushed

1 small egg, beaten

1 tbsp chopped fresh chives, plus extra
   to garnish

flour, for dusting

oil, for frying

salt and pepper

1 Cook the potatoes in a pan of lightly salted boiling water for 10 minutes, or until cooked through

2 Drain the potatoes well, mash with a potato masher or fork and set aside.

3 Meanwhile, melt the butter in a frying pan (skillet). Add the mushrooms and garlic and cook, stirring constantly, for 5 minutes. Drain well.

4 Stir the mushrooms and garlic into the potato, together with the beaten egg and chives.

5 Divide the mixture equally into 4 portions and shape them into round cakes. Toss them in the flour until the outsides of the cakes are completely coated.

6 Heat the oil in a frying pan (skillet). Add the potato cakes and fry over a medium heat for 10 minutes until they are golden brown, turning them over halfway through. Serve the cakes at once, with a simple crisp salad.

COOK'S TIP

Prepare the cakes in advance, cover and leave to chill in the refrigerator for up to 24 hours, if you wish.

Stuffed Vegetable Snacks

In this recipe, aubergines (eggplants) are filled with a spicy bulgur wheat and vegetable stuffing for a delicious light meal.

NUTRITIONAL INFORMATION

Calories 360   Sugars 17g
Protein . . . . .9g   Fat 16g
Carbohydrate . . .50g   Saturates 2g

40 MINS   30 MINS

SERVES 4

I N G R E D I E N T S

4 medium aubergines (eggplants)

salt

175 g/6 oz/¾ cup bulgur wheat

300 ml/½ pint/1¼ cups boiling water

3 tbsp olive oil

2 garlic cloves, crushed

2 tbsp pine nuts

½ tsp turmeric

1 tsp chilli powder

2 celery sticks, chopped

4 spring onions (scallions), chopped

1 carrot, grated

50 g/1¾ oz/¾ cup button
   mushrooms, chopped

2 tbsp raisins

2 tbsp chopped coriander (cilantro)

green salad, to serve

1 Cut the aubergines (eggplants) in half lengthways and scoop out the flesh with a teaspoon. Chop the flesh and set aside. Rub the insides of the aubergines (eggplants) with a little salt and leave to stand for 20 minutes.

2 Meanwhile, put the bulgur wheat in a mixing bowl and pour the boiling water over the top. Leave to stand for 20 minutes, or until the water has been completely absorbed.

3 Heat the oil in a frying pan (skillet). Add the garlic, pine nuts, turmeric, chilli powder, celery, spring onions (scallions), carrot, mushrooms and raisins and cook for 2–3 minutes.

4 Stir in the reserved aubergine (eggplant) flesh and cook for a further 2–3 minutes. Add the chopped coriander (cilantro), mixing well.

5 Remove the pan from the heat and stir in the bulgur wheat. Rinse the aubergine (eggplant) shells under cold water and pat dry with kitchen paper (paper towels).

6 Spoon the bulgur filling into the aubergines (eggplants) and place in a roasting tin (pan). Pour in a little boiling water and cook in a preheated oven, 180°C/350°F/Gas Mark 4, for about 15–20 minutes, until piping hot. Remove from the oven and serve hot with a green salad.

Vegetable Samosas

These Indian snacks are perfect for a quick or light meal. Served with a salad they can be made in advance and frozen for ease.

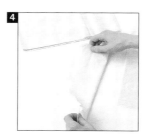

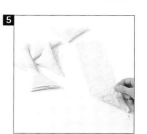

NUTRITIONAL INFORMATION

Calories 291   Sugars 2g
Protein . . . . .4g   Fat 23g
Carbohydrate . . .18g   Saturates 3g

 20 MINS   30 MINS

MAKES 12

I N G R E D I E N T S

FILLING

2 tbsp vegetable oil

1 onion, chopped

½ tsp ground coriander

½ tsp ground cumin

pinch of turmeric

½ tsp ground ginger

½ tsp garam masala

1 garlic clove, crushed

225 g/8 oz/1½ cups potatoes, diced

100 g/3½ oz/1 cup frozen peas, thawed

150 g/5½ oz/2 cups spinach, chopped

PASTRY

12 sheets filo pastry

oil, for deep-frying

1 To make the filling, heat the oil in a frying pan (skillet). Add the onion and sauté, stirring frequently, for 1–2 minutes, until softened. Stir in all of the spices and garlic and cook for 1 minute.

2 Add the potatoes and cook over a low heat, stirring frequently, for 5 minutes, until they begin to soften.

3 Stir in the peas and spinach and cook for a further 3–4 minutes.

4 Lay the filo pastry sheets out on a clean work surface (counter) and fold each sheet in half lengthways.

5 Place 2 tablespoons of the vegetable filling at one end of each folded pastry sheet. Fold over one corner to make a triangle. Continue folding in this way to make a triangular package and seal the edges with water.

6 Repeat with the remaining pastry and the remaining filling.

7 Heat the oil for deep-frying to 180°C/350°F or until a cube of bread browns in 30 seconds. Fry the samosas, in batches, for 1–2 minutes until golden. Drain on absorbent kitchen paper (paper towels) and keep warm while cooking the remainder. Serve immediately.

Stuffed Paratas

This bread can be quite rich and is usually made for special occasions. It can be eaten on its own or with a vegetable curry.

NUTRITIONAL INFORMATION

Calories . . . . . . .391 Sugars 2g
Protein . . . . .6g Fat 24g
Carbohydrate . . .40g Saturates 2.5g

 25 MINS   30-35 MINS

SERVES 6

INGREDIENTS

DOUGH

225 g/8 oz/1¾ cups wholemeal flour (ata
  or chapati flour)

½ tsp salt

200 ml/7 fl oz/scant 1 cup water

100 g/3½ oz/8 tbsp vegetable ghee

2 tbsp ghee, for frying

FILLING

3 medium potatoes

½ tsp turmeric

1 tsp garam masala

1 tsp finely chopped root ginger

fresh coriander (cilantro) leaves

3 green chillies, finely chopped

1 tsp salt

1 To make the paratas, mix the flour, salt, water and ghee in a bowl to form a dough.

2 Divide the dough into 6-8 equal portions. Roll each portion out on to a floured work surface. Brush the middle of the dough portions with ½ tsp ghee. Fold the dough portions in half, roll into a pipe-like shape, flatten with the palms of your hand, then roll around your finger to form a coil. Roll out again, using flour to dust as and when necessary, to form a round about 18 cm/7 inches in diameter.

3 Place the potatoes in a saucepan of boiling water and cook until soft enough to be mashed.

4 Blend the turmeric, garam masala, ginger, coriander (cilantro), chillies and salt together in a bowl.

5 Add the spice mixture to the mashed potato and mix well. Spread about 1 tablespoon of the spicy potato mixture on each dough portion and cover with another rolled-out piece of dough. Seal the edges well.

6 Heat 2 teaspoons ghee in a heavy-based frying-pan (skillet). Place the paratas gently in the pan, in batches, and fry, turning and moving them about gently with a flat spoon, until golden.

7 Remove the paratas from the frying pan (skillet) and serve immediately.

Bombay Bowl

You can use dried chickpeas (garbanzo beans) for this popular snack, but the canned sort are quick and easy without sacrificing much flavour.

NUTRITIONAL INFORMATION

Calories 183   Sugars 6g
Protein ....9g   Fat 3g
Carbohydrate ...33g   Saturates 0.3g

15 MINS   15 MINS

SERVES 4

INGREDIENTS

400 g/14 oz can chickpeas (garbanzo
   beans), drained

2 medium potatoes

1 medium onion

2 tbsp tamarind paste

6 tbsp water

1 tsp chilli powder

2 tsp sugar

1 tsp salt

TO GARNISH

1 tomato, sliced

2 fresh green chillies, chopped

fresh coriander (cilantro) leaves

COOK'S TIP

Cream-coloured and resembling a hazelnut in appearance, chickpeas (garbanzo beans) have a nutty flavour and slightly crunchy texture. Indian cooks grind these to make a flour called gram or besan, which is used to make breads and thicken sauces.

 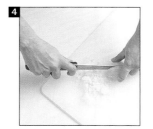

1 Place the drained chickpeas (garbanzo beans) in a bowl.

2 Using a sharp knife, cut the potatoes into even-size dice.

3 Place the diced potatoes in a saucepan of water and boil until cooked through. Test by inserting the tip of a knife into the potatoes – they should feel soft and tender. Drain and set the potatoes aside until required.

4 Using a sharp knife, finely chop the onion. Set aside until required.

5 Mix together the tamarind paste and water in a small mixing bowl.

6 Add the chilli powder, sugar and salt to the tamarind paste mixture and mix together. Pour the mixture over the chickpeas (garbanzo beans).

7 Add the onion and the diced potatoes, and stir to mix. Season to taste with a little salt.

8 Transfer to a serving bowl and garnish with tomatoes, chillies and coriander (cilantro) leaves.

Brown Rice Gratin

This dish is extremely versatile and could be made with any vegetables that you have to hand.

NUTRITIONAL INFORMATION

Calories . . . . .321 Sugars 6g
Protein . . . . .10g Fat 18g
Carbohydrate . . .32g Saturates 9g

15 MINS   1 HOUR

SERVES 4

I N G R E D I E N T S

100 g/3½ oz/⅓ cup brown rice

2 tbsp butter or margarine, plus extra
   for greasing

1 red onion, chopped

2 garlic cloves, crushed

1 carrot, cut into matchsticks

1 courgette (zucchini), sliced

75 g/2¾ oz baby corn cobs,
   halved lengthways

2 tbsp sunflower seeds

3 tbsp chopped mixed herbs

100 g/3½ oz/1 cup grated
   mozzarella cheese

2 tbsp wholemeal (whole
   wheat) breadcrumbs

salt and pepper

VARIATION

Use an alternative rice, such
as basmati, and flavour the
dish with curry spices, if
you prefer.

1 Cook the rice in a saucepan of boiling lightly salted water for 20 minutes. Drain well.

2 Lightly grease a 850 ml/1½ pint/3¾ cup ovenproof dish with butter.

3 Heat the butter in a frying pan (skillet). Add the onion and cook, stirring constantly, for 2 minutes, or until soft and translucent.

4 Add the garlic, carrot, courgette (zucchini) and corn cobs and cook, stirring constantly, for a further 5 minutes.

5 Mix the rice with the sunflower seeds and mixed herbs and stir into the pan.

6 Stir in half of the mozzarella cheese and season with salt and pepper to taste.

7 Spoon the mixture into the prepared dish and top with the breadcrumbs and remaining cheese. Cook in a preheated oven, 180°C/350°F/Gas Mark 4, for about 25–30 minutes, or until the cheese has begun to turn golden. Serve immediately.

Cheese & Onion Rosti

These grated potato cakes are also known as straw cakes, as they resemble a straw mat! Serve them with a tomato sauce or salad.

NUTRITIONAL INFORMATION

Calories 307	Sugars 4g	
Protein 8g	Fat 13g	
Carbohydrate . . .42g	Saturates 6g	

10 MINS   40 MINS

SERVES 4

INGREDIENTS

900 g/2 lb potatoes

1 onion, grated

50 g/1¾ oz/½ cup grated Gruyère cheese

2 tbsp chopped parsley

1 tbsp olive oil

25 g/1 oz/2 tbsp butter

salt and pepper

TO GARNISH

shredded spring onion (scallion)

1 small tomato, quartered

1 Parboil the potatoes in a pan of lightly salted boiling water for 10 minutes and leave to cool. Peel the potatoes and grate with a coarse grater. Place the grated potatoes in a large mixing bowl.

COOK'S TIP

The potato cakes should be flattened as much as possible during cooking, otherwise the outside will be cooked before the centre.

2 Stir in the onion, cheese and parsley. Season well with salt and pepper. Divide the potato mixture into 4 portions of equal size and form them into cakes.

3 Heat half of the olive oil and butter in a frying pan (skillet) and cook 2 of the potato cakes over a high heat for 1 minute, then reduce the heat and cook for 5 minutes, until they are golden underneath. Turn them over and cook for a further 5 minutes.

4 Repeat with the other half of the oil and the remaining butter to cook the remaining 2 cakes. Transfer to warm individual serving plates, garnish and serve immediately.

Spiced Corn & Nut Mix

A tasty mixture of buttery-spiced nuts, raisins and popcorn to enjoy as a snack or with pre-dinner drinks.

NUTRITIONAL INFORMATION

Calories ....372 Sugars 9g
Protein ....8g Fat 31g
Carbohydrate ...16g Saturates 9g

5 MINS   10 MINS

SERVES 6

INGREDIENTS

2 tbsp vegetable oil

60 g/2 oz/¼ cup popping corn

60 g/2 oz/¼ cup butter

1 garlic clove, crushed

60 g/2 oz/⅓ cup unblanched almonds

60 g/2 oz/½ cup unsalted cashews

60 g/2 oz /½ cup unsalted peanuts

1 tsp vegetarian Worcestershire sauce

1 tsp curry powder or paste

¼ tsp chilli powder

60 g/2 oz/⅓ cup seedless raisins

salt

1 Heat the oil in a saucepan. Add the popping corn, stir well, then cover and cook over a fairly high heat for 3-5 minutes, holding the saucepan lid firmly and shaking the pan frequently until the popping stops.

2 Turn the popped corn into a dish, discarding any unpopped corn kernels.

3 Melt the butter in a frying pan, add the garlic, almonds, cashews and peanuts, then stir in the Worcestershire sauce, curry powder or paste and chilli powder and cook over a medium heat, stirring frequently, for 2–3 minutes.

4 Remove the pan from the heat and stir in the raisins and popped corn. Season with salt to taste and mix thoroughly. Transfer to a serving bowl and serve warm or cold.

VARIATION

Use a mixture of any unsalted nuts of your choice – walnuts, pecans, hazelnuts, Brazils, macadamia and pine nuts. For a less fiery flavour, omit the curry and chilli powder and add 1 tsp cumin seeds, 1 tsp ground coriander and ½ tsp paprika.

Three-Cheese Fondue

A hot cheese dip made from three different cheeses can be prepared easily and with guaranteed success in the microwave oven.

NUTRITIONAL INFORMATION

Calories 565   Sugars 1g
Protein ....29g   Fat 38g
Carbohydrate ...15g   Saturates 24g

 15 MINS   🕐 10 MINS

SERVES 4

I N G R E D I E N T S

1 garlic clove

300 ml/½ pint/1¼ cups dry white wine

250 g/8 oz/2 cups grated mild
  Cheddar cheese

125 g/4½ oz/1 cup grated Gruyère
  (Swiss) cheese

125 g/4½ oz/1 cup grated mozzarella
  cheese

2 tbsp cornflour (cornstarch)

pepper

T O   S E R V E

French bread

vegetables, such as courgettes
  (zucchini), mushrooms, baby corn cobs
  and cauliflower

COOK'S TIP

Make sure you add the cheese to the wine gradually, mixing well in between each addition, otherwise the mixture might curdle.

1 Bruise the garlic by placing the flat side of a knife on top and pressing down with the heel of your hand.

2 Rub the garlic around the inside of a large bowl. Discard the garlic.

3 Pour the wine into the bowl and heat, uncovered, on HIGH power for 3–4 minutes, until hot but not boiling.

4 Gradually add the Cheddar and Gruyère (Swiss) cheeses, stirring well after each addition, then add the mozzarella. Stir until completely melted.

5 Mix the cornflour (cornstarch) with a little water to a smooth paste and stir into the cheese mixture. Season to taste with pepper.

6 Cover and cook on MEDIUM power for 6 minutes, stirring twice during cooking, until the sauce is smooth.

7 Cut the French bread into cubes and the vegetables into batons, slices or florets. To serve, keep the fondue warm over a spirit lamp or reheat as necessary in the microwave oven. Dip in cubes of French bread and batons, slices or florets of vegetables.

Cheese & Potato Slices

This recipe takes a while to prepare but it is well worth the effort. The golden potato slices coated in breadcrumbs and cheese are delicious.

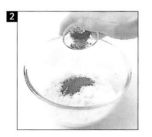

NUTRITIONAL INFORMATION

Calories	560	Sugars	.........3g
Protein	........19g	Fat	..........31g
Carbohydrate	...55g	Saturates	.......7g

🍅 10 MINS   🕐 40 MINS

SERVES 4

I N G R E D I E N T S

3 large waxy potatoes, unpeeled and
   thickly sliced

75 g/2½ oz/1 cup fresh white breadcrumbs

40 g/1½ oz/½ cup grated Parmesan
   cheese

1½ tsp chilli powder

2 eggs, beaten

oil, for deep frying

chilli powder, for dusting (optional)

1 Cook the sliced potatoes in a saucepan of boiling water for about 10-15 minutes, or until the potatoes are just tender. Drain thoroughly.

2 Mix the breadcrumbs, cheese and chilli powder together in a bowl, then transfer to a shallow dish. Pour the beaten eggs into a separate shallow dish.

3 Dip the potato slices first in egg and then roll them in the breadcrumbs to coat completely.

4 Heat the oil in a large saucepan or deep-fryer to 180°C/350°F or until a cube of bread browns in 30 seconds. Cook the cheese and potato slices, in several batches, for 4–5 minutes or until a golden brown colour.

5 Remove the cheese and potato slices from the oil with a slotted spoon and drain thoroughly on kitchen paper (paper towels). Keep the cheese and potato slices warm while you cook the remaining batches.

6 Transfer the cheese and potato slices to warm individual serving plates. Dust lightly with chilli powder, if using, and serve immediately.

COOK'S TIP

The cheese and potato slices may be coated in the breadcrumb mixture in advance and then stored in the refrigerator until ready to use.

Pasta, Grains & Pulses

Grains and pulses (legumes) are universally important staple foods. They are highly nutritious as they are an excellent source of protein, iron, calcium and B vitamins,

and are virtually fat-free. Grains include wheat, corn, barley, rye, oats, buckwheat and many different varieties of rice, as well as associated flours. Pulses (legumes) include chickpeas (garbanzo beans), yellow and green split peas, a fascinating variety of beans, together with many types of lentil. Grains and pulses (legumes) form a substantial base to which other ingredients can be added. Each has its own flavour and texture, so it's worth experimenting.

Baked Pasta

This pasta dish is baked in a pudding basin (bowl) and served cut into slices. It looks and tastes terrific and is great when you want to impress.

NUTRITIONAL INFORMATION

Calories ....179 Sugars 6g
Protein ....8g Fat 10g
Carbohydrate ...16g Saturates 3g

10 MINS   1 HR 5 MINS

SERVES 8

INGREDIENTS

100 g/3½ oz/1 cup dried pasta shapes,
    such as penne or casareccia

1 tbsp olive oil

1 leek, chopped

3 garlic cloves, crushed

1 green (bell) pepper, seeded and chopped

400 g/14 oz can chopped tomatoes

2 tbsp chopped, pitted black olives

2 eggs, beaten

1 tbsp chopped basil

TOMATO SAUCE

1 tbsp olive oil

1 onion, chopped

225 g/8 oz can chopped tomatoes

1 tsp caster (superfine) sugar

2 tbsp tomato purée (paste)

150 ml/¼ pint/¾ cup vegetable stock

salt and pepper

1 Cook the pasta in a saucepan of boiling lightly salted water for 8 minutes. Drain thoroughly.

2 Meanwhile, heat the oil in a saucepan. Add the leek and garlic and sauté, stirring constantly, for 2 minutes. Add the (bell) pepper, tomatoes and olives and cook for a further 5 minutes.

3 Remove the pan from the heat and stir in the pasta, beaten eggs and basil. Season well, and spoon into a lightly greased 1 litre/2 pint/4 cup ovenproof pudding basin (ovenproof bowl).

4 Place the pudding basin (bowl) in a roasting tin (pan) and half-fill the tin (pan) with boiling water. Cover and cook in a preheated oven, 180°C/350°F/Gas Mark 6, for 40 minutes, until set.

5 To make the sauce, heat the oil in a pan and sauté the onion for 2 minutes. Add the remaining ingredients and cook for 10 minutes. Put the sauce in a food processor or blender and process until smooth. Return to a clean saucepan and heat through.

6 Turn the pasta out of the pudding basin (bowl) on to a warm plate. Slice and serve with the tomato sauce.

Vegetable Cannelloni

This dish is made with prepared cannelloni tubes, but may also be made by rolling ready-bought lasagne sheets.

NUTRITIONAL INFORMATION

Calories 594   Sugars 12g
Protein ....13g   Fat 38g
Carbohydrate ...52g   Saturates 7g

10 MINS   45 MINS

SERVES 4

INGREDIENTS

1 aubergine (eggplant)

125 ml/4 fl oz/½ cup olive oil

225 g/8 oz spinach

2 garlic cloves, crushed

1 tsp ground cumin

75 g/2¾oz/1 cup mushrooms, chopped

12 cannelloni tubes

salt and pepper

TOMATO SAUCE

1 tbsp olive oil

1 onion, chopped

2 garlic cloves, crushed

2 x 400 g/14 oz cans chopped tomatoes

1 tsp caster (superfine) sugar

2 tbsp chopped basil

50 g/1¾ oz/½ cup sliced mozzarella

COOK'S TIP

You can prepare the tomato sauce in advance and store it in the refrigerator for up to 24 hours.

1 Cut the aubergine (eggplant) into small dice.

2 Heat the oil in a frying pan (skillet). Add the aubergine (eggplant) and cook over a moderate heat, stirring frequently, for 2–3 minutes.

3 Add the spinach, garlic, cumin and mushrooms. Season and cook, stirring, for 2–3 minutes. Spoon the mixture into the cannelloni tubes and place in an ovenproof dish in a single layer.

4 To make the sauce, heat the olive oil in a saucepan and sauté the onion and garlic for 1 minute. Add the tomatoes, caster (superfine) sugar and chopped basil and bring to the boil. Reduce the heat and simmer for about 5 minutes. Pour the sauce over the cannelloni tubes.

5 Arrange the sliced mozzarella on top of the sauce and cook in a preheated oven, 190°C/375°F/Gas Mark 5, for 30 minutes, or until the cheese is bubbling and golden brown. Serve immediately.

Vegetable Lasagne

This colourful and tasty lasagne has layers of vegetables in tomato sauce and aubergines (eggplants), all topped with a rich cheese sauce.

NUTRITIONAL INFORMATION

Calories ....544 Sugars 18g
Protein ....20g Fat 26g
Carbohydrate ...61g Saturates 12g

35 MINS   55 MINS

SERVES 4

INGREDIENTS

1 aubergine (eggplant), sliced

3 tbsp olive oil

2 garlic cloves, crushed

1 red onion, halved and sliced

3 mixed (bell) peppers, seeded and diced

225 g/8 oz mixed mushrooms, sliced

2 celery sticks, sliced

1 courgette (zucchini), diced

½ tsp chilli powder

½ tsp ground cumin

2 tomatoes, chopped

300 ml/½ pint/1¼ cups passata
   (sieved tomatoes)

2 tbsp chopped basil

8 no pre-cook lasagne verdi sheets

salt and pepper

CHEESE SAUCE

2 tbsp butter or margarine

1 tbsp flour

150 ml/¼ pint/⅔ cup vegetable stock

300 ml/½ pint/1¼ cups milk

75 g/2¾ oz/¾ cup grated Cheddar cheese

1 tsp Dijon mustard

1 tbsp chopped basil

1 egg, beaten

1 Place the aubergine (eggplant) slices in a colander, sprinkle with salt and leave for 20 minutes. Rinse under cold water, drain and reserve.

2 Heat the oil in a pan and sauté the garlic and onion for 1–2 minutes. Add the (bell) peppers, mushrooms, celery and courgette (zucchini) and cook, stirring constantly, for 3–4 minutes.

3 Stir in the spices and cook for 1 minute. Mix in the tomatoes, passata (sieved tomatoes) and basil and season to taste with salt and pepper.

4 For the sauce, melt the butter in a pan, stir in the flour and cook for 1 minute. Remove from the heat, stir in the stock and milk, return to the heat and add half the cheese and the mustard. Boil, stirring, until thickened. Stir in the basil. Remove from the heat and stir in the egg.

5 Place half the lasagne in an ovenproof dish. Top with half the vegetable mixture then half the aubergines (eggplants). Repeat and spoon the cheese sauce on top. Sprinkle with cheese and cook in a preheated oven, 180°C/350°F/ Gas 4, for 40 minutes.

Penne & Vegetables

The sweet cherry tomatoes in this recipe add colour and flavour and are complemented by the black olives and (bell) peppers.

NUTRITIONAL INFORMATION

Calories ....380 Sugars 6g
Protein ....8g Fat 16g
Carbohydrate ...48g Saturates 7g

 10 MINS   25 MINS

SERVES 4

INGREDIENTS

225 g/8 oz/2 cups dried penne

2 tbsp olive oil

25 g/1 oz/2 tbsp butter

2 garlic cloves, crushed

1 green (bell) pepper, seeded and
    thinly sliced

1 yellow (bell) pepper, seeded and
    thinly sliced

16 cherry tomatoes, halved

1 tbsp chopped oregano

125 ml/4 fl oz/½ cup dry white wine

2 tbsp quartered, pitted black olives

75 g/2¾ oz/1 bunch rocket (arugula)

salt and pepper

oregano sprigs, to garnish

VARIATION

If rocket (arugula) is unavailable, spinach makes a good substitute. Follow the same cooking instructions as for rocket (arugula).

1 Cook the pasta in a saucepan of boiling salted water for 8–10 minutes or until al dente. Drain thoroughly.

2 Heat the oil and butter in a pan until the butter melts. Sauté the garlic for 30 seconds. Add the (bell) peppers and cook, stirring, for 3–4 minutes.

3 Stir in the cherry tomatoes, oregano, wine and olives and cook for 3–4 minutes. Season well with salt and pepper and stir in the rocket (arugula) until just wilted.

4 Transfer the pasta to a serving dish, spoon over the sauce and garnish.

Pear & Walnut Pasta

This is quite an unusual combination of ingredients in a savoury dish, but is absolutely wonderful tossed into a fine pasta, such as spaghetti.

NUTRITIONAL INFORMATION

Calories	508	Sugars	.........9g
Protein	........15g	Fat	..........27g
Carbohydrate	...50g	Saturates	......11g

 10 MINS   20 MINS

SERVES 4

I N G R E D I E N T S

225 g/8 oz dried spaghetti

2 small ripe pears, peeled and sliced

150 ml/¼ pint/¾ cup vegetable stock

6 tbsp dry white wine

25 g/1 oz/2 tbsp butter

1 tbsp olive oil

1 red onion, quartered and sliced

1 garlic clove, crushed

50 g/1¾ oz/½ cup walnut halves

2 tbsp chopped oregano

1 tbsp lemon juice

75 g/2¾ oz dolcelatte cheese

salt and pepper

oregano sprigs, to garnish

1 Cook the pasta in a saucepan of boiling lightly salted water for about 8–10 minutes, or until al dente. Drain thoroughly and keep warm until required.

2 Meanwhile, place the pears in a pan and pour over the stock and wine. Poach the pears over a low heat for 10 minutes. Drain and reserve the cooking liquid and set the pears aside.

3 Heat the butter and oil in a saucepan until the butter melts. Add the onion and garlic and sauté over a low heat, stirring frequently for 2–3 minutes.

4 Stir in the walnut halves, oregano and lemon juice.

5 Stir in the reserved pears with 4 tablespoons of the poaching liquid.

6 Crumble the dolcelatte cheese into the pan and cook over a low heat, stirring occasionally, for 1–2 minutes, or until the cheese is just beginning to melt. Season with salt and pepper to taste.

7 Add the pasta and toss in the sauce, using two forks. Garnish and serve.

Spinach & Nut Pasta

Use any pasta shapes that you have for this recipe. Multi-coloured tricolore pasta is visually the most attractive to use.

NUTRITIONAL INFORMATION

Calories ....603 Sugars 5g
Protein ....12g Fat 41g
Carbohydrate ...46g Saturates 6g

 5 MINS   15 MINS

SERVES 4

I N G R E D I E N T S

225 g/8 oz/2 cups dried pasta shapes

125 ml/4 fl oz/½ cup olive oil

2 garlic cloves, crushed

1 onion, quartered and sliced

3 large flat mushrooms, sliced

225 g/8 oz spinach

2 tbsp pine nuts

75 ml/3 fl oz/6 tbsp dry white wine

salt and pepper

Parmesan shavings, to garnish

1 Cook the pasta in a saucepan of boiling salted water for 8–10 minutes, or until al dente. Drain well.

2 Meanwhile, heat the oil in a large saucepan and sauté the garlic and onion for 1 minute.

COOK'S TIP

Grate a little nutmeg over the dish for extra flavour, as this spice has a particular affinity with spinach.

3 Add the sliced mushrooms to the pan and cook over a medium heat, stirring occasionally, for 2 minutes.

4 Lower the heat, add the spinach to the pan and cook, stirring occasionally, for 4–5 minutes, or until the spinach has wilted.

5 Stir in the pine nuts and wine, season to taste with salt and pepper and cook for 1 minute.

6 Transfer the pasta to a warm serving bowl and toss the sauce into it, mixing well. Garnish with shavings of Parmesan cheese and serve.

Thai-Style Stir-Fried Noodles

This dish is considered the Thai national dish, as it is made and eaten everywhere – a one-dish, fast food for eating on the move.

NUTRITIONAL INFORMATION

Calories . . . . .407 Sugars 11g
Protein . . . . .14g Fat 16g
Carbohydrate . . .56g Saturates 3g

 15 MINS   5 MINS

SERVES 4

INGREDIENTS

225 g/8 oz dried rice noodles

2 red chillies, seeded and
finely chopped

2 shallots, finely chopped

2 tbsp sugar

2 tbsp tamarind water

1 tbsp lime juice

2 tbsp light soy sauce

1 tbsp sunflower oil

1 tsp sesame oil

175 g/6 oz/¾ cup diced smoked tofu
(bean curd)

pepper

2 tbsp chopped roasted peanuts,
to garnish

1 Cook the rice noodles as directed on the pack, or soak them in boiling water for 5 minutes.

2 Grind together the chillies, shallots, sugar, tamarind water, lime juice, light soy sauce and pepper to taste.

3 Heat both the oils together in a preheated wok or large, heavy frying pan (skillet) over a high heat. Add the tofu (bean curd) and stir for 1 minute.

4 Add the chilli mixture, bring to the boil, and cook, stirring constantly, for about 2 minutes, until thickened.

5 Drain the rice noodles and add them to the chilli mixture. Use 2 spoons to lift and stir them until they are no longer steaming. Serve immediately, garnished with the peanuts.

COOK'S TIP

This is a quick one-dish meal that is very useful if you are catering for a single vegetarian in the family.

Stir-Fried Japanese Noodles

This quick dish is an ideal lunchtime meal, packed with whatever mixture of mushrooms you like in a sweet sauce.

NUTRITIONAL INFORMATION

Calories	379	Sugars	.........8g
Protein	........12g	Fat	..........13g
Carbohydrate	...53g	Saturates	.......3g

15 MINS   15 MINS

SERVES 4

I N G R E D I E N T S

225 g/8 oz Japanese egg noodles

2 tbsp sunflower oil

1 red onion, sliced

1 garlic clove, crushed

500 g/1 lb 2 oz mixed mushrooms, such as
   shiitake, oyster, brown cap

350 g/12 oz pak choi

2 tbsp sweet sherry

6 tbsp soy sauce

4 spring onions (scallions), sliced

1 tbsp toasted sesame seeds

1 Place the egg noodles in a large bowl. Pour over enough boiling water to cover and leave to soak for 10 minutes.

2 Heat the sunflower oil in a large preheated wok.

COOK'S TIP

The variety of mushrooms in supermarkets has greatly improved and a good mixture should be easily obtainable. If not, use the more common button and flat mushrooms.

3 Add the red onion and garlic to the wok and stir-fry for 2–3 minutes, or until softened.

4 Add the mushrooms to the wok and stir-fry for about 5 minutes, or until the mushrooms have softened.

5 Drain the Japanese egg noodles thoroughly and set aside.

6 Add the the pak choi, noodles, sweet sherry and soy sauce to the wok. Toss all of the ingredients together to mix well and stir-fry for 2–3 minutes, or until the liquid is just bubbling.

7 Transfer the mushroom noodles to warm serving bowls and scatter with sliced spring onions (scallions) and toasted sesame seeds. Serve immediately.

Spicy Fried Noodles

This is a simple idea to add an extra kick to noodles, which accompany many main course dishes in Thailand.

NUTRITIONAL INFORMATION

Calories	568	Sugars	.........3g
Protein	........16g	Fat	..........19g
Carbohydrate	...90g	Saturates	.......4g

 15 MINS   3–5 MINS

SERVES 4

INGREDIENTS

500 g/1 lb 2 oz medium egg noodles

60 g/2 oz/1 cup beansprouts

15 g/½ oz chives

3 tbsp sunflower oil

1 garlic clove, crushed

4 fresh green chillies, seeded, sliced and
    soaked in 2 tbsp rice vinegar

salt

1 Place the noodles in a bowl, cover with boiling water and soak for 10 minutes. Drain and set aside.

2 Pick over the beansprouts and soak in cold water while you cut the chives into 2.5cm/1 inch pieces. Set a few chives aside for the garnish. Drain the beansprouts thoroughly.

3 Heat the oil in a preheated wok or large, heavy-based frying pan (skillet). Add the crushed garlic and stir; then add the chillies and stir-fry for about 1 minute, until fragrant.

4 Add the beansprouts, stir and then add the noodles. Stir in salt to taste and add the chives. Using 2 spoons or a wok scoop, lift and toss the noodles for 1 minute.

5 Transfer the noodles to a warm serving dish, garnish the with the reserved chives and serve immediately.

COOK'S TIP

Soaking a chilli in rice vinegar has the effect of distributing the hot chilli flavour throughout the dish. To reduce the heat, you can slice the chilli more thickly before soaking.

Special Fried Rice

In this simple recipe, cooked rice is fried with vegetables and cashew nuts. It can either be eaten on its own or served as an accompaniment.

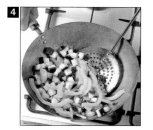

NUTRITIONAL INFORMATION

Calories 355	Sugars 6g
Protein 9g	Fat 15g
Carbohydrate ...48g	Saturates 3g

 10 MINS   30 MINS

SERVES 4

I N G R E D I E N T S

175 g/6 oz/generous ¾ cup long grain rice

60 g/2 oz/½ cup cashew nuts

1 carrot

½ cucumber

1 yellow (bell) pepper

2 spring onions (scallions)

2 tbsp vegetable oil

1 garlic clove, crushed

125 g/4½ oz/¾ cup frozen peas, thawed

1 tbsp soy sauce

1 tsp salt

coriander (cilantro) leaves, to garnish

1 Bring a large pan of water to the boil. Add the rice and simmer for 15 minutes. Tip the rice into a strainer and rinse; drain thoroughly.

COOK'S TIP

You can replace any of the vegetables in this recipe with others suitable for a stir-fry, and using leftover rice makes this a perfect last-minute dish.

2 Heat a wok or large, heavy-based frying pan (skillet), add the cashew nuts and dry-fry until lightly browned. Remove and set aside.

3 Cut the carrot in half along the length, then slice thinly into semi-circles. Halve the cucumber and remove the seeds, using a teaspoon, then dice the flesh. Seed and slice the (bell) pepper and chop the spring onions (scallions).

4 Heat the oil in a wok or large frying pan (skillet). Add the prepared vegetables and the garlic. Stir-fry for 3 minutes. Add the rice, peas, soy sauce and salt. Continue to stir-fry until well mixed and thoroughly heated.

5 Stir in the reserved cashew nuts. Transfer to a warmed serving dish, garnish with coriander (cilantro) leaves and serve immediately.

Chow Mein

Egg noodles are cooked and then fried with a colourful variety of vegetables to make this well-known and ever-popular dish.

NUTRITIONAL INFORMATION

Calories ....669 Sugars 9g
Protein ....19g Fat 23g
Carbohydrate ..100g Saturates 4g

15 MINS   10 MINS

SERVES 4

INGREDIENTS

500 g/1 lb 2 oz egg noodles

4 tbsp vegetable oil

1 onion, thinly sliced

2 carrots, cut into thin sticks

125 g/4½ oz/1⅓cups button
   mushrooms, quartered

125 g/4½ oz mangetout (snow peas)

½ cucumber, cut into sticks

125 g/4½ oz/2 cups spinach, shredded

125 g/4½ oz/2 cups beansprouts

2 tbsp dark soy sauce

1 tbsp sherry

1 tsp salt

1 tsp sugar

1 tsp cornflour (cornstarch)

1 tsp sesame oil

COOK'S TIP

For a spicy hot chow mein,
add 1 tablespoon chilli sauce or
substitute chilli oil for the
sesame oil.

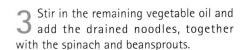

1 Cook the noodles according to the instructions on the packet. Drain and rinse under cold running water until cool. Set aside.

2 Heat 3 tablespoons of the vegetable oil in a preheated wok or frying pan (skillet). Add the onion and carrots, and stir-fry for 1 minute. Add the mushrooms, mangetout (snow peas) and cucumber and stir-fry for 1 minute.

3 Stir in the remaining vegetable oil and add the drained noodles, together with the spinach and beansprouts.

4 Blend together all the remaining ingredients and pour over the noodles and vegetables.

5 Stir-fry until the noodle mixture is thoroughly heated through, transfer to a warm serving dish and serve.

Risotto Verde

Risotto is an Italian dish which is easy to make and uses arborio rice, onion and garlic as a base for a range of savoury recipes.

NUTRITIONAL INFORMATION

Calories	374	Sugars	.........5g
Protein	........10g	Fat	..........9g
Carbohydrate	...55g	Saturates	.......2g

5 MINS   35 MINS

SERVES 4

I N G R E D I E N T S

1.75 litres/3 pints/7½ cups vegetable stock

2 tbsp olive oil

2 garlic cloves, crushed

2 leeks, shredded

225 g/8 oz/1¼ cups arborio rice

300 ml/½ pint/1¼ cups dry white wine

4 tbsp chopped mixed herbs

225 g/8 oz baby spinach

3 tbsp natural (unsweetened) yogurt

salt and pepper

shredded leek, to garnish

1 Pour the stock into a large saucepan and bring to the boil. Reduce the heat to a simmer.

2 Meanwhile, heat the oil in a separate pan. Add the garlic and leeks and sauté over a low heat, stirring occasionally, for 2–3 minutes, until softened.

3 Stir in the rice and cook for 2 minutes, stirring until each grain is coated with oil.

4 Pour in half of the wine and a little of the hot stock. Cook over a low heat until all of the liquid has been absorbed. Add the remaining stock and the wine, a little at a time, and cook over a low heat for 25 minutes, or until the rice is creamy.

5 Stir in the chopped mixed herbs and baby spinach, season to taste with salt and pepper and cook for 2 minutes.

6 Stir in the natural (unsweetened) yogurt. Transfer to a warm serving dish, garnish with the shredded leek and serve immediately.

COOK'S TIP

Do not try to hurry the process of cooking the risotto as the rice must absorb the liquid slowly in order for it to reach the correct consistency.

Risotto in Shells

An aubergine (eggplant) is halved and filled with a risotto mixture, topped with cheese and baked to make a snack or quick meal for two.

NUTRITIONAL INFORMATION

Calories	444	Sugars	........20g
Protein	........13g	Fat	..........23g
Carbohydrate	...50g	Saturates	.......8g

 20 MINS   🕐 55 MINS

SERVES 2

I N G R E D I E N T S

60 g/2 oz/¼ cup mixed long grain and
   wild rice

1 aubergine (eggplant), about 350 g/12 oz

1 tbsp olive oil

1 small onion, finely chopped

1 garlic clove, crushed

½ small red (bell) pepper, seeded
   and chopped

2 tbsp water

25 g/1 oz/3 tbsp raisins

25 g/1 oz/¼ cup cashew nuts,
   roughly chopped

½ tsp dried oregano

40 g/1½ oz/⅓ cup grated mature (sharp)
   Cheddar or Parmesan cheese

salt and pepper

oregano or parsley to garnish

1 Cook the rice in boiling salted water for about 15 minutes, until just tender. Drain, rinse and drain again.

2 Bring a large saucepan of water to the boil. Cut the stem off the aubergine (eggplant) and cut in half lengthways. Cut out the flesh from the centre carefully, leaving about a 1.5 cm/½ inch shell.

Blanch the shells in the boiling water for 3–4 minutes. Drain thoroughly. Chop the aubergine (eggplant) flesh finely.

3 Heat the oil in a saucepan or frying pan (skillet). Add the onion and garlic and fry over a low heat until beginning to soften, then add the (bell) pepper and aubergine (eggplant) flesh and continue cooking for a 2–3 minutes before adding the water and cooking for a further 2–3 minutes.

4 Stir the raisins, cashew nuts, dried oregano and rice into the aubergine

(eggplant) mixture and season to taste with salt and pepper.

5 Place the aubergine (eggplant) shells in an ovenproof dish and spoon in the rice mixture, piling it up well. Cover and cook in a preheated oven, 190°C/375°F/ Gas Mark 5, for 20 minutes.

6 Remove the lid and sprinkle the cheese over the rice. Place under a preheated moderate grill (broiler) and cook for 3–4 minutes, until golden brown and bubbling. Serve hot garnished with oregano or parsley.

Rice with Fruit & Nuts

Here is a tasty and filling rice dish that is nice and spicy and includes fruits for a refreshing flavour and toasted nuts for a crunchy texture.

NUTRITIONAL INFORMATION

Calories	423	Sugars	........19g
Protein	........10g	Fat	..........17g
Carbohydrate	...62g	Saturates	.......2g

🕒 20 MINS   🕐 1 HOUR

SERVES 6

I N G R E D I E N T S

4 tbsp vegetable ghee or oil

1 large onion, chopped

2 garlic cloves, crushed

2.5 cm/1 inch piece root ginger, chopped

1 tsp chilli powder

1 tsp cumin seeds

1 tbsp mild or medium curry powder
   or paste

300 g/10½ oz/1½ cups brown rice

850 ml/1½ pints/3½ cups boiling
   vegetable stock

400 g/14 oz can chopped tomatoes

salt and pepper

175 g/6 oz ready-to-eat dried apricots or
   peaches, cut into slivers

1 red (bell) pepper, seeded and diced

90 g/3 oz/¾ cup frozen peas

1-2 small, slightly green bananas

60-90g/2-3 oz/⅓-½ cup toasted nuts,
   such as almonds, cashews and hazelnuts
   or pine kernels

coriander (cilantro) sprigs, to garnish

1 Heat the ghee or oil in a large saucepan. Add the onion and fry over a low heat for 3 minutes. Stir in the garlic, ginger, spices and rice and cook gently, stirring constantly, for 2 minutes, until the rice is coated in the spiced oil.

2 Pour in the boiling stock, add the chopped tomatoes and season with salt and pepper to taste. Bring to the boil, then reduce the heat, cover and simmer gently for 40 minutes, or until the rice is almost cooked and most of the liquid has been absorbed.

3 Add the slivered apricots or peaches, diced red (bell) pepper and peas. Cover and continue cooking for 10 minutes. Remove from the heat and allow to stand for 5 minutes without uncovering.

4 Peel and slice the bananas. Uncover the rice mixture and fork through to mix the ingredients together. Add the toasted nuts and sliced banana and toss lightly. Transfer to a warm serving platter and garnish with coriander (cilantro) sprigs. Serve hot.

Deep South Rice & Beans

Cajun spices add a flavour of the American Deep South to this colourful rice and red kidney bean salad.

NUTRITIONAL INFORMATION

Calories ....336 Sugars 8g
Protein ....7g Fat 13g
Carbohydrate ...51g Saturates 2g

  10 MINS   15 MINS

SERVES 4

INGREDIENTS

175 g/6 oz/scant 1 cup long grain rice

4 tbsp olive oil

1 small green (bell) pepper, seeded
   and chopped

1 small red (bell) pepper, seeded
   and chopped

1 onion, finely chopped

1 small red or green chilli, seeded and
   finely chopped

2 tomatoes, chopped

125 g/4½ oz/½ cup canned red kidney
   beans, rinsed and drained

1 tbsp chopped fresh basil

2 tsp chopped fresh thyme

1 tsp Cajun spice

salt and pepper

fresh basil leaves, to garnish

1 Cook the rice in plenty of boiling, lightly salted water for about 12 minutes, until just tender. Rinse with cold water and drain well.

2 Meanwhile, heat the olive oil in a frying pan (skillet) and fry the green and red (bell) peppers and onion gently for about 5 minutes, until softened.

3 Add the chilli and tomatoes, and cook for a further 2 minutes.

4 Add the vegetable mixture and red kidney beans to the rice. Stir well to combine thoroughly.

5 Stir the chopped herbs and Cajun spice into the rice mixture. Season to taste with salt and pepper, and serve, garnished with basil leaves.

Spiced Basmati Pilau

The whole spices are not meant to be eaten and may be removed before serving. Omit the broccoli and mushrooms for a plain, spiced pilau.

20 MINS   25 MINS

SERVES 6

INGREDIENTS

500 g/1 lb 2 oz/2½ cups basmati rice

175 g/6 oz broccoli, trimmed

6 tbsp vegetable oil

2 large onions, chopped

225 g/8 oz/3 cups sliced mushrooms

2 garlic cloves, crushed

6 cardamom pods, split

6 whole cloves

8 black peppercorns

1 cinnamon stick or piece of cassia bark

1 tsp ground turmeric

1.2 litres/2 pints/5 cups boiling vegetable
   stock or water

salt and pepper

60 g/2 oz/⅓ cup seedless raisins

60 g/2 oz/½ cup unsalted pistachios,
   coarsely chopped

VARIATION

For added richness, you could stir a spoonful of vegetable ghee through the rice mixture just before serving. A little diced red (bell) pepper and a few cooked peas forked through at step 4 add a colourful touch.

1 Place the rice in a strainer and wash well under cold running water. Drain. Trim off most of the broccoli stalk and cut into small florets, then quarter the stalk lengthways and cut diagonally into 1 cm/½ inch pieces.

2 Heat the oil in a large saucepan. Add the onions and broccoli stalks and cook over a low heat, stirring frequently, for 3 minutes. Add the mushrooms, rice, garlic and spices and cook for 1 minute, stirring, until the rice is coated in oil.

3 Add the boiling stock and season to taste with salt and pepper. Stir in the broccoli florets and return the mixture to the boil. Cover, reduce the heat and cook over a low heat for 15 minutes without uncovering the pan.

4 Remove from the heat and leave to stand for 5 minutes without uncovering. Add the raisins and pistachios and gently fork through to fluff up the grains. Serve hot.

Thai Jasmine Rice

Every Thai meal has as its centrepiece a big bowl of steaming, fluffy Thai jasmine rice, to which salt should not be added.

NUTRITIONAL INFORMATION

Calories	239	Sugars	.........0g
Protein	.........5g	Fat	...........2g
Carbohydrate	...54g	Saturates	.....0.6g

5 MINS   10-15 MINS

SERVES 4

I N G R E D I E N T S

OPEN PAN METHOD

225 g/8 oz/generous 1 cup
 Thai jasmine rice

1 litre/1¾ pints/4 cups water

ABSORPTION METHOD

225 g/8 oz/generous 1 cup
 Thai jasmine rice

450 ml/16 fl oz/scant 2 cups water

COOK'S TIP

Thai jasmine rice can be frozen. Freeze in a plastic sealed container. Frozen rice is ideal for stir-fry dishes, as the process seems to separate the grains.

1 For the open pan method, rinse the rice in a strainer under cold running water and leave to drain.

2 Bring the water to the boil. Add the rice, stir once and return to a medium boil. Cook, uncovered, for 8–10 minutes, until tender.

3 Drain thoroughly and fork through lightly before serving.

4 For the absorption method, rinse the rice under cold running water.

5 Put the rice and water into a saucepan and bring to the boil. Stir once and then cover the pan tightly. Lower the heat as much as possible. Cook for 10 minutes. Leave to rest for 5 minutes.

6 Fork through lightly and serve the rice immediately.

Vegetable Couscous

Couscous is a semolina grain which is very quick and easy to cook, and it makes a pleasant change from rice or pasta.

NUTRITIONAL INFORMATION

Calories 280   Sugars 13g
Protein ....10g   Fat 7g
Carbohydrate ...47g   Saturates 1g

20 MINS   40 MINS

SERVES 4

INGREDIENTS

2 tbsp vegetable oil

1 large onion, coarsely chopped

1 carrot, chopped

1 turnip, chopped

600 ml/1 pint/2½ cups vegetable stock

175 g/6 oz/1 cup couscous

2 tomatoes, peeled and quartered

2 courgettes (zucchini), chopped

1 red (bell) pepper, seeded and chopped

125 g/4½ oz French (green) beans, chopped

grated rind of 1 lemon

pinch of ground turmeric (optional)

1 tbsp finely chopped fresh coriander
   (cilantro) or parsley

salt and pepper

fresh flat leaf parsley sprigs,
   to garnish

1 Heat the oil in a large saucepan and fry the onion, carrot and turnip for 3–4 minutes. Add the stock, bring to the boil, cover and simmer for 20 minutes.

2 Meanwhile, put the couscous in a bowl and moisten with a little boiling water, stirring, until the grains have swollen and separated.

3 Add the tomatoes, courgettes (zucchini), (bell) pepper and French (green) beans to the saucepan.

4 Stir the lemon rind into the couscous and add the turmeric, if using, and mix thoroughly. Put the couscous in a steamer and position it over the saucepan of vegetables. Simmer the vegetables so that the couscous steams for about 8–10 minutes.

5 Pile the couscous on to warmed serving plates. Ladle the vegetables and some of the liquid over the top. Scatter with the coriander (cilantro) or parsley and serve at once, garnished with parsley sprigs.

Couscous Royale

Serve this stunning dish as a centrepiece for a North African-style feast; it will prove to be a truly memorable meal.

NUTRITIONAL INFORMATION

Calories 329   Sugars 31g
Protein ....6g   Fat 13g
Carbohydrate ...50g   Saturates 6g

25 MINS   45 MINS

SERVES 6

I N G R E D I E N T S

3 carrots

3 courgettes (zucchini)

350 g/12 oz pumpkin or squash

1.25 litres/2¼ pints/5 cups vegetable stock

2 cinnamon sticks, broken in half

2 tsp ground cumin

1 tsp ground coriander

pinch of saffron strands

2 tbsp olive oil

pared rind and juice of 1 lemon

2 tbsp clear honey

500 g/1 lb 2 oz/2¾ cups pre-
    cooked couscous

60 g/2 oz/¼ cup butter or, softened

175 g/6 oz/1 cup large
    seedless raisins

salt and pepper

coriander (cilantro), to garnish

  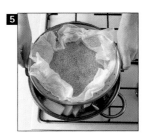

1 Cut the carrots and courgettes (zucchini) into 7 cm/3 inch pieces and cut in half lengthways.

2 Trim the pumpkin or squash and discard the seeds. Peel and cut into pieces the same size as the carrots and courgettes (zucchini).

3 Put the stock, spices, saffron and carrots in a large saucepan. Bring to the boil, skim off any scum and add the olive oil. Simmer for 15 minutes.

4 Add the lemon rind and juice to the pan, together with the honey, courgettes (zucchini) and pumpkin or squash. Season well. Bring back to the boil and simmer for a further 10 minutes.

5 Meanwhile, soak the couscous according to the packet instructions. Transfer to a steamer or large strainer lined with muslin (cheesecloth) and place over the vegetable pan. Cover and steam as directed. Stir in the butter.

6 Pile the couscous on to a warmed serving plate. Drain the vegetables, reserving the stock, lemon rind and cinnamon. Arrange the vegetables on top of the couscous. Put the raisins on top and spoon over 6 tablespoons of the reserved stock. Keep warm.

7 Return the remaining stock to the heat and boil for 5 minutes to reduce slightly. Discard the lemon rind and cinnamon. Garnish with sprigs of coriander (cilantro) and serve immediately, handing the sauce separately.

Bulgur Pilau

Bulgur wheat is very easy to use and, as well as being full of nutrients, it is a delicious alternative to rice, having a distinctive nutty flavour.

NUTRITIONAL INFORMATION

Calories	637	Sugars	........25g
Protein	........16g	Fat	..........26g
Carbohydrate	...90g	Saturates	......11g

15 MINS   35–40 MINS

SERVES 4

I N G R E D I E N T S

75 g/2¾ oz/6 tbsp butter or margarine

1 red onion, halved and sliced

2 garlic cloves, crushed

350 g/12 oz/2 cups bulgur wheat

175 g/6 oz tomatoes, seeded and chopped

50 g/1¾ oz baby corn cobs,
   halved lengthways

75 g/2¾ oz small broccoli florets

850 ml/1½ pints/3¾ cups vegetable stock

2 tbsp clear honey

50 g/1¾ oz sultanas (golden raisins)

50 g/1¾ oz/½ cup pine nuts

½ tsp ground cinnamon

½ tsp ground cumin

salt and pepper

sliced spring onions (scallions), to garnish

COOK'S TIP

The dish is left to stand for 10 minutes so that the bulgur can finish cooking and the flavours will mingle.

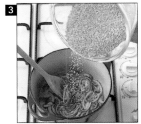

1 Melt the butter or margarine in a large flameproof casserole.

2 Add the onion and garlic and sauté for 2–3 minutes, stirring occasionally.

3 Add the bulgur wheat, tomatoes, corn cobs, broccoli and stock and bring to the boil. Reduce the heat, cover and cook, stirring occasionally, for 15–20 minutes.

4 Stir in the honey, sultanas (golden raisins), pine nuts, ground cinnamon and cumin and season with salt and pepper to taste, mixing well. Remove the casserole from the heat, cover and set aside for 10 minutes.

5 Spoon the bulgur pilau into a warmed serving dish.

6 Garnish the bulgur pilau with thinly sliced spring onions (scallions) and serve immediately.

Tabbouleh Salad

This kind of salad is eaten widely throughout the Middle East. The flavour improves as it is kept, so it tastes even better on the second day.

NUTRITIONAL INFORMATION

Calories	637	Sugars	. . . . .8g
Protein	. . . . .20g	Fat	. . . . .41g
Carbohydrate	. . .50g	Saturates	. . . . . .11g

1½ HOURS   5-10 MINS

SERVES 2

I N G R E D I E N T S

125 g/4½ oz/1 cup bulgar wheat

600 ml/1 pint/2½ cups boiling water

1 red (bell) pepper, seeded and halved

3 tbsp olive oil

1 garlic clove, crushed

grated rind of ½ lime

about 1 tbsp lime juice

1 tbsp chopped mint

1 tbsp chopped parsley

3–4 spring onions (scallions), trimmed and
    thinly sliced

8 pitted black olives, halved

40 g/1½ oz/½cup large salted peanuts or
    cashew nuts

1–2 tsp lemon juice

60–90 g/2–3 oz Gruyère cheese

salt and pepper

mint sprigs, to garnish

warm pitta (pocket) bread or crusty rolls,
    to serve

1 Put the bulgar wheat into a bowl and cover with the boiling water to reach about 2.5 cm/1 inch above the bulgar. Set aside to soak for up to 1 hour, until most of the water is absorbed and is cold.

2 Meanwhile, put the halved red (bell) pepper, skin side upwards, on a grill (broiler) rack and cook under a preheated moderate grill (broiler) until the skin is thoroughly charred and blistered. Leave to cool slightly.

3 When cool enough to handle, peel off the skin and discard the seeds. Cut the (bell) pepper flesh into narrow strips.

4 Whisk together the oil, garlic and lime rind and juice. Season to taste and whisk until thoroughly blended. Add 4½ teaspoons of the dressing to the (bell) peppers and mix lightly.

5 Drain the soaked bulgar wheat thoroughly, squeezing it in a dry cloth to make it even drier, then place in a bowl.

6 Add the chopped herbs, spring onions (scallions), olives and peanuts or cashew nuts to the bulgar and toss . Add the lemon juice to the remaining dressing, and stir through the salad. Spoon the salad on to 2 serving plates.

7 Cut the cheese into narrow strips and mix with the (bell) pepper strips. Spoon alongside the bulgar salad. Garnish with mint sprigs and serve with warm pitta (pocket) bread or crusty rolls.

Rice & Nuts

Here is a tasty and filling rice dish that is nice and spicy and includes fruits for a refreshing flavour and toasted nuts for a crunchy texture.

NUTRITIONAL INFORMATION

Calories 612   Sugars 31g
Protein . . . . .15g   Fat 21g
Carbohydrate . . .96g   Saturates 3g

20 MINS   55 MINS

SERVES 4

INGREDIENTS

4 tbsp vegetable ghee or oil

1 large onion, chopped

2 garlic cloves, crushed

2.5 cm/1 inch ginger root, chopped finely

1 tsp chilli powder

1 tsp cumin seeds

1 tbsp mild or medium curry powder
  or paste

300 g/10½ oz/1½ cups brown rice

850 ml/1½ pints/3½ cups boiling
  vegetable stock

400 g/14 oz can chopped tomatoes

175 g/6 oz ready-soaked dried apricots or
  peaches, cut into slivers

1 red (bell) pepper, cored, seeded and diced

90 g/3 oz frozen peas

1-2 small, slightly green bananas

60-90 g/2-3oz/⅓-½ cup toasted mixed nuts

salt and pepper

 Heat the ghee or oil in a large saucepan, add the onion and fry gently for 3 minutes.

 Stir in the garlic, ginger, chilli powder, cumin seeds, curry powder or paste and rice. Cook gently for 2 minutes, stirring all the time, until the rice is coated in the spiced oil.

3 Pour in the boiling stock, stirring to mix. Add the tomatoes and season with salt and pepper to taste. Bring the mixture to the boil, then reduce the heat, cover the pan and leave to simmer gently for 40 minutes or until the rice is almost cooked and most of the liquid is absorbed.

4 Add the apricots or peaches, red (bell) pepper and peas to the rice mixture in the pan. Cover and cook for 10 minutes.

5 Remove the pan from the heat and leave to stand for 5 minutes without uncovering.

6 Peel and slice the bananas. Uncover the rice mixture and toss with a fork to mix. Add the toasted nuts and sliced banana and toss lightly.

7 Transfer the brown rice and fruit and nuts to a serving platter and serve piping hot.

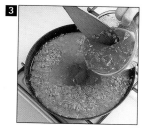

Stuffed Rice Pancakes

Dosas (pancakes) are widely eaten in southern India. The rice and urid dhal need to soak and ferment, so prepare well in advance.

NUTRITIONAL INFORMATION

Calories ....748 Sugars 1g
Protein ....10g Fat 47g
Carbohydrate ...76g Saturates 5g

6¼ HOURS   40-45 MINS

SERVES 4

INGREDIENTS

200 g/7 oz/1 cup rice and 50 g/1¾ oz/
  ¼ cup urid dhal, or 200 g/7 oz/1¾ cups
  ground rice and 50 g/1¾ oz/7 tbsp urid
  dhal flour (ata)

425–600 ml/¾–1 pint/2–2½ cups water

1 tsp salt

4 tbsp vegetable oil

FILLING

4 medium potatoes, diced

3 fresh green chillies, chopped

½ tsp turmeric

1 tsp salt

150 ml/¼ pint/⅔ cup oil

1 tsp mixed mustard and onion seeds

3 dried chillies

4 curry leaves

2 tbsp lemon juice

1 To make the dosas (pancakes), soak the rice and urid dhal for 3 hours. Grind the rice and urid dhal to a smooth consistency, adding water if necessary. Set aside for a further 3 hours to ferment. Alternatively, if you are using ground rice and urid dhal flour (ata), mix together in a bowl. Add the water and salt and stir until a batter is formed.

2 Heat about 1 tbsp of oil in a large, non-stick, frying-pan (skillet). Using a ladle, spoon the batter into the frying-pan (skillet). Tilt the frying-pan (skillet) to spread the mixture over the base. Cover and cook over a medium heat for about 2 minutes. Remove the lid and turn the dosa over very carefully. Pour a little oil around the edge, cover and cook for a further 2 minutes. Repeat with the remaining batter.

3 To make the filling, cook the potatoes in a pan of boiling water. Add the chillies, turmeric and salt and cook until the potatoes are just soft. Drain and mash lightly with a fork.

4 Heat the oil in a saucepan and fry the mustard and onion seeds, dried red chillies and curry leaves, stirring constantly, for about 1 minute. Pour the spice mixture over the mashed potatoes, then sprinkle over the lemon juice and mix well. Spoon the potato filling on one half of each of the dosas (pancakes) and fold the other half over it. Transfer to a warmed serving dish and serve hot.

Pilau Rice

Plain boiled rice is eaten by most people in India every day, but for entertaining, a more interesting rice dish, such as this, is served.

NUTRITIONAL INFORMATION

Calories 265	Sugars 0g	
Protein 4g	Fat 10g	
Carbohydrate ...43g	Saturates 6g	

5 MINS   25 MINS

SERVES 4

INGREDIENTS

200 g/7 oz/1 cup basmati rice

2 tbsp vegetable ghee

3 green cardamoms

2 cloves

3 peppercorns

½ tsp salt

½ tsp saffron

400 ml/14 fl oz/scant 2 cups water

1 Rinse the rice twice under running water and set aside until required.

2 Heat the ghee in a saucepan. Add the cardamoms, cloves and peppercorns to the pan and fry, stirring constantly, for about 1 minute.

3 Add the rice and stir-fry over a medium heat for a further 2 minutes.

4 Add the salt, saffron and water to the rice mixture and reduce the heat. Cover the pan and simmer over a low heat until the water has been absorbed.

5 Transfer the pilau rice to a serving dish and serve hot.

COOK'S TIP

The most expensive of all spices, saffron strands are the stamens of a type of crocus. They give dishes a rich, golden colour, as well as adding a distinctive, slightly bitter taste. Saffron is sold as a powder or in the more expensive strands.

Tomato Rice

Rice cooked with tomatoes and onions will add colour to your table, especially when garnished with green chillies and coriander (cilantro).

NUTRITIONAL INFORMATION

Calories 866   Sugars 7g
Protein . . . . .15g   Fat 46g
Carbohydrate ..106g   Saturates 6g

 10 MINS   35 MINS

SERVES 4

I N G R E D I E N T S

150 ml/¼ pint/⅔ cup vegetable oil

2 medium onions, sliced

1 tsp onion seeds

1 tsp, finely chopped root ginger

1 tsp crushed garlic

½ tsp turmeric

1 tsp chilli powder

1½ tsp salt

400 g/14 oz can tomatoes

500 g/1 lb 2 oz/2¼ cups basmati rice

600 ml/1 pint/2½ cups water

TO GARNISH

3 fresh green chillies, finely chopped

fresh coriander (cilantro) leaves, chopped

3 hard-boiled (hard-cooked) eggs

1 Heat the oil in a saucepan. Add the onions and fry over a moderate heat, stirring frequently, for 5 minutes, until golden brown.

2 Add the onion seeds, ginger, garlic, turmeric, chilli powder and salt, stirring to combine.

3 Reduce the heat, add the tomatoes and stir-fry for 10 minutes, breaking them up.

4 Add the rice to the tomato mixture, stirring gently to coat the rice completely in the mixture. Stir in the water. Cover the pan and cook over a low heat until the water has been absorbed and the rice is cooked.

5 Transfer the tomato rice to a warmed serving dish. Garnish with the finely chopped green chillies, (cilantro) leaves and hard-boiled (hard-cooked) eggs. Serve the tomato rice immediately.

COOK'S TIP

Onion seeds are always used whole in Indian cooking. They are often used in pickles and often sprinkled over the top of naan breads. Onion seeds don't have anything to do with the vegetable, but they look similar to the plant's seed, hence the name.

Green Rice

Based on the Mexican dish *Arroz Verde*, this recipe is perfect for (bell) pepper and chilli lovers. Serve with iced lemonade to quell the fire!

NUTRITIONAL INFORMATION

Calories 445   Sugars 6g
Protein ....13g   Fat 12g
Carbohydrate ...76g   Saturates 2g

25 MINS   30 MINS

SERVES 4

I N G R E D I E N T S

2 large green (bell) peppers

2 fresh green chillies

2 tbsp, plus 1 tsp vegetable oil

1 large onion, finely chopped

1 garlic clove, crushed

1 tbsp ground coriander

300 g/10½ oz/1½ cups long grain rice

700 ml/1¼ pints/3 cups Vegetable stock

225 g/8 oz/2 cups frozen peas

6 tbsp chopped coriander (cilantro)

1 egg, beaten

salt and pepper

coriander (cilantro), to garnish

TO SERVE

tortilla chips

lime wedges

COOK'S TIP

There are hundreds of varieties of chillies, many of them very similar in appearance, so it is not always easy to tell how hot they are. As a general rule, small, pointed chillies are hotter than larger, more rounded ones, but this is not invariable.

1 Halve, core and seed the (bell) peppers. Cut the flesh into small cubes. Seed and finely chop the chillies.

2 Heat 2 tablespoons of the oil in a saucepan and fry the onion, garlic, (bell) peppers and chillies for 5–6 minutes, until softened, but not browned.

3 Stir in the ground coriander, rice, and stock. Bring to the boil, cover and simmer for 10 minutes. Add the peas, bring back to the boil, cover and simmer for a further 5 minutes, until the rice is tender. Remove from the heat and leave to stand, covered, for 10 minutes.

4 Season to taste with salt and pepper and mix in the fresh coriander (cilantro). Pile into a warmed serving dish and keep warm.

5 Heat the remaining oil in a small omelette pan. Pour in the egg and cook over a medium heat for 1–2 minutes on each side, until set. Slide the omelette on to a plate, roll up loosely and slice into thin rounds.

6 Arrange the omelette strips on top of the rice. Garnish with coriander (cilantro) and serve immediately with tortilla chips and lime wedges.

Spinach & Nut Pilau

Fragrant basmati rice is cooked with porcini (cep) mushrooms, spinach and pistachio nuts in this easy microwave recipe.

NUTRITIONAL INFORMATION

Calories	403	Sugars	.........7g
Protein	........10g	Fat	..........15g
Carbohydrate	...62g	Saturates	.......2g

  55 MINS 15-20 MINS

SERVES 4

I N G R E D I E N T S

10 g/⅓ oz dried porcini
  (cep) mushrooms

300 ml/½ pint/1¼ cups hot water

1 onion, chopped

1 garlic clove, crushed

1 tsp grated root ginger

½ fresh green chilli, seeded
  and chopped

2 tbsp oil

225 g/8 oz/generous 1 cup basmati rice

1 large carrot, grated

175 ml/6 fl oz/¾ cup vegetable stock

½ tsp ground cinnamon

4 cloves

½ tsp saffron strands

225 g/8 oz/6 cups fresh spinach, long
  stalks removed

60 g/2 oz/½ cup pistachio nuts

1 tbsp chopped coriander (cilantro)

salt and pepper

coriander (cilantro) leaves
  to garnish

1 Place the porcini (cep) mushrooms in a small bowl. Pour over the hot water and leave to soak for 30 minutes.

2 Place the onion, garlic, ginger, chilli and oil in a large bowl. Cover and cook on HIGH power for 2 minutes. Rinse the rice, then stir it into the bowl, together with the carrot. Cover and cook on HIGH power for 1 minute.

3 Strain and coarsely chop the mushrooms. Add the mushroom soaking liquid to the stock to make 425 ml/¾ pint/scant 2 cups. Pour on to the rice. Stir in the mushrooms, cinnamon, cloves, saffron and ½ teaspoon salt. Cover and cook on HIGH power for 10 minutes, stirring once. Leave to stand, covered, for 10 minutes.

4 Place the spinach in a large bowl. Cover and cook on HIGH power for 3½ minutes, stirring once. Drain well and chop coarsely.

5 Stir the spinach, pistachio nuts and chopped coriander (cilantro) into the rice. Season to taste with salt and pepper and garnish with coriander (cilantro) leaves. Serve immediately.

Kitchouri

The traditional breakfast plate of kedgeree reputedly has its roots in this Indian flavoured rice dish, which English colonists adopted.

NUTRITIONAL INFORMATION

Calories 318   Sugars 5g
Protein . . . . .12g   Fat 10g
Carbohydrate . . .48g   Saturates 6g

10 MINS   30 MINS

SERVES 4

I N G R E D I E N T S

2 tbsp vegetable ghee or butter

1 red onion, finely chopped

1 garlic clove, crushed

½ celery stick, finely chopped

1 tsp turmeric

½ tsp garam masala

1 green chilli, seeded and finely chopped

½ tsp cumin seeds

1 tbsp chopped coriander (cilantro)

125 g/4½ oz/generous ½ cup basmati rice, rinsed under cold water

125 g/4½ oz/½ cup green lentils

300 ml/½ pint/1¼ cups vegetable juice

600 ml/1 pint/2½ cups vegetable stock

1 Heat the ghee or butter in a large heavy-based saucepan. Add the onion, garlic and celery and cook for about 5 minutes, until soft.

2 Add the turmeric, garam masala, green chilli, cumin seeds and coriander (cilantro). Cook over a moderate heat, stirring constantly, for about 1 minute, until fragrant.

3 Add the rice and lentils and cook for 1 minute, until the rice is translucent.

4 Pour the vegetable juice and stock into the saucepan and bring to the boil over a medium heat. Cover and simmer over a low heat, stirring occasionally, for about 20 minutes, or until the lentils are cooked. (They should be tender when pressed between two fingers.)

5 Transfer the kitchouri to a warmed serving dish and serve piping hot.

COOK'S TIP

This is a versatile dish, and can be served as a great-tasting and satisfying one-pot meal. It can also be served as a winter lunch dish with tomatoes and yogurt.

Vegetable Biryani

The Biryani originated in the North of India, and was a dish reserved for festivals. The vegetables are marinated in a yogurt-based marinade.

NUTRITIONAL INFORMATION

Calories 449   Sugars 18g
Protein ....12g   Fat 12g
Carbohydrate ...79g   Saturates 6g

  2¼ HOURS   1 HR 5 MINS

SERVES 4

I N G R E D I E N T S

1 large potato, cubed

100 g/3½ oz baby carrots

50 g/1¾ oz okra, thickly sliced

2 celery sticks, sliced

75 g/2¾ oz baby button mushrooms, halved

1 aubergine (eggplant), halved and sliced

300 ml/½ pint/1¼ cups natural
   (unsweetened) yogurt

1 tbsp grated root ginger

2 large onions, grated

4 garlic cloves, crushed

1 tsp turmeric

1 tbsp curry powder

25 g/1 oz/2 tbsp butter

2 onions, sliced

225 g/8 oz/1¼ cups basmati rice

chopped coriander (cilantro),
   to garnish

1 Cook the potato cubes, carrots and okra in a pan of boiling salted water for 7–8 minutes. Drain well and place in a large bowl. Mix with the celery, mushrooms and aubergine (eggplant).

2 Mix the natural (unsweetened) yogurt, ginger, grated onions, garlic, turmeric and curry powder and spoon over the vegetables. Set aside in a cool place to marinate for at least 2 hours.

3 Heat the butter in a heavy-based frying pan (skillet). Add the sliced onions and cook over a medium heat for 5–6 minutes, until golden brown. Remove a few onions from the pan and reserve for the garnish.

4 Cook the rice in a large pan of boiling water for 7 minutes. Drain thoroughly and set aside.

5 Add the marinated vegetables to the onions and cook for 10 minutes.

6 Put half of the rice in a 2 litre/ 3½ pint/8¾ cup casserole dish. Spoon the vegetables on top and cover with the remaining rice. Cover and cook in a preheated oven, 190°C/375°F/Gas Mark 5, for 20–25 minutes, or until the rice is tender.

7 Spoon the biryani on to a serving plate, garnish with the reserved onions and coriander (cilantro) and serve.

Mooli (White Radish) Curry

This is rather an unusual recipe for a vegetarian curry. The dish is good served hot with chapatis

NUTRITIONAL INFORMATION

Calories	384	Sugars	........4g
Protein	.........3g	Fat	..........38g
Carbohydrate	....9g	Saturates	.......4g

🍲 10 MINS   🕐 20 MINS

SERVES 4

I N G R E D I E N T S

500 g/1 lb 2 oz mooli (white radish), preferably with leaves

1 tbsp moong dhal

600 ml/1 pint/2½ cups water

150 ml/¼ pint/⅔cup vegetable oil

1 medium onion, thinly sliced

1 tsp crushed garlic

1 tsp crushed dried red chillies

1 tsp salt

1 Rinse, peel and roughly slice the mooli (white radish), together with its leaves, if using.

2 Place the mooli (white radish), the leaves, if using, and the moong dhal in a large saucepan and pour over the water. Bring to the boil and cook over a medium heat until the mooli (white radish) has softened enough to handle.

3 Drain the mooli (white radish) thoroughly and squeeze out any excess water, using your hands.

4 Heat the vegetable oil in a heavy-based saucepan. Add the onion, garlic, crushed red chillies and salt and fry over a medium heat, stirring from time to time, for about 5–7 minutes, until the onions have softened and turned light golden brown in colour.

5 Stir the mooli (white radish) mixture into the spiced onion mixture and combine well. Reduce the heat and continue cooking, stirring frequently, for about 3–5 minutes.

6 Transfer the mooli (white radish) curry to individual serving plates and serve hot with chapatis.

COOK'S TIP

The vegetable used in this recipe, mooli (white radish), looks a bit like a parsnip without the tapering end and is now sold in most supermarkets, as well as in Indian grocers.

Aloo Chat

Aloo Chat is one of a variety of Indian foods served at any time of the day. The chickpeas (garbanzo beans) need to be soaked overnight.

NUTRITIONAL INFORMATION

Calories 262   Sugars 6g
Protein ....13g   Fat 4g
Carbohydrate ...46g   Saturates 0.5g

 35 MINS   1 HR 5 MINS

SERVES 4

I N G R E D I E N T S

125 g/4½ oz/generous ½ cup chickpeas
   (garbanzo beans), soaked overnight in
   cold water and drained

1 dried red chilli

500 g/1 lb 2 oz waxy potatoes, boiled in
   their skins and peeled

1 tsp cumin seeds

2 tsp salt

1 tsp black peppercorns

½ tsp dried mint

½ tsp chilli powder

½ tsp ground ginger

2 tsp mango powder

125 ml/4 fl oz/½ cup natural
   (unsweetened) yogurt

oil, for deep frying

4 poppadoms

VARIATION

Instead of chickpeas (garbanzo beans), diced tropical fruits can be stirred into the potatoes and spice mix; add a little lemon juice to balance the sweetness.

1 Boil the chickpeas (garbanzo beans) with the chilli in plenty of water for about 1 hour, until tender. Drain.

2 Cut the potatoes into 2.5 cm/1 inch dice and mix into the chickpeas (garbanzo beans) while they are still warm. Set aside.

3 Grind together the cumin, salt and peppercorns in a spice grinder or with a pestle and mortar. Stir in the mint, chilli powder, ginger and mango powder.

4 Put a small saucepan or frying pan (skillet) over a low heat and add the spice mix. Stir until the spices give off their aroma and then immediately remove the pan from the heat.

5 Stir half of the spice mix into the chickpea (garbanzo bean) and potato mixture and stir the other half into the yogurt.

6 Cook the poppadoms according to the instructions on the packet. Drain on plenty of kitchen paper (paper towels). Break into bite-size pieces and stir into the potatoes and chickpeas (garbanzo beans), spoon over the spiced yogurt and serve immediately.

Tarka Dhal

This is just one version of many dhals that are served throughout India; as many people are vegetarian, they form a staple part of the diet.

NUTRITIONAL INFORMATION

Calories	183	Sugars	........4g
Protein	........8g	Fat	..........8g
Carbohydrate	...22g	Saturates	.......5g

 10 MINS   25 MINS

SERVES 4

I N G R E D I E N T S

2 tbsp ghee

2 shallots, sliced

1 tsp yellow mustard seeds

2 garlic cloves, crushed

8 fenugreek seeds

1 cm/½ inch piece of root ginger, grated

½ tsp salt

125 g/4½ oz/½ cup red lentils

1 tbsp tomato purée (paste)

600 ml/1 pint/2½ cups water

2 tomatoes, peeled and chopped

1 tbsp lemon juice

4 tbsp chopped coriander (cilantro)

½ tsp chilli powder

½ tsp garam masala

1 Heat half of the ghee in a large saucepan and add the shallots. Cook for 2–3 minutes over a high heat, then add the mustard seeds. Cover the pan until the seeds begin to pop.

2 Immediately remove the lid from the pan and add the garlic, fenugreek, ginger and salt.

3 Stir once and add the lentils, tomato purée (paste) and water. Bring to the boil, then lower the heat and simmer for 10 minutes.

4 Stir in the tomatoes, lemon juice, and coriander (cilantro) and simmer for 4–5 minutes, until the lentils are tender.

5 Transfer to a serving dish. Heat the remaining ghee in a pan. Remove from the heat and stir in the garam masala and chilli powder. Pour over the tarka dhal; serve.

COOK'S TIP

The flavours in a dhal can be altered to suit your taste; for extra heat, add more chilli powder or chillies, or add fennel seeds for an aniseed flavour.

Channa Dhal

Dried pulses and lentils can be cooked in similar ways, but the soaking and cooking times do vary, so check the pack for instructions.

NUTRITIONAL INFORMATION

Calories	195	Sugars	.........4g
Protein	........11g	Fat	...........5g
Carbohydrate	...28g	Saturates	.......3g

1 HR 10 MINS   50 MINS

SERVES 6

INGREDIENTS

2 tbsp vegetable ghee

1 large onion, finely chopped

1 garlic clove, crushed

1 tbsp grated root ginger

1 tbsp cumin seeds, ground

2 tsp coriander seeds, ground

1 dried red chilli

2.5 cm/1 inch piece of cinnamon stick

1 tsp salt

½ tsp ground turmeric

225 g/8 oz/1 cup split yellow peas, soaked
   in cold water for 1 hour and drained

400 g/14 oz can plum tomatoes

300 ml/½ pint/1¼ cups water

2 tsp garam masala

1 Heat the ghee in a large saucepan, add the onion, garlic and ginger and fry for 3–4 minutes, until the onion has softened slightly.

2 Add the cumin, coriander, chilli, cinnamon, salt and turmeric, then stir in the split peas until well mixed.

3 Add the tomatoes, together with their can juices, breaking the tomatoes up slightly with the back of a spoon.

4 Add the water and bring to the boil. Reduce the heat to very low and simmer, uncovered, stirring occasionally, for about 40 minutes, until most of the liquid has been absorbed and the split peas are tender. Skim the surface occasionally with a slotted spoon to remove any scum.

5 Gradually stir in the garam masala, tasting after each addition, until it is of the required flavour. Serve hot.

COOK'S TIP

Use a non-stick saucepan if you have one, because the mixture is quite dense and does stick to the base of the pan occasionally. If the dhal is overstirred the split peas will break up and the dish will not have much texture or bite.

Kofta Kebabs (Kabobs)

Traditionally, koftas are made from a spicy meat mixture, but this bean and wheat version makes a tasty vegetarian alternative.

NUTRITIONAL INFORMATION

Calories 598   Sugars 7g
Protein . . . . .26g   Fat 17g
Carbohydrate . . .90g   Saturates 3g

1 HR 20 MINS   1½ HOURS

SERVES 4

I N G R E D I E N T S

175 g/6 oz/1 cup aduki beans

175 g/6 oz/1 cup bulgur wheat

450 ml/16 fl oz/scant 2 cups vegetable
    stock

3 tbsp olive oil, plus extra for brushing

1 onion, finely chopped

2 garlic cloves, crushed

1 tsp ground coriander

1 tsp ground cumin

2 tbsp chopped fresh coriander (cilantro)

3 eggs, beaten

125 g/4½ oz/¾ cup dried breadcrumbs

salt and pepper

T A B B O U L E H

175 g/6 oz/1 cup bulgur wheat

2 tbsp lemon juice

1 tbsp olive oil

6 tbsp chopped parsley

4 spring onions (scallions), finely chopped

60 g/2 oz cucumber, finely chopped

3 tbsp chopped mint

1 extra-large tomato, finely chopped

TO SERVE

black olives

pitta (pocket) bread

1 Cook the aduki beans in boiling water for 40 minutes, until tender. Drain, rinse and leave to cool. Cook the bulgur wheat in the stock for 10 minutes, until the stock is absorbed. Set aside.

2 Heat 1 tablespoon of the oil in a frying pan (skillet) and fry the onion, garlic and spices for 4–5 minutes.

3 Transfer to a bowl, together with the beans, coriander (cilantro), seasoning and eggs and mash with a potato masher or fork. Add the breadcrumbs and bulgur wheat and stir well. Cover and chill for 1 hour, until firm.

4 To make the tabbouleh, soak the bulgur wheat in 425 ml/¾ pint/scant 2 cups of boiling water for 15 minutes. Combine with the remaining ingredients. Cover and chill.

5 With wet hands, mould the kofta mixture into 32 oval shapes.

6 Press on to skewers, brush with oil and grill (broil) for 5–6 minutes until golden. Turn, brush with oil again and cook for 5–6 minutes. Drain on kitchen paper (paper towels). Garnish and serve with the tabbouleh, black olives and pitta (pocket) bread.

Black-Eye Beans (Peas)

This is very good served with chapatis and a vegetable curry. The beans (peas) need to be soaked overnight so prepare well in advance.

NUTRITIONAL INFORMATION

Calories	757	Sugars	.........5g
Protein	........10g	Fat	..........69g
Carbohydrate	...26g	Saturates	.......7g

 5 MINS   1 HOUR

SERVES 4

I N G R E D I E N T S

150 g/5½ oz/1 cup black-eye beans (peas)

300 ml/½ pint/1¼ cups vegetable oil

2 medium onions, sliced

1 tsp finely chopped root ginger

1 tsp crushed garlic

1 tsp chilli powder

1½ tsp salt

1½ tsp ground coriander

1½ tsp ground cumin

150 ml/¼ pint/⅔ cup water

2 green chillies

coriander (cilantro) leaves

1 tbsp lemon juice

1 Rinse the black-eye beans (peas), place them in a bowl, cover with cold water and set aside to soak overnight.

2 Drain the black-eye beans (peas), place in a pan of water and bring to the boil over a low heat. Simmer for about 30 minutes. Drain the beans (peas) thoroughly and set aside.

3 Heat the oil in a heavy-based pan. Add the onions and fry, stirring frequently, for 5–8 minutes, until golden brown. Add the ginger, garlic, chilli powder, salt, ground coriander and ground cumin and stir-fry the mixture for 3–5 minutes.

4 Add the water to the pan, cover and simmer until all of the water has completely evaporated.

5 Add the black-eye beans (peas), green chillies and coriander (cilantro) leaves to the onions and stir-fry for 3-5 minutes.

6 Transfer the black-eye beans (peas) to a serving dish, sprinkle over the lemon juice and serve immediately. Alternatively, allow the beans (peas) to cool and serve cold.

COOK'S TIP

Black-eye beans (peas) are oval-shaped, grey or beige beans (peas) with a dark dot in the centre. They have a slightly smoky flavour. They are sold canned, as well as dried.

White Lentils

This dhal is dry when cooked, so give it a baghaar (seasoned oil dressing). It makes an excellent accompaniment to any meal of kormas.

NUTRITIONAL INFORMATION

Calories	129	Sugars	.........1g
Protein	.........6g	Fat	...........6g
Carbohydrate	...14g	Saturates	.......1g

 5 MINS   45 MINS

SERVES 4

I N G R E D I E N T S

100 g/3½ oz/½ cup urid dhal

1 tsp finely chopped root ginger

600 ml/1 pint/2½ cups water

1 tsp salt

1 tsp pepper

2 tbsp vegetable ghee

2 garlic cloves

2 fresh red chillies, finely chopped

mint leaves, to garnish

chapatis, to serve

1 Rinse the lentils thoroughly and put them in a large saucepan, together with the ginger.

2 Add the water and bring to a boil. Cover and simmer over a medium heat for about 30 minutes. Check to see whether the lentils are cooked by rubbing them between your finger and thumb. If they are still a little hard in the middle, cook for a further 5–7 minutes. If necessary, remove the lid and cook until any remaining water has evaporated.

3 Add the salt and pepper to the lentils, mix well and set aside.

4 To make the baghaar, heat the ghee in a separate saucepan. Add the cloves of garlic and chopped red chillies and stir well to mix thoroughly.

5 Pour the garlic and chilli mixture over the lentils and then garnish with the fresh mint leaves.

6 Transfer the white lentils to warm individual serving dishes and serve hot with chapatis.

COOK'S TIP

Ghee was traditionally made from clarified butter, which can withstand higher temperatures than ordinary butter. Vegetable ghee has largely replaced it now because it is lower in saturated fats.

Stir-Fries & Sautés

Stir-frying is one of the most convenient and nutritious ways of cooking vegetarian food as ingredients are cooked quickly over a very high heat in very little oil. The high

heat seals in the natural juices and helps preserve nutrients. The short cooking time makes the vegetables more succulent and preserves texture as well as the natural flavour and colour.

A round-bottomed wok is ideal for stir-frying as it conducts and retains heat evenly and requires the use of less oil. You need a flat-bottomed pan for sautéing so that the food can be easily tossed and stirred. A brisk heat is essential so that the food turns golden brown and crisp.

Vegetable Curry

This colourful and interesting mixture of vegetables, cooked in a spicy sauce, is excellent served with pulao rice and naan bread

NUTRITIONAL INFORMATION

Calories 421   Sugars 20g
Protein . . . . .12g   Fat 24g
Carbohydrate . . .42g   Saturates 3g

 15 MINS   🕐 45 MINS

SERVES 4

I N G R E D I E N T S

225 g/8 oz turnips or swede (rutabaga)

1 aubergine (eggplant)

350 g/12 oz new potatoes

225 g/8 oz cauliflower

225 g/8 oz button mushrooms

1 large onion

225 g/8 oz carrots

6 tbsp vegetable ghee or oil

2 garlic cloves, crushed

5 cm/2 inch piece of ginger root,
   finely chopped

1-2 fresh green chillies,
   seeded and chopped

1 tbsp paprika

2 tsp ground coriander

1 tbsp mild or medium curry powder
   or paste

450 ml/16 fl oz/1¾ cups vegetable stock

400 g/14 oz can chopped tomatoes

1 green (bell) pepper, seeded and sliced

1 tbsp cornflour (cornstarch)

150 ml/¼ pint/⅔ cup coconut milk

2-3 tbsp ground almonds

salt

coriander (cilantro) sprigs, to garnish

1 Cut the turnips or swede (rutabaga), aubergine (eggplant) and potatoes into 1 cm/½ inch cubes. Divide the cauliflower into small florets. Leave the mushrooms whole, or slice thickly if preferred. Slice the onion and carrots.

2 Heat the ghee or oil in a large saucepan. Add the onion, turnip or swede (rutabaga), potato and cauliflower and cook over a low heat, stirring frequently, for 3 minutes.

3 Add the garlic, ginger, chillies, paprika, ground coriander and curry powder or paste and cook, stirring, for 1 minute.

4 Add the stock, tomatoes, aubergine (eggplant) and mushrooms and season with salt. Cover and simmer, stirring occasionally, for about 30 minutes, or until tender. Add the green (bell) pepper and carrots, cover and continue cooking for a further 5 minutes.

5 Blend the cornflour (cornstarch) with the coconut milk to a smooth paste and stir into the mixture. Add the ground almonds and simmer, stirring constantly, for 2 minutes. Season if necessary. Transfer the curry to serving plates and serve hot, garnished with sprigs of fresh coriander (cilantro).

Potato Curry

Very little meat is eaten in India, their diet being mainly vegetarian. This potato curry with added vegetables makes a very substantial main meal.

NUTRITIONAL INFORMATION

Calories	.301	Sugars	.10g
Protein	.9g	Fat	.12g
Carbohydrate	.41g	Saturates	.1g

 15 MINS 45 MINS

SERVES 4

INGREDIENTS

4 tbsp vegetable oil

675 g/1½ lb waxy potatoes,
    cut into large chunks

2 onions, quartered

3 garlic cloves, crushed

1 tsp garam masala

½ tsp turmeric

½ tsp ground cumin

½ tsp ground coriander

2.5 cm/1 inch piece of root ginger, grated

1 fresh red chilli, chopped

225 g/8 oz cauliflower florets

4 tomatoes, peeled and quartered

75 g/2¾ oz/¾ cup frozen peas

2 tbsp chopped coriander (cilantro)

300 ml/½ pint/1¼ cups vegetable stock

shredded coriander (cilantro), to garnish

COOK'S TIP

Use a large heavy-based saucepan or frying pan (skillet) for this recipe to ensure that the potatoes are cooked thoroughly.

1 Heat the vegetable oil in a large heavy-based saucepan or frying pan (skillet). Add the potato chunks, onion and garlic and fry over a low heat, stirring frequently, for 2–3 minutes.

2 Add the garam masala, turmeric, ground cumin, ground coriander, grated ginger and chopped chilli to the pan, mixing the spices into the vegetables. Fry over a low heat, stirring constantly, for 1 minute.

3 Add the cauliflower florets, tomatoes, peas, chopped coriander (cilantro) and vegetable stock to the curry mixture.

4 Cook the potato curry over a low heat for 30–40 minutes, or until the potatoes are tender and completely cooked through.

5 Garnish the potato curry with fresh coriander (cilantro) and serve with plain boiled rice or warm Indian bread.

Potato & Cauliflower Curry

Potatoes and cauliflower go very well together. Served with a dhal and rice or bread, this dish makes a perfect vegetarian meal.

NUTRITIONAL INFORMATION

Calories 426   Sugars 6g
Protein ....4g   Fat 35g
Carbohydrate ...26g   Saturates 4g

10 MINS   25 MINS

SERVES 4

I N G R E D I E N T S

150 ml/¼ pint/⅔ cup vegetable oil

½ tsp white cumin seeds

4 dried red chillies

2 medium onions, sliced

1 tsp finely chopped root ginger

1 tsp crushed garlic

1 tsp chilli powder

1 tsp salt

pinch of turmeric

3 medium potatoes, chopped

½ cauliflower, cut into small florets

2 green chillies (optional)

coriander (cilantro) leaves

150 ml/¼ pint/⅔ cup water

1 Heat the oil in a large heavy-based saucepan. Add the white cumin seeds and dried red chillies to the pan, stirring to mix.

2 Add the onions to the pan and fry over a medium heat, stirring occasionally, for about 5–8 minutes, until golden brown.

3 Mix the ginger, garlic, chilli powder, salt and turmeric together. Add the spice mixture to the onions and stir-fry for about 2 minutes.

4 Add the potatoes and cauliflower to the pan and stir to coat thoroughly with the spice mixture. Reduce the heat and add the green chillies (if using), coriander (cilantro) leaves and water to the pan. Cover and simmer for about 10-15 minutes, until the vegetables are cooked through and tender.

5 Transfer the potato and cauliflower curry to warmed serving plates and serve immediately.

COOK'S TIP

Ground ginger is no substitute for the fresh root. It is less aromatic and flavoursome and cannot be used in fried or sautéed dishes, as it burns easily at the high temperatures required.

Muttar Paneer

Paneer is a delicious fresh, soft cheese frequently used in Indian cooking. It is easily made at home, but must be made the day before it's required.

NUTRITIONAL INFORMATION

Calories	550	Sugars	.......25g
Protein	........19g	Fat	.........39g
Carbohydrate	...33g	Saturates	......12g

15 MINS   25 MINS

SERVES 6

I N G R E D I E N T S

150 ml/¼ pint/⅔ cup vegetable oil

2 onions, chopped

2 garlic cloves, crushed

2.5 cm/1 inch piece of root ginger, chopped

1 tsp garam masala

1 tsp ground turmeric

1 tsp chilli powder

500 g/1 lb 2 oz/4 cups frozen peas

225 g/8 oz can chopped tomatoes

125 ml/4 fl oz/½ cup vegetable stock

salt and pepper

2 tbsp chopped coriander (cilantro)

P A N E E R

2.5 litres/4½ pints/10 cups pasteurized full-cream milk

5 tbsp lemon juice

1 garlic clove, crushed (optional)

1 tbsp chopped coriander (cilantro) (optional)

1 To make the paneer, bring the milk to a rolling boil in a pan. Remove from the heat and stir in the lemon juice. Return to the heat for about 1 minute until the curds and whey separate. Remove from the heat. Line a colander with double thickness muslin and pour the mixture through the muslin, adding the garlic and coriander, if using. Squeeze all the liquid from the curds and leave to drain.

2 Transfer to a dish, cover with a plate and a heavy weight and leave overnight in the refrigerator.

3 Cut the pressed paneer into small cubes. Heat the oil in a large frying pan (skillet). Add the paneer and fry until golden on all sides. Remove from the pan and drain on kitchen paper (paper towels).

4 Pour off some of the oil, leaving about 4 tablespoons in the pan. Add the onions, garlic and ginger and fry gently, stirring frequently, for 5 minutes. Stir in the spices and fry gently for 2 minutes. Add the peas, tomatoes and stock and season with salt and pepper. Cover and simmer, stirring occasionally, for 10 minutes, until the onion is tender. Add the fried paneer cubes and cook for a further 5 minutes. Taste and adjust the seasoning, if necessary. Sprinkle with the coriander (cilantro) and serve at once.

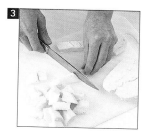

Tomato Curry

This vegetarian tomato curry is served topped with a few hard-boiled (hard-cooked) eggs. It is a lovely accompaniment to any Indian meal.

NUTRITIONAL INFORMATION

Calories 170   Sugars 3g
Protein . . . . .6g   Fat 15g
Carbohydrate . . . .3g   Saturates 2g

 25 MINS   15 MINS

SERVES 4

I N G R E D I E N T S

400 g/14 oz can tomatoes

1 tsp finely chopped root ginger

1 tsp crushed garlic

1 tsp chilli powder

1 tsp salt

½ tsp ground coriander

½ tsp ground cumin

4 tbsp oil

½ tsp onion seeds

½ tsp mustard seeds

½ tsp fenugreek seeds

pinch of white cumin seeds

3 dried red chillies

2 tbsp lemon juice

3 eggs, hard-boiled (hard-cooked)

fresh coriander (cilantro) leaves

1 Place the tomatoes in a large mixing bowl. Add the ginger, garlic, chilli powder, salt, ground coriander and ground cumin and blend well.

2 Heat the oil in a saucepan. Add the onion, mustard, fenugreek and white cumin seeds, and the dried red chillies, and stir-fry for about 1 minute, until they give off their aroma. Remove the pan from the heat.

3 Add the tomato mixture to the spicy oil mixture and return the pan to the heat. Stir-fry for about 3 minutes, then reduce the heat and cook, half covered with a lid, stirring frequently, for 7-10 minutes.

4 Sprinkle over 1 tablespoon of the lemon juice. Taste the curry and add the remaining lemon juice, if required.

5 Transfer the tomato curry to a warmed serving dish, set aside and keep warm until required.

6 Shell the hard-boiled (hard-cooked) eggs and cut them into quarters. Gently add them, yolk end downwards, to the tomato curry.

7 Garnish with fresh coriander (cilantro) leaves and serve hot.

Green Pumpkin Curry

The Indian pumpkin used in this curry is long and green and sold by weight. It can easily be bought from any Indian or Pakistani grocers.

NUTRITIONAL INFORMATION

Calories	347	Sugars	.........6g
Protein	.........2g	Fat	..........34g
Carbohydrate	....8g	Saturates	.......4g

 10 MINS   30 MINS

SERVES 4

INGREDIENTS

150 ml/¼ pint/⅔ cup vegetable oil

2 medium-sized onions, sliced

½ tsp white cumin seeds

500 g/1 lb 2 oz green pumpkin, cubed

1 tsp dried mango powder

1 tsp finely chopped root ginger

1 tsp crushed garlic

1 tsp crushed red chilli

½ tsp salt

300 ml/½ pint/1¼ cups water

chapatis or naan bread,
   to serve

1 Heat the oil in a large heavy-based frying pan (skillet). Add the onions and cumin seeds and fry over a medium heat, stirring occasionally, for about 5 minutes, until the onions are a light golden brown colour.

2 Add the cubed pumpkin to the pan and stir-fry over a low heat for 3–5 minutes.

3 Mix the dried mango powder, ginger, garlic, chilli and salt together. Add the spice mixture to the pan, stirring well to combine with the vegetables.

4 Add the water, cover and cook over a low heat, stirring occasionally, for 10–15 minutes.

5 Transfer to serving plates and serve with chapatis or naan bread.

COOK'S TIP

Cumin seeds are popular with Indian cooks because of their warm, pungent flavour and aroma. The seeds are sold whole or ground, and are usually included as one of the flavourings in garam masala.

Okra Curry

This is a delicious dry bhujia (vegetarian curry) which should be served hot with chapatis As okra is such a tasty vegetable it needs few spices.

NUTRITIONAL INFORMATION

Calories 371	Sugars 8g	
Protein 4g	Fat 35g	
Carbohydrate . . .10g	Saturates 4g	

10 MINS   30 MINS

SERVES 4

I N G R E D I E N T S

450 g/1 lb okra (lady's fingers)

150 ml/¼ pint/⅔ cup oil

2 medium onions, sliced

3 green chillies, finely chopped

2 curry leaves

1 tsp salt

1 tomato, sliced

2 tbsp lemon juice

coriander (cilantro) leaves

1 Rinse the okra (lady's fingers) and drain thoroughly. Using a sharp knife, chop and discard the ends of the okra (lady's fingers). Cut the okra (lady's fingers) into 2.5 cm/1 inch long pieces.

2 Heat the oil in a large, heavy-based frying pan (skillet). Add the onions, green chillies, curry leaves and salt and mix together. Stir-fry the vegetables for 5 minutes.

3 Gradually add the okra (lady's fingers), mixing in gently with a slotted spoon. Stir-fry the vegetable mixture over a medium heat for 12–15 minutes.

4 Add the sliced tomato to the pan and sprinkle over half the lemon juice. taste and add more if required.

5 Garnish with coriander (cilantro) leaves, cover and simmer for a further 3–5 minutes.

6 Transfer to warmed serving plates and serve hot.

COOK'S TIP

Okra (lady's fingers) have a remarkable glutinous quality which naturally thickens curries and casseroles.

Red Curry with Cashews

This is a wonderfully quick dish to prepare. If you don't have time to prepare the curry paste, it can be bought ready-made.

NUTRITIONAL INFORMATION

Calories ....274 Sugars 5g
Protein ....10g Fat 10g
Carbohydrate ...38g Saturates 3g

25 MINS   15 MINS

SERVES 4

INGREDIENTS

250 ml/9 fl oz/1 cup coconut milk

1 kaffir lime leaf

¼ tsp light soy sauce

60 g/2 oz/4 baby corn cobs,
   halved lengthways

125 g/4½ oz/1¼ cups broccoli florets

125 g/4½ oz French (green) beans, cut into
   5 cm/2 inch pieces

25 g/1 oz/¼ cup cashew nuts

15 fresh basil leaves

1 tbsp chopped coriander (cilantro)

1 tbsp chopped roast peanuts, to garnish

RED CURRY PASTE

7 fresh red chillies, halved, seeded
   and blanched

2 tsp cumin seeds

2 tsp coriander seeds

2.5 cm/1 inch piece galangal, chopped

½ stalk lemon grass, chopped

1 tsp salt

grated rind of 1 lime

4 garlic cloves, chopped

3 shallots, chopped

2 kaffir lime leaves, shredded

1 tbsp vegetable oil

1 To make the curry paste, grind all the ingredients together in a large mortar with a pestle or a grinder. Alternatively, process briefly in a food processor. The quantity of red curry paste is more than required for this recipe. However, it will keep for up to 3 weeks in a sealed container in the refrigerator.

2 Put a wok or large, heavy-based frying pan (skillet) over a high heat, add 3 tablespoons of the red curry paste and stir until it gives off its aroma. Reduce the heat to medium.

3 Add the coconut milk, kaffir lime leaf, light soy sauce, baby corn cobs, broccoli florets, French (green) beans and cashew nuts. Bring to the boil and simmer for about 10 minutes, until the vegetables are cooked, but still firm and crunchy.

4 Remove and discard the lime leaf and stir in the basil leaves and coriander (cilantro). Transfer to a warmed serving dish, garnish with peanuts and serve immediately.

Egg Curry

This curry can be made very quickly. It can either be served as a side dish or, with parathas, as a light lunch.

NUTRITIONAL INFORMATION

Calories	189	Sugars	.........3g
Protein	........7g	Fat	..........16g
Carbohydrate	....4g	Saturates	.......3g

10 MINS   15 MINS

SERVES 4

I N G R E D I E N T S

4 tbsp vegetable oil

1 medium onion, sliced

1 fresh red chilli, finely chopped

½ tsp chilli powder

½ tsp fresh root ginger, finely chopped

½ tsp fresh garlic, crushed

4 medium eggs

1 firm tomato, sliced

fresh coriander (cilantro) leaves

parathas, to serve (optional)

1 Heat the oil in a large heavy-based saucepan. Add the sliced onion to the pan and fry over a medium heat, stirring occasionally, for about 5 minutes, until it is just softened and a light golden colour.

2 Lower the heat. Add the red chilli, chilli powder, chopped ginger and crushed garlic and fry over a low heat, stirring constantly, for about 1 minute.

3 Add the eggs and tomatoes to the pan and continue cooking, stirring to break up the eggs when they begin to cook, for 3–5 minutes.

4 Sprinkle over the fresh coriander (cilantro) leaves.

5 Transfer the egg curry to warm serving plates and serve hot with parathas, if you wish.

COOK'S TIP

Both the leaves and finely chopped stems of coriander (cilantro) are used in Indian cooking, to flavour dishes and as edible garnishes. It has a very distinctive and pronounced taste.

Spicy Mixed Vegetable Curry

You can vary the vegetables used in this recipe according to personal preferences – experiment!

NUTRITIONAL INFORMATION

Calories 408   Sugars 20
Protein . . . . .11g   Fat 24g
Carbohydrate . . .39g   Saturates 3g

30 MINS   45 MINS

SERVES 4

I N G R E D I E N T S

225 g/8 oz turnips or swede, peeled

1 aubergine (eggplant), leaf end trimmed

350 g/12 oz new potatoes, scrubbed

225 g/8 oz cauliflower

225 g/8 oz button mushrooms, wiped

1 large onion, peeled

225 g/8 oz carrots, peeled

6 tbsp vegetable ghee or oil

2 garlic cloves, peeled and crushed

5 cm/2 inch piece of ginger root, peeled and chopped

1-2 fresh green chillies, seeded and chopped

1 tbsp paprika

2 tsp ground coriander

1 tbsp mild or medium curry powder or paste

450 ml/16 fl oz/1¾ cups vegetable stock

400 g/14 oz can chopped tomatoes

salt

1 green (bell) pepper, seeded and sliced

1 tbsp cornflour (cornstarch)

150 ml/¼ pint/⅔ cup coconut milk

2-3 tbsp ground almonds

coriander (cilantro) sprigs, to garnish

1 Using a sharp knife, cut the turnips or swede, aubergine (eggplant) and potatoes into 1 cm (½ inch) cubes.

2 Divide the cauliflower into small florets. Leave the mushrooms whole, or slice thickly. Slice the onion and carrots.

3 Heat the ghee or oil in a large saucepan, add the onion, turnip, potato and cauliflower and cook gently for 3 minutes, stirring frequently.

4 Add the garlic, ginger, chilli and spices and cook for 1 minute, stirring.

5 Add the stock, tomatoes, aubergine (eggplant) and mushrooms and season with salt. Cover and simmer gently for about 30 minutes or until tender, stirring occasionally. Add the green (bell) pepper, cover and continue cooking for a further 5 minutes.

6 Smoothly blend the cornflour (cornstarch) with the coconut milk and stir into the mixture. Add the ground almonds and simmer for 2 minutes, stirring all the time. Taste and adjust the seasoning, if necessary. Serve hot, garnished with coriander sprigs.

Green Curry with Tempeh

Green curry paste will keep for up to three weeks in the refrigerator. Serve the curry over rice or noodles.

NUTRITIONAL INFORMATION

Calories . . . . . . .237 Sugars 4g
Protein . . . . .16g Fat 17g
Carbohydrate . . . .5g Saturates 3g

 20 MINS   15–20 MINS

SERVES 4

I N G R E D I E N T S

1 tbsp sunflower oil

175 g/6 oz marinated or plain tempeh, cut
    into diamonds

6 spring onions (scallions), cut into
    2.5 cm/1 inch pieces

150 ml/¼ pint/⅔ cup coconut milk

grated rind of 1 lime

15 g/½ oz/¼ cup fresh basil leaves

¼ tsp liquid seasoning, such as Maggi

GREEN CURRY PASTE

2 tsp coriander seeds

1 tsp cumin seeds

1 tsp black peppercorns

4 large green chillies, seeded

2 shallots, quartered

2 garlic cloves,

2 tbsp chopped coriander (cilantro)

grated rind of 1 lime

1 tbsp roughly chopped galangal

1 tsp ground turmeric

salt

2 tbsp oil

TO GARNISH

coriander (cilantro) leaves

2 green chillies, thinly sliced

1 To make the green curry paste, grind together the coriander and cumin seeds and the peppercorns in a food processor or in a mortar with a pestle.

2 Blend the remaining ingredients together and add the ground spice mixture. Store in a clean, dry jar for up to 3 weeks in the refrigerator, or freeze in a suitable container.

3 Heat the oil in a wok or large, heavy frying pan (skillet). Add the tempeh and stir over a high heat for about 2 minutes until sealed on all sides. Add the spring onions (scallions) and stir-fry for 1 minute. Remove the tempeh and spring onions (scallions) and reserve.

4 Put half the coconut milk into the wok or pan (skillet) and bring to the boil. Add 6 tablespoons of the curry paste and the lime rind, and cook for 1 minute, until fragrant. Add the reserved tempeh and spring onions (scallions).

5 Add the remaining coconut milk and simmer for 7–8 minutes. Stir in the basil leaves and liquid seasoning. Leave to simmer for 1 minute before serving, garnished with coriander (cilantro) leaves and chillies.

Green Bean & Potato Curry

You can use fresh or canned green beans for this semi-dry vegetable curry. Serve an oil-dressed dhal for contrasting flavours and colours.

NUTRITIONAL INFORMATION

Calories	690	Sugars	.........4g
Protein	.........3g	Fat	..........69g
Carbohydrate	...16g	Saturates	.......7g

  15 MINS   30 MINS

SERVES 4

INGREDIENTS

300 ml/½ pint/1¼ cups oil

1 tsp white cumin seeds

1 tsp mustard and onion seeds

4 dried red chillies

3 fresh tomatoes, sliced

1 tsp salt

1 tsp finely chopped root ginger

1 tsp crushed garlic

1 tsp chilli powder

200 g/7 oz green cut beans

2 medium potatoes, diced

300 ml/½ pint/1¼ cups water

coriander (cilantro) leaves, chopped

2 green chillies, finely chopped

boiled rice, to serve

1 Heat the oil in a large, heavy-based saucepan. Lower the heat and add the white cumin seeds, mustard and onion seeds and dried red chillies to the saucepan, stirring well.

2 Add the tomatoes to the pan and stir-fry the mixture for 3–5 minutes.

3 Mix together the salt, ginger, garlic and chilli powder and spoon into the pan. Blend the mixture together.

4 Add the green beans and potatoes to the pan and stir-fry for about 5 minutes.

5 Add the water to the pan, reduce the heat to low and simmer for 10–15 minutes, stirring occasionally.

6 Garnish the green bean and potato curry with chopped coriander (cilantro) leaves and green chillies and serve hot with boiled rice.

COOK'S TIP

Mustard seeds are often fried in oil or ghee to bring out their flavour before being combined with other ingredients.

Fried Rice with Spicy Beans

This rice is really colourful and crunchy with the addition of sweetcorn and red kidney beans.

NUTRITIONAL INFORMATION

Calories	363	Sugars	.........3g
Protein	........10g	Fat	...........11g
Carbohydrate	...61g	Saturates	.......2g

 10 MINS   25 MINS

SERVES 4

INGREDIENTS

3 tbsp sunflower oil

1 onion, finely chopped

225 g/8 oz/1 cup long-grain white rice

1 green (bell) pepper, deseeded and diced

1 tsp chilli powder

600 ml/1 pint/2½ cups boiling water

100 g/3½ oz canned sweetcorn

225 g/8 oz canned red kidney beans

2 tbsp chopped fresh coriander (cilantro)

1 Heat the sunflower oil in a large preheated wok.

2 Add the finely chopped onion to the wok and stir-fry for about 2 minutes or until the onion has softened.

COOK'S TIP

For perfect fried rice, the raw rice should ideally be soaked in a bowl of water for a short time before cooking to remove excess starch. Short-grain Oriental rice can be substituted for the long-grain rice.

3 Add the long-grain rice, diced (bell) pepper and chilli powder to the wok and stir-fry for 1 minute.

4 Pour 600 ml/1 pint/2½ cups of boiling water into the wok. Bring to the boil, then reduce the heat and leave the mixture to simmer for 15 minutes.

5 Add the sweetcorn, kidney beans and coriander (cilantro) to the wok and heat through, stirring occasionally.

6 Transfer to a serving bowl and serve hot, scattered with extra coriander (cilantro), if wished.

Pan Potato Cake

This tasty meal is made with sliced potatoes, tofu (bean curd) and vegetables cooked in the pan from which it is served.

NUTRITIONAL INFORMATION

Calories 452   Sugars 6g
Protein . . . . .17g   Fat 28g
Carbohydrate . . .35g   Saturates 13g

15 MINS   30 MINS

SERVES 4

INGREDIENTS

675 g/1½ lb waxy potatoes,
   unpeeled and sliced

1 carrot, diced

225 g/8 oz small broccoli florets

60 g/2 oz/½ cup butter

2 tbsp vegetable oil

1 red onion, quartered

2 garlic cloves, crushed

175 g/6 oz tofu (bean curd), diced

2 tbsp chopped sage

75 g/2¾ oz/¾ cup grated mature
   (sharp) cheese

COOK'S TIP

Make sure that the mixture fills the whole width of your frying pan (skillet) to enable the layers to remain intact.

1 Cook the sliced potatoes in a large saucepan of boiling water for 10 minutes. Drain thoroughly.

2 Meanwhile, cook the carrot and broccoli florets in a separate pan of boiling water for 5 minutes. Drain with a slotted spoon.

3 Heat the butter and oil in a 23 cm/ 9 inch frying pan (skillet). Add the onion and garlic and fry over a low heat for 2-3 minutes. Add half of the potatoes slices to the frying pan (skillet), covering the base of the pan (skillet).

4 Cover the potato slices with the carrot, broccoli and the tofu (bean curd). Sprinkle with half of the sage and cover with the remaining potato slices. Sprinkle the grated cheese over the top.

5 Cook over a moderate heat for 8-10 minutes. Then place the pan under a preheated medium grill (broiler) for 2-3 minutes, or until the cheese melts and browns.

6 Garnish with the remaining sage and serve immediately, straight from the pan (skillet).

Potato Hash

This is a variation of the American dish, beef hash, which was made with salt beef and leftovers, and served to seagoing New Englanders.

NUTRITIONAL INFORMATION

Calories	302	Sugars	.........5g
Protein	........15g	Fat	..........10g
Carbohydrate	...40g	Saturates	.......4g

10 MINS   30 MINS

SERVES 4

INGREDIENTS

25 g/1 oz/2 tbsp butter

1 red onion, halved and sliced

1 carrot, diced

25 g/1 oz French (green) beans, halved

3 large waxy potatoes, diced

2 tbsp plain (all purpose) flour

600 ml/1 pint/1¼ cups vegetable stock

225 g/8 oz tofu (bean curd), diced

salt and pepper

chopped parsley, to garnish

1 Melt the butter in a large, heavy-based frying pan (skillet). Add the onion, carrot, French (green) beans and potatoes and fry over a fairly low heat, stirring constantly, for about 5–7 minutes, or until the vegetables begin to turn golden brown.

2 Add the flour to the frying pan (skillet) and cook, stirring constantly, for 1 minute. Gradually pour in the stock, stirring constantly.

3 Reduce the heat to low and simmer for 15 minutes, or until the potatoes are tender.

4 Add the diced tofu (bean curd) to the pan and cook for a further 5 minutes. Season to taste with salt and pepper.

5 Sprinkle the chopped parsley over the top of the potato hash to garnish and then serve hot straight from the frying pan (skillet).

COOK'S TIP

Hash is an American term meaning to chop food into small pieces. Therefore a traditional hash dish is made from chopped fresh ingredients, such as (bell) peppers, onion and celery.

Kidney Bean Kiev

This is a vegetarian version of chicken Kiev – the bean patties are topped with garlic and herb butter and coated in breadcrumbs.

NUTRITIONAL INFORMATION

Calories ....688 Sugars 8g
Protein ....17g Fat 49g
Carbohydrate ...49g Saturates 20g

  25 MINS   20 MINS

SERVES 4

I N G R E D I E N T S

GARLIC BUTTER

100 g/3½ oz/ 7 tbsp butter

3 garlic cloves, crushed

1 tbsp chopped parsley

BEAN PATTIES

675 g/1½ lb canned red kidney beans

150 g/5½ oz/1¼ cups fresh
   white breadcrumbs

25 g/1 oz/2 tbsp butter

1 leek, chopped

1 celery stick, chopped

1 tbsp chopped parsley

1 egg, beaten

salt and pepper

vegetable oil, for shallow frying

1 To make the garlic butter, put the butter, garlic and parsley in a bowl and blend together with a wooden spoon. Place the garlic butter on to a sheet of baking parchment, roll into a cigar shape and wrap in the baking parchment. Chill in the refrigerator until required.

2 Using a potato masher, mash the red kidney beans in a mixing bowl and stir in 75 g/ 2¾ oz/¾ cup of the breadcrumbs until thoroughly blended.

3 Melt the butter in a heavy-based frying pan (skillet). Add the leek and celery and sauté over a low heat, stirring constantly, for 3–4 minutes.

4 Add the bean mixture to the pan, together with the parsley, season with salt and pepper to taste and mix thoroughly. Remove the pan from the heat and set aside to cool slightly.

5 Divide the kidney bean mixture into 4 equal portions and shape them into ovals.

6 Slice the garlic butter into 4 pieces and place a slice in the centre of each bean patty. With your hands, mould the bean mixture around the garlic butter to encase it completely.

7 Dip each bean patty into the beaten egg to coat and then roll in the remaining breadcrumbs.

8 Heat a little oil in a frying pan (skillet) and fry the patties, turning once, for 7–10 minutes. or until golden brown. Serve immediately.

Bubble & Squeak

Bubble and squeak is best known as fried mashed potato and leftover greens served as an accompaniment.

NUTRITIONAL INFORMATION

Calories	.301	Sugars	.5g
Protein	.11g	Fat	.18g
Carbohydrate	.24g	Saturates	.2g

 15 MINS   40 MINS

SERVES 4

INGREDIENTS

450 g/1 lb floury (mealy) potatoes, diced

225 g/8 oz Savoy cabbage, shredded

5 tbsp vegetable oil

2 leeks, chopped

1 garlic clove, crushed

225 g/8 oz smoked tofu (bean curd), cubed

salt and pepper

shredded cooked leek, to garnish

1 Cook the diced potatoes in a saucepan of lightly salted boiling water for 10 minutes, until tender. Drain and mash the potatoes.

2 Meanwhile, in a separate saucepan, blanch the cabbage in boiling water for 5 minutes. Drain well and add to the potato.

COOK'S TIP

This vegetarian version is a perfect main meal, as the smoked tofu (bean curd) cubes added to the basic bubble and squeak mixture make it very substantial and nourishing.

3 Heat the oil in a heavy-based frying pan (skillet). Add the leeks and garlic and fry gently for 2-3 minutes. Stir into the potato and cabbage mixture.

4 Add the smoked tofu (bean curd) and season well with salt and pepper. Cook over a moderate heat for 10 minutes.

5 Carefully turn the whole mixture over and continue to cook over a moderate heat for a further 5-7 minutes, until crispy underneath. Serve immediately, garnished with shredded leek.

Cheese Potato Cakes

Make these tasty potato cakes for a quick and simple supper dish. Serve them with scrambled eggs if you're very hungry.

NUTRITIONAL INFORMATION

Calories 766   Sugars 7g
Protein . . . . .22g   Fat 50g
Carbohydrate . . .60g   Saturates 20g

25 MINS   35 MINS

SERVES 4

I N G R E D I E N T S

1 kg/2 lb 4 oz potatoes

4 tbsp milk

60 g/2 oz/¼ cup butter or margarine

2 leeks, finely chopped

1 onion, finely chopped

175 g/6 oz/1½ cups grated mature (sharp) Cheddar cheese

1 tbsp chopped parsley or chives

1 egg, beaten

2 tbsp water

90 g/3 oz/1½ cups fresh white or brown breadcrumbs

vegetable oil, for shallow frying

salt and pepper

fresh flat leaf parsley sprigs, to garnish

mixed salad (greens), to serve

1 Cook the potatoes in lightly salted boiling water until tender. Drain and mash them with the milk and the butter or margarine.

2 Cook the leeks and onion in a small quantity of lightly salted boiling water for about 10 minutes until tender. Drain well.

3 In a large mixing bowl, combine the leeks and onion with the mashed potato, cheese and parsley or chives. Season to taste with salt and pepper.

4 Beat together the egg and water in a shallow bowl. Sprinkle the breadcrumbs into a separate shallow bowl. Shape the potato mixture into 12 even-sized cakes, brushing each with the egg mixture, then coating all over with the breadcrumbs.

5 Heat the oil in a large frying pan (skillet). Add the potato cakes, in batches if necessary, and fry over a low heat for about 2–3 minutes on each side, until light golden brown. Garnish with flat leaf parsley and serve with a mixed salad (greens).

Sauté of Summer Vegetables

The freshness of lightly cooked summer vegetables is enhanced by the aromatic flavour of a tarragon and white wine dressing.

NUTRITIONAL INFORMATION

Calories . . . . .217 Sugars 8g
Protein . . . . .2g Fat 18g
Carbohydrate . . . .9g Saturates 9g

  10 MINS 10–15 MINS

SERVES 4

I N G R E D I E N T S

225 g/8 oz baby carrots, scrubbed

125 g/4½ oz runner (string) beans

2 courgettes (zucchini), trimmed

1 bunch large spring onions (scallions)

1 bunch radishes

60 g/2 oz/¼ cup butter

2 tbsp light olive oil

2 tbsp white wine vinegar

4 tbsp dry white wine

1 tsp caster (superfine) sugar

1 tbsp chopped tarragon

salt and pepper

tarragon sprigs, to garnish

1 Cut the carrots in half lengthways, slice the beans and courgettes (zucchini), and halve the spring onions (scallions) and radishes, so that all the vegetables are cut to even-size pieces.

2 Melt the butter in a large, heavy-based frying pan (skillet) or wok. Add all the vegetables and fry them over a medium heat, stirring frequently, until they are tender, but still crisp and firm to the bite.

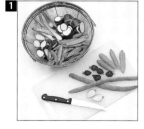

3 Heat the olive oil, vinegar, white wine and sugar in a small saucepan over a low heat, stirring until the sugar has dissolved. Remove from the heat and add the chopped tarragon.

4 When the vegetables are just cooked, pour over the 'dressing'. Stir through, tossing the vegetables well to coat, and then transfer to a warmed serving dish. Garnish with sprigs of fresh tarragon and serve at once.

Cashew Nut Paella

Paella traditionally contains chicken and fish, but this recipe is packed with vegetables and nuts for a truly delicious and simple vegetarian dish.

NUTRITIONAL INFORMATION

Calories 406   Sugars 8g
Protein ....10g   Fat 22g
Carbohydrate ...44g   Saturates 6g

15 MINS   35 MINS

SERVES 4

INGREDIENTS

2 tbsp olive oil

1 tbsp butter

1 red onion, chopped

150 g/5½ oz/1 cup arborio rice

1 tsp ground turmeric

1 tsp ground cumin

½ tsp chilli powder

3 garlic cloves, crushed

1 green chilli, sliced

1 green (bell) pepper, seeded and diced

1 red (bell) pepper, seeded and diced

75 g/2¾ oz baby corn cobs,
   halved lengthways

2 tbsp pitted black olives

1 large tomato, seeded and diced

450 ml/16 fl oz/2 cups vegetable stock

75 g/2¾ oz/¾ cup unsalted cashew nuts

50 g/1¾ oz/¼ cup frozen peas

2 tbsp chopped parsley

pinch of cayenne pepper

salt and pepper

herbs, to garnish

1 Heat the olive oil and butter in a large frying pan (skillet) or paella pan until the butter has melted.

2 Add the chopped onion to the pan and sauté over a medium heat, stirring constantly, for 2–3 minutes, until the onion has softened.

3 Stir in the rice, ground turmeric, ground cumin, chilli powder, garlic, sliced chilli, (bell) peppers, corn cobs, black olives and diced tomato and cook over a medium heat, stirring occasionally, for 1–2 minutes.

4 Pour in the stock and bring the mixture to the boil. Reduce the heat and cook, stirring constantly, for 20 minutes.

5 Add the cashew nuts and peas and cook, stirring occasionally, for 5 minutes. Season to taste with salt and pepper and sprinkle with parsley and cayenne pepper. Transfer to warm serving plates, garnish and serve immediately.

Vegetable Medley

Serve this as a crisp and colourful dish, with pitta bread, chapattis or naan, or as an accompaniment to baked pasta dishes.

NUTRITIONAL INFORMATION

Calories 190	Sugars 17g	
Protein 7g	Fat 7g	
Carbohydrate ...27g	Saturates 1g	

  15 MINS   🕐 10 MINS

SERVES 4

I N G R E D I E N T S

150 g/5½ oz young, French (green) beans

8 baby carrots

6 baby turnips

½ small cauliflower

2 tbsp vegetable oil

2 large onions, sliced

2 garlic cloves, finely chopped

300 ml/½ pint/1¼ cups natural
   (unsweetened) yogurt

1 tbsp cornflour (cornstarch)

2 tbsp tomato purée (paste)

pinch of chilli powder

salt

1 Top and tail the beans and snap them in half. Cut the carrots in half and the turnips in quarters. Divide the cauliflower into florets, discarding the thick stalk.

2 Steam the vegetables over boiling, salted water for 3 minutes, then turn them into a colander and plunge them at once in a large bowl of cold water to prevent further cooking.

3 Heat the oil in a pan and fry the onions over a medium heat until they are translucent. Stir in the garlic and cook for 1 minute.

4 Mix together the yogurt, cornflour (cornstarch) and tomato purée (paste) to form a smooth paste. Stir this paste into the onions and cook for 1–2 minutes, until the sauce is thoroughly blended.

5 Drain the vegetables well, then gradually stir them into the sauce, taking care not to break them up. Season with salt and chilli powder to taste, cover and simmer over a low heat for 5 minutes, until the vegetables are just tender. Taste and adjust the seasoning if necessary. Serve immediately.

Vegetable Pasta Stir-Fry

East meets West in this delicious dish. Prepare all the vegetables and cook the pasta in advance, then the dish can be cooked in a few minutes.

NUTRITIONAL INFORMATION

Calories 383	Sugars 18g	
Protein 14g	Fat 23g	
Carbohydrate ...32g	Saturates 8g	

 20 MINS   30 MINS

SERVES 4

I N G R E D I E N T S

400 g/14 oz/4⅔ cups dried wholewheat
   pasta·shells, or other short pasta shapes

1 tbsp olive oil

2 carrots, thinly sliced

115 g/4 oz baby corn cobs

3 tbsp peanut oil

2.5-cm/1-inch piece fresh ginger root,
   thinly sliced

1 large onion, thinly sliced

1 garlic clove, thinly sliced

3 celery sticks, thinly sliced

1 small red (bell) pepper, seeded and sliced
   into matchstick strips

1 small green (bell) pepper,
   seeded and sliced into matchstick strips

salt

steamed mangetouts (snow peas),
   to serve

S A U C E

1 tsp cornflour (cornstarch)

2 tbsp water

3 tbsp soy sauce

3 tbsp dry sherry

1 tsp clear honey

dash of hot pepper sauce (optional)

1 Cook the pasta in a large pan of boiling lightly salted water, adding the tablespoon of olive oil. When tender, but still firm to the bite, drain the pasta in a colander, return to the pan, cover and keep warm.

2 Cook the carrots and baby corn cobs in boiling, salted water for 2 minutes. Drain them in a colander, plunge into cold water to prevent further cooking and drain again.

3 Heat the peanut oil in a large frying pan (skillet) over medium heat. Add the ginger and stir-fry for 1 minute, to flavour the oil. Remove with a slotted spoon and discard.

4 Add the onion, garlic, celery and (bell) peppers to the oil and stir-fry over a medium heat for 2 minutes. Add the carrots and baby corn cobs, and stir-fry for a further 2 minutes, then stir in the reserved pasta.

5 Put the cornflour (cornstarch) in a small bowl and mix to a smooth paste with the water. Stir in the soy sauce, sherry and honey.

6 Pour the sauce into the pan, stir well and cook for 2 minutes, stirring once or twice. Taste the sauce and season with hot pepper sauce if wished. Serve with a steamed green vegetable, such as mangetouts (snow peas).

Sweet & Sour Vegetables

Serve this dish with plain noodles or fluffy white rice for a filling, and flavoursome oriental meal.

NUTRITIONAL INFORMATION

Calories . . . . .401 Sugars 16g
Protein . . . . .14g Fat 9g
Carbohydrate . . .70g Saturates 2g

 10 MINS   15 MINS

SERVES 4

I N G R E D I E N T S

1 tbsp peanut oil

2 garlic cloves, crushed

1 tsp grated root ginger

50 g/1¾ oz baby corn cobs

50 g/1¾ oz mangetout (snow peas)

1 carrot, cut into matchsticks

1 green (bell) pepper, seeded and cut
   into matchsticks

8 spring onions (scallions)

50 g/1¾ oz canned bamboo shoots

225 g/8 oz marinated firm tofu (bean
   curd), cubed

2 tbsp dry sherry or Chinese rice wine

2 tbsp rice vinegar

2 tbsp clear honey

1 tbsp light soy sauce

150 ml/¼ pint/⅔ cup vegetable stock

1 tbsp cornflour (cornstarch)

noodles or boiled rice, to serve

1 Heat the oil in a preheated wok until almost smoking. Add the garlic and grated root ginger and cook over a medium heat, stirring frequently, for 30 seconds.

2 Add the baby corn cobs, mangetout (snow peas), carrot and (bell) pepper matchsticks and stir-fry for about 5 minutes, or until the vegetables are tender, but still crisp.

3 Add the spring onions (scallions), bamboo shoots and tofu (bean curd) and cook for 2 minutes.

4 Stir in the sherry or Chinese rice wine, rice vinegar, honey, soy sauce, vegetable stock and cornflour (cornstarch) and bring to the boil. Reduce the heat to low and simmer for 2 minutes, until heated through. Transfer to warmed serving dishes and serve immediately.

Feta Cheese Patties

Grated carrots, courgettes (zucchini) and feta cheese are combined with cumin seeds, poppy seeds, curry powder and chopped fresh parsley.

NUTRITIONAL INFORMATION

Calories 217   Sugars 6g
Protein . . . . .6g   Fat 16g
Carbohydrate . . .12g   Saturates 7g

15 MINS   20 MINS

SERVES 4

INGREDIENTS

2 large carrots

1 large courgette (zucchini)

1 small onion

60 g/2 oz feta cheese

25 g/1 oz/½ cup plain (all-purpose) flour

¼ tsp cumin seeds

½ tsp poppy seeds

1 tsp medium curry powder

1 tbsp chopped fresh parsley

1 egg, beaten

25 g/1 oz/2 tbsp butter

2 tbsp vegetable oil

salt and pepper

herb sprigs, to garnish

1 Grate the carrots, courgette (zucchini), onion and feta cheese coarsely, either by hand or process in a food processor.

2 Mix together the flour, cumin seeds, poppy seeds, curry powder and parsley in a large bowl. Season to taste with salt and pepper.

3 Add the carrot mixture to the seasoned flour, tossing well to combine. Stir in the beaten egg.

4 Heat the butter and oil in a large, heavy-based frying pan (skillet). Place heaped tablespoonfuls of the carrot mixture in the pan, flattening them slightly with the back of the spoon. Fry gently for about 2 minutes on each side, until crisp and golden brown. Drain on kitchen paper (paper towels) and keep warm until all the mixture is used.

5 Serve immediately, garnished with sprigs of fresh herbs.

Casseroles & Bakes

Anyone who ever thought that vegetarian meals were dull will be proved wrong by the rich variety of dishes in this chapter. You'll recognize influences from Mexican and Chinese cooking, but there are also

traditional stews and casseroles, as well as hearty bakes and roasts. They all make exciting meals, at any time of year, and for virtually any occasion. Don't be afraid to substitute your own personal favourite ingredients where appropriate. There is no reason why you cannot enjoy experimenting and adding your own touch to these imaginative ideas.

Lentil & Rice Casserole

This is a really hearty dish, perfect for cold days when a filling hot dish is just what you need.

NUTRITIONAL INFORMATION

Calories 312   Sugars 9g
Protein . . . . .20g   Fat 2g
Carbohydrate . . .51g   Saturates 0.4g

15 MINS   40 MINS

SERVES 4

INGREDIENTS

225 g/8 oz/1 cup split red lentils

50 g/1¾ oz/⅓ cup long grain white rice

1.2 litres/2 pints/5 cups vegetable stock

1 leek, cut into chunks

3 garlic cloves, crushed

400 g/14 oz can chopped tomatoes

1 tsp ground cumin

1 tsp chilli powder

1 tsp garam masala

1 red (bell) pepper, seeded and sliced

100 g/3½ oz small broccoli florets

8 baby corn cobs, halved lengthways

50 g/1¾ oz French (green) beans, halved

1 tbsp shredded basil

salt and pepper

fresh basil sprigs, to garnish

VARIATION

You can vary the rice in this recipe – use brown or wild rice, if you prefer.

1 Place the lentils, rice and vegetable stock in a large flameproof casserole and cook over a low heat, stirring occasionally, for 20 minutes.

2 Add the leek, garlic, tomatoes and their can juice, ground cumin, chilli powder, garam masala, sliced (bell) pepper, broccoli, corn cobs and French (green) beans to the pan .

3 Bring the mixture to the boil, reduce the heat, cover and simmer for a further 10–15 minutes, or until the vegetables are tender.

4 Add the shredded basil and season with salt and pepper to taste.

5 Garnish with fresh basil sprigs and serve immediately.

Winter Vegetable Casserole

This hearty supper dish is best served with plenty of warm crusty bread to mop up the delicious juices.

NUTRITIONAL INFORMATION

Calories	211	Sugars	.........6g
Protein	.........11g	Fat	...........6g
Carbohydrate	...26g	Saturates	.....0.8g

 10 MINS   40 MINS

SERVES 4

I N G R E D I E N T S

1 tbsp olive oil

1 red onion, halved and sliced

3 garlic cloves, crushed

225 g/8 oz spinach

1 fennel bulb, cut into eight

1 red (bell) pepper, seeded and cubed

1 tbsp plain (all-purpose) flour

450 ml/16 fl oz/1¾ cups vegetable stock

6 tbsp dry white wine

400 g/14 oz can chickpeas
   (garbanzo beans), drained

1 bay leaf

1 tsp ground coriander

½ tsp paprika

salt and pepper

fennel fronds, to garnish

1 Heat the olive oil in a large flameproof casserole. Add the onion and garlic and sauté over a low heat, stirring frequently, for 1 minute. Add the spinach and cook, stirring occasionally, for 4 minutes, or until wilted.

2 Add the fennel pieces and red (bell) pepper and cook, stirring constantly, for 2 minutes.

3 Stir in the flour and cook, stirring constantly, for 1 minute.

4 Add the vegetable stock, white wine, chickpeas (garbanzo beans), bay leaf, ground coriander and paprika, cover and simmer for 30 minutes. Season to taste with salt and pepper, garnish with fennel fronds and serve immediately straight from the casserole.

COOK'S TIP

Use other canned pulses or mixed beans instead of the chickpeas (garbanzo beans), if you prefer.

Winter Vegetable Cobbler

Seasonal fresh vegetables are casseroled with lentils, then topped with a ring of fresh cheese scones (biscuits) to make this tasty cobbler.

NUTRITIONAL INFORMATION

Calories	734	Sugars	........22g
Protein	........27g	Fat	..........30g
Carbohydrate	...96g	Saturates	......16g

20 MINS   40 MINS

SERVES 4

I N G R E D I E N T S

1 tbsp olive oil

1 garlic clove, crushed

8 small onions, halved

2 celery sticks, sliced

225 g/8 oz swede (rutabaga), chopped

2 carrots, sliced

½ small cauliflower, broken into florets

225 g/8 oz mushrooms, sliced

400 g/14 oz can chopped tomatoes

60 g/2 oz/¼ cup red lentils

2 tbsp cornflour (cornstarch)

3–4 tbsp water

300 ml/½ pint/1¼ cups vegetable stock

2 tsp Tabasco sauce

2 tsp chopped oregano

oregano sprigs, to garnish

C O B B L E R T O P P I N G

225 g/8 oz/2 cups self-raising flour

60 g/2 oz/¼ cup butter

125 g/4½ oz/1 cup grated mature (sharp) Cheddar cheese

2 tsp chopped oregano

1 egg, beaten

150 ml/¼ pint/⅔ cup milk

salt

1 Heat the oil in a large saucepan. Fry the garlic and onions for 5 minutes. Add the celery, swede (rutabaga), carrots and cauliflower and fry for 2–3 minutes. Add the mushrooms, tomatoes and lentils.

2 Mix the cornflour (cornstarch) and water and add to the pan with the stock, Tabasco and oregano. Bring to the boil, stirring. Transfer to an ovenproof dish, cover and bake in a preheated oven, 180°C/350°F/Gas Mark 4, for 20 minutes.

3 To make the topping, sift the flour and salt into a bowl. Rub in the butter, then stir in most of the cheese and the chopped herbs. Beat together the egg and milk and add enough to the dry ingredients to make a soft dough. Knead lightly, roll out to 1 cm/½ inch thick and cut into 5 cm/2 inch rounds.

4 Remove the dish from the oven and increase the temperature to 200°C/400°F/Gas Mark 6. Arrange the rounds around the edge of the dish, brush with the remaining egg and milk and sprinkle with the reserved cheese. Cook for a further 10–12 minutes, until the topping is risen and golden. Garnish and serve.

Lentil Roast

The perfect dish to serve for Sunday lunch. Roast vegetables make a succulent accompaniment.

  15 MINS   1 HR 20 MINS

SERVES 6

I N G R E D I E N T S

225 g/8 oz/1 cup red lentils

450 ml/16 fl oz/2 cups vegetable stock

1 bay leaf

15 g/½ oz/1 tbsp butter or
   margarine, softened

2 tbsp dried wholemeal
   (whole wheat) breadcrumbs

225 g/8 oz/2 cups grated mature
   (sharp) Cheddar cheese

1 leek, finely chopped

125 g/4½ oz button mushrooms,
   finely chopped

90 g/3 oz/1½ cups fresh wholemeal
   (whole wheat) breadcrumbs

2 tbsp chopped parsley

1 tbsp lemon juice

2 eggs, lightly beaten

salt and pepper

flat leaf parsley sprigs, to garnish

mixed roast vegetables, to serve

1 Put the lentils, stock and bay leaf in a saucepan. Bring to the boil, cover and simmer gently for 15–20 minutes, until all the liquid is absorbed and the lentils have softened. Discard the bay leaf.

2 Base-line a 1 kg/2 lb 4 oz loaf tin (pan) with baking parchment. Grease with the butter or margarine and sprinkle with the dried breadcrumbs.

3 Stir the cheese, leek, mushrooms, fresh breadcrumbs and parsley into the lentils.

4 Bind the mixture together with the lemon juice and eggs. Season with salt and pepper. Spoon into the prepared loaf tin (pan) and smooth the top.

5 Bake in a preheated oven, 190°C/375°F/Gas Mark 5, for about 1 hour, until golden.

6 Loosen the loaf with a palette knife (spatula) and turn on to a warmed serving plate. Garnish with parsley and serve sliced, with roast vegetables.

Almond & Sesame Nut Roast

Toasted almonds are combined with sesame seeds, rice and vegetables in this tasty roast. Serve it with a delicious onion and mushroom sauce.

NUTRITIONAL INFORMATION

Calories	612	Sugars	. . . . .7g
Protein	. . . . .22g	Fat	. . . . .46g
Carbohydrate	. . .29g	Saturates	. . . . . .13g

30–40 MINS   35 MINS

SERVES 4

INGREDIENTS

2 tbsp sesame or olive oil

1 small onion, finely chopped

60 g/2 oz/scant ¼ cup risotto rice

300 ml/½ pint/1¼ cups vegetable stock

1 large carrot, grated

1 large leek, finely chopped

2 tsp sesame seeds, toasted

90 g/3 oz/¾ cup chopped almonds, toasted

60 g/2 oz/½ cup ground almonds

90 g/3 oz/¾ cup grated mature (sharp)
   Cheddar cheese

2 eggs, beaten

1 tsp dried mixed herbs

salt and pepper

flat leaf parsley sprigs, to garnish

fresh vegetables, to serve

SAUCE

25 g/1 oz/2 tbsp butter

1 small onion, finely chopped

125 g/4½ oz/1½ cups finely
   chopped mushrooms

25 g/1 oz/¼ cup plain (all-purpose) flour

300 ml/½ pint/1½ cups vegetable stock

1 Heat the oil in a large frying pan (skillet) and fry the onion gently for 2–3 minutes. Add the rice and cook gently for 5–6 minutes, stirring frequently.

2 Add the stock, bring to the boil, lower the heat and simmer for 15 minutes, or until the rice is tender. Add a little extra water if necessary. Remove from the heat and transfer to a large mixing bowl.

3 Add the carrot, leek, sesame seeds, almonds, cheese, beaten eggs and herbs. Mix well and season with salt and pepper. Transfer the mixture to a greased 500 g/1 lb 2 oz loaf tin (pan), levelling the

surface. Bake in a preheated oven, 180°C/350°F/Gas Mark 4, for 1 hour, until set and firm. Leave in the tin (pan) for 10 minutes.

4 To make the sauce, melt the butter in a small saucepan and fry the onion until dark golden brown. Add the mushrooms and cook for 2 minutes. Stir in the flour, cook gently for 1 minute, then gradually add the stock. Bring to the boil, stirring constantly, until thickened and blended. Season to taste.

5 Turn out the nut roast, slice and serve, garnished with parsley, with fresh vegetables, accompanied by the sauce.

Potato-Topped Lentil Bake

A wonderful mixture of red lentils, tofu (bean curd) and vegetables is cooked beneath a crunchy potato topping for a really hearty meal.

NUTRITIONAL INFORMATION

Calories 627	Sugars 7g	
Protein 26g	Fat 30g	
Carbohydrate ...66g	Saturates 13g	

10 MINS   1½ HOURS

SERVES 4

I N G R E D I E N T S

TOPPING

675 g/1½ lb floury (mealy) potatoes, diced

25 g/1 oz/2 tbsp butter

1 tbsp milk

50 g/1¾ oz/½ cup chopped pecan nuts

2 tbsp chopped thyme

thyme sprigs, to garnish

FILLING

225 g/8 oz/1 cup red lentils

60 g/2 oz/½ cup butter

1 leek, sliced

2 garlic cloves, crushed

1 celery stick, chopped

125 g/4½ oz broccoli florets

175 g/6 oz smoked tofu (bean curd), cubed

2 tsp tomato purée (paste)

salt and pepper

1 To make the topping, cook the potatoes in a saucepan of boiling water for 10–15 minutes, or until cooked through. Drain well, add the butter and milk and mash thoroughly. Stir in the pecan nuts and chopped thyme and set aside.

2 Cook the lentils in boiling water for 20–30 minutes, or until tender. Drain and set aside.

3 Melt the butter in a frying pan (skillet). Add the leek, garlic, celery and broccoli. Fry over a medium heat, stirring frequently, for 5 minutes, until softened. Add the tofu (bean curd) cubes. Stir in the lentils, together with the tomato purée (paste). Season with salt and pepper to taste, then turn the mixture into the base of a shallow ovenproof dish.

4 Spoon the mashed potato on top of the lentil mixture, spreading to cover it completely.

5 Cook in a preheated oven, 200°C/ 400°F/Gas Mark 6, for about 30–35 minutes, or until the topping is golden. Garnish with sprigs of fresh thyme and serve hot.

VARIATION

You can use almost any combination of your favourite vegetables in this dish.

Mexican Chilli Corn Pie

This bake of sweetcorn (corn) and kidney beans, flavoured with chilli and fresh coriander (cilantro), is topped with crispy cheese cornbread.

 25 MINS   20 MINS

SERVES 4

INGREDIENTS

1 tbsp corn oil

2 garlic cloves, crushed

1 red (bell) pepper, seeded and diced

1 green (bell) pepper, seeded and diced

1 celery stick, diced

1 tsp hot chilli powder

400 g/14 oz can chopped tomatoes

325 g/11½ oz can sweetcorn (corn),
    drained

215 g/7½ oz can kidney beans,
    drained and rinsed

2 tbsp chopped coriander (cilantro)

salt and pepper

coriander (cilantro) sprigs, to garnish

tomato and avocado salad, to serve

TOPPING

125 g/4½ oz/⅔ cup cornmeal

1 tbsp plain (all-purpose) flour

½ tsp salt

2 tsp baking powder

1 egg, beaten

6 tbsp milk

1 tbsp corn oil

125 g/4½ oz/1 cup grated mature
    (sharp) Cheddar cheese

1 Heat the oil in a large frying pan (skillet) and gently fry the garlic (bell) peppers and celery for 5–6 minutes until just softened.

2 Stir in the chilli powder, tomatoes, sweetcorn, beans and seasoning. Bring to the boil and simmer for 10 minutes. Stir in the coriander (cilantro) and spoon into an ovenproof dish.

3 To make the topping, mix together the cornmeal, flour, salt and baking powder. Make a well in the centre, add the egg, milk and oil and beat until a smooth batter is formed.

4 Spoon over the (bell) pepper and sweetcorn mixture and sprinkle with the cheese. Bake in a preheated oven, at 220°C/425°F/Gas Mark 7, for 25–30 minutes until golden and firm.

5 Garnish with coriander (cilantro) sprigs and serve immediately with a tomato and avocado salad.

Vegetable Hot Pot

In this recipe, a variety of vegetables are cooked under a layer of potatoes, topped with cheese and cooked until golden brown.

NUTRITIONAL INFORMATION

Calories	279	Sugars	........12g
Protein	........10g	Fat	...........11g
Carbohydrate	...34g	Saturates	.......4g

25 MINS   1 HOUR

SERVES 4

INGREDIENTS

2 large potatoes, thinly sliced

2 tbsp vegetable oil

1 red onion, halved and sliced

1 leek, sliced

2 garlic cloves, crushed

1 carrot, cut into chunks

100 g/3½ oz broccoli florets

100 g/3½ oz cauliflower florets

2 small turnips, quartered

1 tbsp plain (all-purpose) flour

700 ml/1¼ pints/3 cups vegetable stock

150 ml/¼ pint/⅔ cup dry cider

1 eating apple, cored and sliced

2 tbsp chopped sage

pinch of cayenne pepper

50 g/1¾ oz/½ cup grated
   Cheddar cheese

salt and pepper

1 Cook the potato slices in a saucepan of boiling water for 10 minutes. Drain thoroughly and reserve.

2 Heat the oil in a flameproof casserole. Add the onion, leek and garlic and sauté, stirring occasionally, for 2–3 minutes. Add the remaining vegetables and cook, stirring constantly, for a further 3–4 minutes.

3 Stir in the flour and cook for 1 minute. Gradually add the stock and cider and bring to the boil. Add the apple, sage and cayenne pepper and season well. Remove from the heat and transfer the vegetables to an ovenproof dish.

4 Arrange the potato slices on top of the vegetable mixture to cover.

5 Sprinkle the cheese on top of the potato slices and cook in a preheated oven, 190°C/375°F/Gas Mark 5, for 30–35 minutes or until the potato is golden brown and beginning to crispen around the edges. Serve immediately.

Brazil Nut & Mushroom Pie

The button mushrooms give this wholesome vegan pie a wonderful aromatic flavour. The pie can be frozen uncooked and baked from frozen.

NUTRITIONAL INFORMATION

Calories 530	Sugars 4g	
Protein 12g	Fat 38g	
Carbohydrate ...38g	Saturates 8g	

 1 HOUR   50 MINS

SERVES 6

INGREDIENTS

PASTRY (PIE DOUGH)

225 g/8 oz/1¾ cups plain (all-purpose)
  wholemeal (whole wheat) flour

100 g/3½ oz/⅓ cup margarine,
  cut into small pieces

4 tbsp water

soya milk, to glaze

FILLING

25 g/1 oz/2 tbsp margarine

1 onion, chopped

1 garlic clove, finely chopped

125 g/4½ oz button mushrooms, sliced

1 tbsp plain (all-purpose) flour

150 ml/¼ pint/⅔ cup vegetable stock

175 g/6 oz Brazil nuts

1 tbsp tomato purée (paste)

75 g/2¾ oz fresh wholemeal
  (whole wheat) breadcrumbs

2 tbsp chopped parsley

½ tsp pepper

1 To make the pastry (pie dough), place the flour in a mixing bowl and rub in the margarine with your fingertips until the mixture resembles fine breadcrumbs. Stir in the water and bring together to form a smooth dough. Knead lightly, then wrap and chill in the refrigerator for 30 minutes.

2 To make the filling, melt half of the margarine in a pan. Add the onion, garlic and mushrooms and fry over a medium heat, stirring occasionally, for 5 minutes, until softened. Add the flour and cook for 1 minute, stirring frequently. Gradually add the stock, stirring until the sauce is smooth and beginning to thicken. Chop the Brazil nuts. Stir in the tomato purée (paste), nuts, breadcrumbs, parsley and pepper. Set aside to cool slightly.

3 On a lightly floured surface, roll out two-thirds of the pastry (pie dough) and use to line a 20 cm/8 inch loose-based flan tin (pan) or pie dish. Spread the filling in the pastry case (pie shell). Brush the edges of the pastry (pie dough) with soya milk. Roll out the remaining pastry (pie dough) to fit the top of the pie. Seal the edges, make a slit in the top of the pastry (pie dough) and brush with soya milk to glaze.

4 Bake in a preheated oven, 200°C/400°F/Gas Mark 6, for 30–40 minutes, until golden brown. Serve immediately.

Layered Pies

These individual pies of layered potato, aubergine (eggplant) and courgettes (zucchini) baked in a tomato sauce can be made in advance.

NUTRITIONAL INFORMATION

Calories 427   Sugars 8g
Protein . . . . .22g   Fat 21g
Carbohydrate . . .41g   Saturates 8g

🥘 40 MINS   🕐 1 HR 20 MINS

SERVES 4

I N G R E D I E N T S

3 large waxy potatoes, thinly sliced

1 small aubergine (eggplant), thinly sliced

1 courgette (zucchini), sliced

3 tbsp vegetable oil

1 onion, diced

1 green (bell) pepper, seeded and diced

1 tsp cumin seeds

2 tbsp chopped basil

200 g/7 oz can chopped tomatoes

175 g/6 oz mozzarella cheese, sliced

225 g/8 oz tofu (bean curd), sliced

60 g/2 oz/1 cup fresh white breadcrumbs

2 tbsp grated Parmesan cheese

salt and pepper

basil leaves, to garnish

1 Cook the sliced potatoes in a saucepan of boiling water for 5 minutes. Drain and set aside.

2 Put the aubergine (eggplant) slices on a plate, sprinkle with salt and leave for 20 minutes. Meanwhile, blanch the courgette (zucchini) in a saucepan of boiling water for 2-3 minutes. Drain and set aside.

3 Meanwhile, heat 2 tbsp of the oil in a frying pan (skillet). Add the onion and fry over a low heat, stirring occasionally, for 2-3 minutes, until softened. Add the (bell) pepper, cumin seeds, basil and canned tomatoes. Season to taste with salt and pepper and simmer for 30 minutes.

4 Rinse the aubergine (eggplant) slices and pat dry. Heat the remaining oil in a large frying pan (skillet) and fry the aubergine (eggplant) slices for 3-5 minutes, turning to brown both sides. Drain and set aside.

5 Arrange half of the potato slices in the base of 4 small loose-based flan tins (pans). Cover with half of the courgette (zucchini) slices, half of the aubergine (eggplant) slices and half of the mozzarella slices. Lay the tofu (bean curd) on top and spoon over the tomato sauce. Repeat the layers of vegetables and cheese in the same order.

6 Mix the breadcrumbs and Parmesan together and sprinkle over the top. Cook in a preheated oven,190°C/375°F/Gas Mark 5, for 25-30 minutes, or until golden. Garnish with basil leaves.

3

5

6

Curry Pasties

These pasties, which are suitable for vegans, are a delicious combination of vegetables and spices. They can be eaten either hot or cold.

NUTRITIONAL INFORMATION

Calories ....455 Sugars 5g
Protein ....8g Fat 27g
Carbohydrate ...48g Saturates 5g

1 HOUR   1 HOUR

SERVES 4

INGREDIENTS

225 g/8 oz/2 cups plain (all-purpose)
   wholemeal (whole wheat) flour

100 g/3½ oz/ ⅓ cup margarine,
   cut into small pieces

4 tbsp water

2 tbsp oil

225 g/8 oz diced root vegetables, such as
   potatoes, carrots and parsnips

1 small onion, chopped

2 garlic cloves, finely chopped

½ tsp curry powder

½ tsp ground turmeric

½ tsp ground cumin

½ tsp wholegrain mustard

5 tbsp vegetable stock

soya milk, to glaze

1 Place the flour in a mixing bowl and rub in the margarine with your fingertips until the mixture resembles breadcrumbs. Stir in the water and bring together to form a soft dough. Wrap and set aside to chill in the refrigerator for 30 minutes.

2 To make the filling, heat the oil in a large saucepan. Add the diced root vegetables, chopped onion and garlic and fry, stirring occasionally, for 2 minutes. Stir in all of the spices, turning the vegetables to coat them thoroughly. Fry the vegetables, stirring constantly, for a further 1 minute.

3 Add the stock to the pan and bring to the boil. Cover and simmer, stirring occasionally, for about 20 minutes, until the vegetables are tender and the liquid has been absorbed. Leave to cool.

4 Divide the pastry (pie dough) into 4 portions. Roll each portion into a 15 cm/6 inch round. Place the filling on one half of each round.

5 Brush the edges of each round with soya milk, then fold over and press the edges together to seal. Place on a baking tray (cookie sheet). Bake in a preheated oven, 200°C/ 400°F/Gas Mark 6, for 25–30 minutes until golden brown.

Mushroom Vol-au-Vent

A simple mixture of creamy, tender mushrooms filling a crisp, rich pastry case, this dish will make an impression at any dinner party.

NUTRITIONAL INFORMATION

Calories 688   Sugars 2g
Protein ....10g   Fat 52g
Carbohydrate ...45g   Saturates 22g

25 MINS   50 MINS

SERVES 4

INGREDIENTS

500 g/1 lb 2 oz puff pastry, thawed if frozen

1 egg, beaten, for glazing

FILLING

25 g/1 oz/2 tbsp butter or margarine

750 g/1 lb 10 oz mixed mushrooms, such
    as open cup, field, button, chestnut
    (crimini), shiitake, pied de mouton, sliced

6 tbsp dry white wine

4 tbsp double (heavy) cream

2 tbsp chopped chervil

salt and pepper

chervil sprigs, to garnish

1 Roll out the pastry on a lightly floured surface to a 20 cm/8 inch square.

2 Using a sharp knife, mark a square 2.5 cm/1 inch from the pastry edge, cutting halfway through the pastry.

3 Score the top in a diagonal pattern. Knock up the edges with a kitchen knife and put on a baking tray (cookie sheet). Brush the top with beaten egg, taking care not to let the egg run into the cut. Bake in a preheated oven, 220°C/425°F/Gas Mark 7, for 35 minutes.

4 Cut out the central square. Discard the soft pastry inside the case, leaving the base intact. Return to the oven, with the square, for 10 minutes.

5 Meanwhile, make the filling. Melt the butter or margarine in a frying pan (skillet) and stir-fry the mushrooms over a high heat for 3 minutes.

6 Add the wine and cook, stirring occasionally, for 10 minutes, until the mushrooms have softened. Stir in the cream and chervil and season to taste with salt and pepper.

7 Pile into the pastry case. Top with the pastry square, garnish with sprigs of chervil and serve.

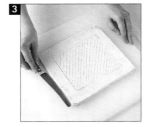

Green Vegetable Gougère

A tasty, simple supper dish of choux pastry and crisp green vegetables. The choux pastry ring can be filled with all kinds of vegetables.

NUTRITIONAL INFORMATION

Calories ....672 Sugars 6g
Protein ....19g Fat 51g
Carbohydrate ...36g Saturates 14g

30 MINS   40 MINS

SERVES 4

INGREDIENTS

150 g/5½ oz/1¼ cups plain (all-purpose) flour

125 g/4½ oz/½ cup butter

300 ml/½ pint/1¼ cups water

4 eggs, beaten

90 g/3 oz/¾ cup grated Gruyère (Swiss) cheese

1 tbsp milk

salt and pepper

FILLING

2 tbsp garlic and herb butter or margarine

2 tsp olive oil

2 leeks, shredded

225 g/8 oz green cabbage, finely shredded

125 g/4½ oz/2 cups beansprouts

½ tsp grated lime rind

1 tbsp lime juice

celery salt and pepper

lime slices, to garnish

1 Sift the flour on to a piece of baking parchment. Cut the butter into dice and put in a saucepan with the water. Heat until the butter has melted.

2 Bring the butter and water to the boil, then tip in the flour all at once. Beat until the mixture becomes thick. Remove from the heat and beat until the mixture is glossy and comes away from the sides of the saucepan.

3 Transfer to a mixing bowl and cool for 10 minutes. Gradually beat in the eggs, a little at a time, making sure they are thoroughly incorporated after each addition. Stir in 60 g/2 oz/½ cup of the cheese and season with salt and pepper.

4 Place spoonfuls of the mixture in a 23 cm/9 inch circle on a dampened baking tray (cookie sheet). Brush with milk and sprinkle with the remaining cheese. Bake in a preheated oven, 220°C/425°F/Gas Mark 7, for 30–35 minutes, until golden and crisp. Transfer to a warmed serving plate.

5 Meanwhile, make the filling. Heat the butter or margarine and the oil in a large frying pan (skillet) and stir-fry the leeks and cabbage for 2 minutes. Add the beansprouts, lime rind and juice and stir-fry for 1 minute. Season to taste.

6 Pile into the centre of the pastry ring. Garnish with lime slices and serve.

Vegetable & Tofu Strudels

These strudels look really impressive and are perfect if friends are coming round or for a more formal dinner party dish.

NUTRITIONAL INFORMATION

Calories 485   Sugars 5g
Protein ....16g   Fat 27g
Carbohydrate ...47g   Saturates 5g

25 MINS   30 MINS

SERVES 4

INGREDIENTS

FILLING

2 tbsp vegetable oil

2 tbsp butter

150 g/5½ oz/⅓ cup potatoes, finely diced

1 leek, shredded

2 garlic cloves, crushed

1 tsp garam masala

½ tsp chilli powder

½ tsp turmeric

50 g/1¾ oz okra, sliced

100 g/3½ oz/1¼ cups sliced button mushrooms

2 tomatoes, diced

225 g/8 oz firm tofu (bean curd), diced

12 sheets filo pastry

2 tbsp butter, melted

salt and pepper

1 To make the filling, heat the oil and butter in a frying pan (skillet). Add the potatoes and leek and fry, stirring constantly, for 2–3 minutes. Add the garlic and spices, okra, mushrooms, tomatoes, and tofu (bean curd) and season to taste with salt and pepper. Cook, stirring, for 5–7 minutes, or until tender.

2 Lay the pastry out on a chopping board and brush each individual sheet with melted butter. Place 3 sheets on top of one another; repeat to make 4 stacks.

3 Spoon a quarter of the filling along the centre of each stack and brush the edges with melted butter. Fold the short edges in and roll up lengthways to form a cigar shape. Brush the outside with melted butter. Place the strudels on a greased baking tray (cookie sheet).

4 Cook in a preheated oven, 190°C/ 375°F/Gas Mark 5, for 20 minutes, or until golden brown and crisp. Transfer to a warm serving dish and serve immediately.

Mushroom & Spinach Puffs

These puff pastry parcels, filled with garlic, mushrooms and spinach are easy to make and simply melt in the mouth.

NUTRITIONAL INFORMATION

Calories ....467 Sugars 4g
Protein ....8g Fat 38g
Carbohydrate ...24g Saturates 18g

20 MINS   30 MINS

SERVES 4

INGREDIENTS

25 g/1/ oz/2 tbsp butter

1 red onion, halved and sliced

2 garlic cloves, crushed

225 g/8 oz/3 cups sliced open-
   cap mushrooms,

175 g/6 oz baby spinach

pinch of nutmeg

4 tbsp double (heavy) cream

225 g/8 oz puff pastry

1 egg, beaten

salt and pepper

2 tsp poppy seeds

1 Melt the butter in a frying pan (skillet). Add the onion and garlic and sauté over a low heat, stirring, for 3–4 minutes, until the onion has softened.

2 Add the mushrooms, spinach and nutmeg and cook over a medium heat, stirring occasionally, for 2–3 minutes.

3 Stir in the double (heavy) cream, mixing thoroughly. Season with salt and pepper to taste and remove the pan from the heat.

4 Roll the pastry out on a lightly floured surface and cut into four 15 cm/ 6 inch rounds.

5 Put a quarter of the filling on to one half of each round and fold the pastry over to encase it. Press down to seal the edges and brush with the beaten egg. Sprinkle with the poppy seeds.

6 Place the parcels on a dampened baking tray (cookie sheet) and cook in a preheated oven, 200°C/400°F/Gas Mark 6, for 20 minutes, until risen and golden brown in colour.

7 Transfer the mushroom and spinach puffs to warmed serving plates and serve immediately.

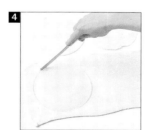

COOK'S TIP

The baking tray (cookie sheet) is dampened so that steam forms with the heat of the oven, which helps the pastry to rise and set.

Italian Vegetable Tart

This mouthwateringly attractive tart is full of Mediterranean flavours – spinach, red (bell) peppers, ricotta cheese and pine nuts.

NUTRITIONAL INFORMATION

Calories 488   Sugars 7g
Protein . . . . .13g   Fat 40g
Carbohydrate . . .21g   Saturates 19g

30 MINS   30 MINS

SERVES 6

INGREDIENTS

225 g/8 oz frozen filo pastry, thawed

125 g/4½ oz/½ cup butter, melted

350 g/12 oz frozen spinach, thawed

2 eggs

150 ml/¼ pint/⅔ cup single (thin) cream

225 g/8 oz/1 cup ricotta cheese

1 red (bell) pepper, seeded and
   sliced into strips

60 g/2 oz/½ cup pine nuts

salt and pepper

1 Use the sheets of filo pastry to line a 20 cm/8 inch flan tin (pan), brushing each layer with melted butter.

2 Put the spinach into a strainer or colander and squeeze out the excess moisture with the back of a spoon or your hand. Form the spinach into 8–9 small balls and arrange them in the prepared flan tin (pan).

3 Beat the eggs, cream and ricotta cheese together until thoroughly blended. Season to taste with salt and pepper and pour over the spinach.

4 Put the remaining butter into a saucepan. Add the red (bell) pepper strips and sauté over a low heat, stirring

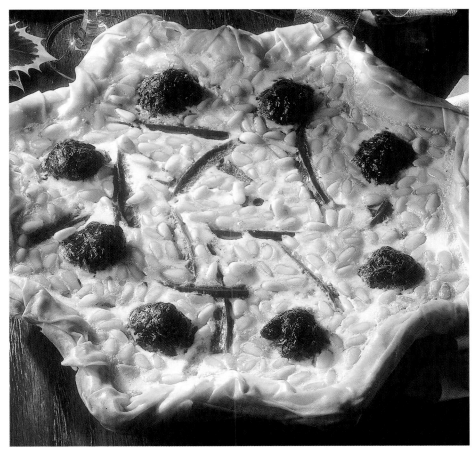

frequently, for about 4–5 minutes, until softened. Arrange the strips on the flan.

5 Scatter the pine nuts over the surface and bake in a preheated oven at 190°C/375°F/Gas Mark 5 for about 20–25 minutes, until the filling has set and the pastry is golden brown. Serve immediately or allow to cool completely and serve at room temperature.

VARIATION

If you are not fond of (bell) peppers, you could mushrooms instead. Wild mushrooms would be especially delicious. Add a few sliced sun-dried tomatoes for extra colour and flavour.

Mushroom & Pine Nut Tarts

Different varieties of mushroom are becoming more widely available in supermarkets, so use this recipe to make the most of them.

NUTRITIONAL INFORMATION

Calories ....494 Sugars 2g
Protein ....9g Fat 35g
Carbohydrate ...38g Saturates 18g

 15 MINS   20 MINS

SERVES 4

INGREDIENTS

500 g/1 lb 2 oz filo pastry

125 g/4½ oz/½ cup butter, melted

1 tbsp hazelnut oil

25 g/1 oz/¼ cup pine nuts

350 g/12 oz mixed mushrooms, such as
    button, chestnut (crimini), oyster
    and shiitake

2 tsp chopped parsley

225 g/8 oz/1 cup soft goat's cheese

salt and pepper

parsley sprigs to garnish

lettuce, tomatoes, cucumber and spring
    onions (scallions), to serve

1 Cut the sheets of filo pastry into pieces about 10 cm/4 inches square and use them to line 4 individual tart tins (pans), brushing each layer of pastry with melted butter. Line the tins (pans) with foil or baking parchment and baking beans. Bake in a preheated oven at 200°C/400°F/Gas Mark 6 for about 6–8 minutes, or until light golden brown.

2 Remove the tarts from the oven and carefully take out the foil or parchment and baking beans. Reduce the oven temperature to 180°C/350°F/Gas Mark 4.

3 Put any remaining butter into a large saucepan with the hazelnut oil and fry the pine nuts gently until golden brown. Lift them out with a slotted spoon and drain on kitchen paper (paper towels).

4 Add the mushrooms to the saucepan and cook them gently, stirring frequently, for about 4–5 minutes. Add the chopped parsley and season to taste with salt and pepper.

5 Spoon one quarter of the goat's cheese into the base of each cooked filo tart. Divide the mushrooms equally between them and scatter the pine nuts over the top.

6 Return the tarts to the oven for 5 minutes to heat through, and then serve them, garnished with sprigs of parsley. Serve with lettuce, tomatoes, cucumber and spring onions (scallions).

Vegetable Cake

This is a savoury version of a cheesecake with a layer of fried potatoes as a delicious base. Use frozen mixed vegetables for the topping, if liked.

NUTRITIONAL INFORMATION

Calories	502	Sugars	.........8g
Protein	........16g	Fat	..........31g
Carbohydrate	...41g	Saturates	......14g

 20 MINS 45 MINS

SERVES 4

INGREDIENTS

BASE

2 tbsp vegetable oil, plus extra for brushing

4 large waxy potatoes, thinly sliced

TOPPING

1 tbsp vegetable oil

1 leek, chopped

1 courgette (zucchini), grated

1 red (bell) pepper, seeded and diced

1 green (bell) pepper, seeded and diced

1 carrot, grated

2 tsp chopped parsley

225 g/8 oz/1 cup full-fat soft cheese

25 g/1 oz/¼ cup grated mature
   (sharp) cheese

2 eggs, beaten

salt and pepper

shredded cooked leek, to garnish

salad, to serve

1 Brush a 20 cm/8 inch springform cake tin (pan) with oil.

2 To make the base, heat the oil in a frying pan (skillet). Cook the potato slices until softened and browned. Drain on kitchen paper (paper towels) and place in the base of the tin (pan).

3 To make the topping, heat the oil in a separate frying pan (skillet). Add the leek and fry over a low heat, stirring frequently, for 3-4 minutes, until softened.

4 Add the courgette (zucchini), (bell) peppers, carrot and parsley to the pan and cook over a low heat for 5-7 minutes, or until the vegetables have softened.

5 Meanwhile, beat the cheeses and eggs together in a bowl. Stir in the vegetables and season to taste with salt and pepper. Spoon the mixture evenly over the potato base.

6 Cook in a preheated oven, 190°C/ 375°F/Gas Mark 5, for 20–25 minutes, until the cake is set.

7 Remove the vegetable cake from the tin (pan), transfer to a warm serving plate, garnish with shredded leek and serve with a crisp salad.

Spinach Pancake Layer

Nutty-tasting buckwheat pancakes are combined with a cheese and spinach mixture and baked with a crispy topping.

NUTRITIONAL INFORMATION

Calories 467   Sugars 10g
Protein ....29g   Fat 26g
Carbohydrate ...31g   Saturates 7g

45 MINS   1 HR 5 MINS

SERVES 4

I N G R E D I E N T S

125 g/4½ oz/1 cup buckwheat flour

1 egg, beaten

1 tbsp walnut oil

300 ml/½ pint/1¼ cups milk

2 tsp vegetable oil

F I L L I N G

1 kg/2 lb 4 oz young spinach leaves

2 tbsp water

1 bunch spring onions (scallions), white
   and green parts, chopped

2 tsp walnut oil

1 egg, beaten

1 egg yolk

225 g/8 oz/1 cup cottage cheese

½ tsp grated nutmeg

25 g/1 oz/¼ cup grated mature
(sharp) Cheddar cheese

25 g/1 oz/¼ cup walnut pieces

salt and pepper

1 Sift the flour into a bowl and add any husks that remain in the strainer.

2 Make a well in the centre and add the egg and walnut oil. Gradually whisk in the milk to make a smooth batter. Leave to stand for 30 minutes.

3 To make the filling, wash the spinach and pack into a saucepan with the water. Cover tightly and cook on a high heat for 5–6 minutes, until soft.

4 Drain well and leave to cool. Gently fry the spring onions (scallions) in the walnut oil for 2–3 minutes, until just soft. Drain on kitchen paper (paper towels) and set aside.

5 Whisk the batter. Brush a small crêpe pan with oil, heat until hot and pour in enough batter just to cover the base. Cook for 1–2 minutes, until set, flip over and cook for 1 minute, until golden on the underside. Turn on to a warmed plate.

Repeat to make 8–10 pancakes, layering them with baking parchment.

6 Chop the spinach and dry with kitchen paper (paper towels). Mix with the spring onions (scallions), beaten egg, egg yolk, cottage cheese and nutmeg and season to taste with salt and pepper.

7 Layer the pancakes and spinach mixture on a baking tray (cookie sheet) lined with baking parchment, finishing with a pancake. Sprinkle with Cheddar cheese and bake in a preheated oven, 190°C/ 375°F/Gas Mark 5, for 20–25 minutes, until firm and golden. Sprinkle with the walnuts and serve immediately.

Leek & Herb Soufflé

Hot soufflés look very impressive if served as soon as they come out of the oven, otherwise they will sink quite quickly.

NUTRITIONAL INFORMATION

Calories	182	Sugars	. . . . .4g
Protein	. . . . .8g	Fat	. . . . .15g
Carbohydrate	. . . .5g	Saturates	. . . . . . .2g

15 MINS   50 MINS

SERVES 4

I N G R E D I E N T S

350 g/12 oz baby leeks

1 tbsp olive oil

125 ml/4 fl oz/½ cup vegetable stock

50 g/1¾ oz/½ cup walnuts

2 eggs, separated

2 tbsp chopped mixed herbs

2 tbsp natural (unsweetened) yogurt

salt and pepper

1 Using a sharp knife, chop the leeks finely. Heat the oil in a frying pan (skillet). Add the leeks and sauté over a medium heat, stirring occasionally, for 2–3 minutes.

2 Add the vegetable stock to the pan, lower the heat and simmer gently for a further 5 minutes.

3 Place the walnuts in a food processor and process until finely chopped. Add the leek mixture to the nuts and process briefly to form a purée. Transfer to a mixing bowl.

4 Mix together the egg yolks, herbs and yogurt until thoroughly combined. Pour the egg mixture into the leek purée. Season with salt and pepper to taste and mix well.

5 In a separate mixing bowl, whisk the egg whites until firm peaks form.

6 Fold the egg whites into the leek mixture. Spoon the mixture into a lightly greased 900 ml/1½ pint/3¾ cup soufflé dish and place on a warmed baking tray (cookie sheet).

7 Cook in a preheated oven, 180°C/ 350°F/Gas Mark 4, for 35–40 minutes, or until risen and set. Serve the soufflé immediately.

COOK'S TIP
Placing the soufflé dish on a warm baking tray (cookie sheet) helps to cook the soufflé from the bottom, thus aiding its cooking and lightness.

Jacket Potatoes with Beans

Baked jacket potatoes, topped with a tasty mixture of beans in a spicy sauce, provide a deliciously filling, high-fibre dish.

NUTRITIONAL INFORMATION

Calories ....378 Sugars 9g
Protein ....15g Fat 9g
Carbohydrate ...64g Saturates 1g

 15 MINS   1¼ HOURS

SERVES 6

INGREDIENTS

6 large potatoes

4 tbsp vegetable ghee or oil

1 large onion, chopped

2 garlic cloves, crushed

1 tsp ground turmeric

1 tbsp cumin seeds

2 tbsp mild or medium curry paste

350 g/12 oz cherry tomatoes

400 g/14 oz can black-eye beans (peas),
    drained and rinsed

400 g/14 oz can red kidney beans,
    drained and rinsed

1 tbsp lemon juice

2 tbsp tomato purée (paste)

150 ml/¼ pint/ ⅔ cup water

2 tbsp chopped fresh mint or coriander

salt and pepper

VARIATION

Instead of cutting the potatoes in half, cut a cross in each and squeeze gently to open out. Spoon some of the prepared filling into the cross and place any remaining filling to the side.

1 Scrub the potatoes and prick several times with a fork. Place in a preheated oven, 180°C/350°F/Gas Mark 4, and cook for 1–1¼ hours, or until the potatoes feel soft when gently squeezed.

2 About 20 minutes before the end of cooking time, prepare the topping. Heat the ghee or oil in a saucepan, add the onion and cook over a low heat, stirring frequently, for 5 minutes. Add the garlic, turmeric, cumin seeds and curry paste and cook gently for 1 minute.

3 Stir in the tomatoes, black-eye beans (peas) and red kidney beans, lemon juice, tomato purée (paste), water and chopped mint. Season to taste with salt and pepper, then cover and simmer over a low heat, stirring frequently, for 10 minutes.

4 When the potatoes are cooked, cut them in half and mash the flesh lightly with a fork. Spoon the prepared bean mixture on top, place on warming serving plates and serve immediately.

Four-Cheese & Potato Layer

This is a quick dish to prepare and it can be left to cook in the oven without requiring any further attention.

NUTRITIONAL INFORMATION

Calories	766	Sugars	........14g
Protein	........44g	Fat	..........40g
Carbohydrate	...60g	Saturates	......23g

25 MINS   45 MINS

SERVES 4

I N G R E D I E N T S

900 g/2 lb unpeeled waxy potatoes,
   cut into wedges

25 g/1 oz/2 tbsp butter

1 red onion, halved and sliced

2 garlic cloves, crushed

25 g/1 oz/¼ cup plain (all-purpose) flour

600 ml/1 pint/2½ cups milk

400 g/14 oz can artichoke hearts in brine,
   drained and halved

150 g/5½ oz frozen mixed
   vegetables, thawed

125 g/4½ oz/1 cup grated Gruyère
   (Swiss) cheese

125 g/4½ oz/1 cup grated mature
   (sharp) cheese

50 g/1¾ oz/½ cup crumbled Gorgonzola

25 g/1 oz/⅓ cup grated Parmesan cheese

225 g/8 oz tofu (bean curd), sliced

2 tbsp chopped thyme

salt and pepper

thyme sprigs, to garnish

1 Cook the potato wedges in a saucepan of boiling water for 10 minutes. Drain thoroughly.

2 Meanwhile, melt the butter in a saucepan. Add the sliced onion and garlic and fry over a low heat, stirring frequently, for 2-3 minutes.

3 Stir the flour into the pan and cook for 1 minute. Gradually add the milk and bring to the boil, stirring constantly.

4 Reduce the heat and add the artichoke hearts, mixed vegetables, half of each of the 4 cheeses and the tofu (bean curd) to the pan, mixing well. Stir in the chopped thyme and season with salt and pepper to taste.

5 Arrange a layer of parboiled potato wedges in the base of a shallow ovenproof dish. Spoon the vegetable mixture over the top and cover with the remaining potato wedges. Sprinkle the rest of the 4 cheeses over the top.

6 Cook in a preheated oven, 200°C/400°F/Gas Mark 6, for 30 minutes or until the potatoes are cooked and the top is golden brown. Serve the bake garnished with fresh thyme sprigs.

Potato & Cheese Soufflé

This soufflé is very simple to make, yet it has a delicious flavour and melts in the mouth. Choose three alternative cheeses, if preferred.

NUTRITIONAL INFORMATION

Calories	447	Sugars	.........1g
Protein	........22g	Fat	..........23g
Carbohydrate	...41g	Saturates	......11g

10 MINS   55 MINS

SERVES 4

I N G R E D I E N T S

25 g/1 oz/2 tbsp butter

2 tsp plain (all-purpose) flour

900 g/2 lb floury (mealy) potatoes

8 eggs, separated

25 g/1 oz/¼ cup grated Gruyère
   (Swiss) cheese

25 g/1 oz/¼ cup crumbled blue cheese

25 g/1 oz/¼ cup grated mature
   (sharp) Cheddar cheese

salt and pepper

1 Butter a 2.4 litre/4 pint/10 cup soufflé dish and dust with the flour. Set aside.

2 Cook the potatoes in a saucepan of boiling water until tender. Mash until very smooth and then transfer to a mixing bowl to cool.

3 Beat the egg yolks into the potato and stir in the Gruyère (Swiss) cheese, blue cheese and Cheddar, mixing well. Season to taste with salt and pepper.

4 Whisk the egg whites until standing in peaks, then gently fold them into the potato mixture with a metal spoon until fully incorporated.

5 Spoon the potato mixture into the prepared soufflé dish.

6 Cook in a preheated oven, 220°C/ 425°F/Gas Mark 7, for 35–40 minutes, until risen and set. Serve immediately.

COOK'S TIP

Insert a fine skewer into the centre of the soufflé; it should come out clean when the soufflé is fully cooked through.

Creamy Baked Fennel

Fennel tastes fabulous in this creamy sauce, flavoured with caraway seeds. A crunchy breadcrumb topping gives an interesting texture.

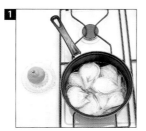
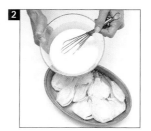

NUTRITIONAL INFORMATION

Calories ....292 Sugars 5g
Protein ....10g Fat 23g
Carbohydrate ...12g Saturates 14g

10 MINS   45 MINS

SERVES 4

I N G R E D I E N T S

2 tbsp lemon juice

2 fennel bulbs, thinly sliced

60 g/2 oz/¼ cup butter, plus extra
   for greasing

125 g/4½ oz/¼ cup low-fat soft cheese

150 ml/¼ pint/⅔ cup single (light) cream

150 ml/¼ pint/⅔ cup milk

1 egg, beaten

2 tsp caraway seeds

60 g/2 oz/1 cup fresh white breadcrumbs

salt and pepper

parsley sprigs, to garnish

1 Bring a saucepan of water to the boil and add the lemon juice and fennel. Cook for 2–3 minutes to blanch, drain and place in a greased ovenproof dish.

2 Beat the soft cheese in a bowl until smooth. Add the cream, milk and beaten egg, and whisk together until combined. Season with salt and pepper and pour the mixture over the fennel.

3 Melt 15 g/½ oz/1 tbsp of the butter in a small frying pan (skillet) and fry the caraway seeds gently for 1–2 minutes, until they release their aroma. Sprinkle them over the fennel.

4 Melt the remaining butter in a frying pan (skillet). Add the breadcrumbs and fry over a low heat, stirring frequently, until lightly browned. Sprinkle them evenly over the surface of the fennel.

5 Place in a preheated oven, 180°C/ 350°F/Gas Mark 4, and bake for 25–30 minutes, or until the fennel is tender. Serve immediately, garnished with sprigs of parsley.

Lentil & Vegetable Shells

These stuffed aubergines (eggplants) are delicious served hot or cold, topped with natural (unsweetened) yogurt or cucumber raita.

NUTRITIONAL INFORMATION

Calories ....386 Sugars 9g
Protein ....14g Fat 24g
Carbohydrate ...30g Saturates 3g

25 MINS   1 HOUR

SERVES 6

INGREDIENTS

225 g/8 oz/1⅓ cup continental lentils

850 ml/1½ pints/3¾ cups water

2 garlic cloves, crushed

3 well-shaped aubergines (eggplants)

150 ml/¼ pint/⅔ cup vegetable oil, plus
    extra for brushing

2 onions, chopped

4 tomatoes, chopped

2 tsp cumin seeds

1 tsp ground cinnamon

2 tbsp mild curry paste

1 tsp minced chilli

2 tbsp chopped mint

salt and pepper

natural (unsweetened) yogurt and
    mint sprigs, to serve

COOK'S TIP

Choose nice plump aubergines (eggplants), rather than thin tapering ones, as they retain their shape better when filled and baked with a stuffing.

1 Rinse the lentils under cold running water. Drain and place in a saucepan with the water and garlic. Cover and simmer for 30 minutes.

2 Cook the aubergines (eggplants) in a saucepan of boiling water for 5 minutes. Drain, then plunge into cold water for 5 minutes. Drain again, then cut the aubergines (eggplants) in half lengthways and scoop out most of the flesh and reserve, leaving a 1 cm/½ inch thick border to form a shell.

3 Place the aubergine (eggplant) shells in a shallow greased ovenproof dish, brush with a little oil and sprinkle with salt and pepper. Cook in a preheated oven, 190°C/375°F/Gas Mark 5, for 10 minutes. Meanwhile, heat half the remaining oil in a frying pan, add the onions and tomatoes and fry gently for 5 minutes. Chop the reserved aubergine (eggplant) flesh, add to the pan with the spices and cook gently for 5 minutes. Season with salt.

4 Stir in the lentils, most of the remaining oil, reserving a little for later, and the mint. Spoon the mixture into the shells. Drizzle with remaining oil and bake for 15 minutes. Serve hot or cold, topped with a spoonful of natural (unsweetened) yogurt and mint sprigs.

Potato & Vegetable Gratin

Similar to a simple moussaka, this recipe is made up of layers of aubergine (eggplant), tomato and potato baked with a yogurt topping.

NUTRITIONAL INFORMATION

Calories 409   Sugars 17g
Protein . . . . .28g   Fat 14g
Carbohydrate . . .45g   Saturates 3g

25 MINS   1¼ HOURS

SERVES 4

I N G R E D I E N T S

500 g/1 lb 2 oz waxy potatoes, sliced

1 tbsp vegetable oil

1 onion, chopped

2 garlic cloves, crushed

500 g/1 lb 2 oz tofu (bean curd), diced

2 tbsp tomato purée (paste)

2 tbsp plain (all-purpose) flour

300 ml/½ pint/1¼ cups vegetable stock

2 large tomatoes, sliced

1 aubergine (eggplant), sliced

2 tbsp chopped fresh thyme

450 ml/16 fl oz/scant 2 cups natural
  (unsweetened) yogurt

2 eggs, beaten

salt and pepper

salad, to serve

VARIATION

You can use marinated or smoked tofu (bean curd) for extra flavour, if you wish.

1 Cook the sliced potatoes in a saucepan of boiling water for 10 minutes, until tender, but not breaking up. Drain and set aside.

2 Heat the oil in a frying pan (skillet). Add the onion and garlic and fry, stirring occasionally, for 2–3 minutes.

3 Add the tofu (bean curd), tomato purée (paste) and flour and cook for 1 minute. Gradually stir in the stock and bring to the boil, stirring. Reduce the heat and simmer for 10 minutes.

4 Arrange a layer of the potato slices in the base of a deep ovenproof dish.

Spoon the tofu (bean curd) mixture evenly on top. Layer the sliced tomatoes, then the aubergine (eggplant) and finally, the remaining potato slices on top of the tofu mixture, making sure that it is completely covered. Sprinkle with thyme.

5 Mix the yogurt and beaten eggs together in a bowl and season to taste with salt and pepper. Spoon the yogurt topping over the sliced potatoes to cover them completely.

6 Bake in a preheated oven, 190°C/375°F/Gas Mark 5, for about 35–45 minutes or until the topping is browned. Serve with a crisp salad.

Potato-Topped Vegetables

This is a very colourful and nutritious dish, packed full of crunchy vegetables in a tasty white wine sauce.

NUTRITIONAL INFORMATION

Calories 413   Sugars 11g
Protein . . . . .19g   Fat 18g
Carbohydrate . . .41g   Saturates 11g

🥔 20 MINS   🕐 1¼ HOURS

SERVES 4

I N G R E D I E N T S

1 carrot, diced

175 g/6 oz cauliflower florets

175 g/6 oz broccoli florets

1 fennel bulb, sliced

75 g/2¾ oz green beans, halved

25 g/1 oz/2 tbsp butter

25 g/1 oz/¼ cup plain (all-purpose) flour

150 ml/¼ pint/⅔ cup vegetable stock

150 ml/¼ pint/⅔ cup dry white wine

150 ml/¼ pint/⅔ cup milk

175 g/6 oz chestnut (crimini)
    mushrooms, quartered

2 tbsp chopped sage

T O P P I N G

4 floury (mealy) potatoes, diced

25 g/1 oz/2 tbsp butter

4 tbsp natural (unsweetened) yogurt

4 tbsp grated Parmesan cheese

1 tsp fennel seeds

salt and pepper

1 Cook the carrot, cauliflower, broccoli, fennel and beans in a large saucepan of boiling water for 10 minutes, until just tender. Drain the vegetables thoroughly and set aside.

2 Melt the butter in a saucepan. Stir in the flour and cook for 1 minute. Remove from the heat and stir in the stock, wine and milk. Return to the heat and bring to the boil, stirring until thickened. Stir in the reserved vegetables, mushrooms and sage.

3 Meanwhile, make the topping. Cook the diced potatoes in a pan of boiling water for 10-15 minutes. Drain and mash with the butter, yogurt and half the cheese. Stir in the fennel seeds.

4 Spoon the vegetable mixture into a 1 litre/1¾ pint/4 cup pie dish. Spoon the potato over the top and sprinkle with the remaining cheese. Cook in a preheated oven, 190°C/375°F/Gas Mark 5, for 30-35 minutes, or until golden. Serve hot.

Vegetable Jalousie

This is a really easy dish to make, but looks impressive. The mixture of vegetables gives the dish a wonderful colour and flavour.

NUTRITIONAL INFORMATION

Calories 660	Sugars 7g
Protein 11g	Fat 45g
Carbohydrate ...53g	Saturates 15g

 25 MINS   45 MINS

SERVES 4

I N G R E D I E N T S

500 g/1 lb 2 oz puff pastry

1 egg, beaten

F I L L I N G

2 tbsp butter or margarine

1 leek, shredded

2 garlic cloves, crushed

1 red (bell) pepper, seeded and sliced

1 yellow (bell) pepper, seeded and sliced

50 g/1¾ oz/½ cup sliced mushrooms

75 g/2¾ oz small asparagus spears

2 tbsp plain (all-purpose) flour

6 tbsp vegetable stock

6 tbsp milk

4 tbsp dry white wine

1 tbsp chopped oregano

salt and pepper

1 Melt the butter or margarine in a frying pan (skillet) and sauté the leek and garlic, stirring frequently, for 2 minutes. Add the remaining vegetables and cook, stirring, for 3-4 minutes.

2 Add the flour and cook for 1 minute. Remove the pan from the heat and stir in the vegetable stock, milk and white wine. Return the pan to the heat and bring to the boil, stirring, until thickened.

Stir in the oregano and season with salt and pepper to taste.

3 Roll out half of the pastry on a lightly floured surface to form a rectangle 38 x 15 cm/15 x 6 inches.

4 Roll out the other half of the pastry to the same shape, but a little larger all round. Put the smaller rectangle on a baking tray (cookie sheet) lined with dampened baking parchment.

5 Spoon the filling evenly on top of the smaller rectangle, leaving a 1 cm/ ½ inch clear margin around the edges.

6 Using a sharp knife, cut parallel diagonal slits across the larger rectangle to within 2.5 cm/1 inch of each of the long edges.

7 Brush the edges of the smaller rectangle with beaten egg and place the larger rectangle on top, pressing the edges firmly together to seal.

8 Brush the whole jalousie with egg to glaze and bake in a preheated oven, 200°C/400°F/Gas Mark 6, for about 30-35 minutes, until risen and golden. Transfer to a warmed serving dish and serve immediately.

Spicy Potato Casserole

This is based on a Moroccan dish in which potatoes are spiced with coriander (cilantro) and cumin and cooked in a lemon sauce.

NUTRITIONAL INFORMATION

Calories 338   Sugars 8g
Protein ....5g   Fat 23g
Carbohydrate ...29g   Saturates 2g

15 MINS   35 MINS

SERVES 4

I N G R E D I E N T S

100 ml/3½ fl oz/½ cup olive oil

2 red onions, cut into eight

3 garlic cloves, crushed

2 tsp ground cumin

2 tsp ground coriander

pinch of cayenne pepper

1 carrot, thickly sliced

2 small turnips, quartered

1 courgette (zucchini), sliced

500 g/1 lb 2 oz potatoes, thickly sliced

juice and rind of 2 large lemons

300 ml/½ pint/1¼ cups vegetable stock

2 tbsp chopped coriander (cilantro)

salt and pepper

COOK'S TIP

Check the vegetables while they are cooking, as they may begin to stick to the pan. Add a little more boiling water or stock if necessary.

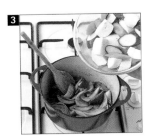

1 Heat the olive oil in a flameproof casserole. Add the onion and sauté over a medium heat, stirring frequently, for 3 minutes.

2 Add the garlic and cook for 30 seconds. Stir in the spices and cook, stirring constantly, for 1 minute.

3 Add the carrot, turnips, courgette (zucchini) and potatoes and stir to coat in the oil.

4 Add the lemon juice and rind and the vegetable stock. Season to taste with salt and pepper. Cover and cook over a medium heat, stirring occasionally, for 20–30 minutes, until tender.

5 Remove the lid, sprinkle in the coriander (cilantro) and stir well. Serve immediately.

Indian Curry Feast

This vegetable curry is quick and easy to prepare and it tastes superb. A colourful Indian salad and mint raita make perfect accompaniments.

NUTRITIONAL INFORMATION

Calories 473	Sugars 18g	
Protein 19g	Fat 9g	
Carbohydrate ...84g	Saturates 1g	

25-30 MINS 55 MINS

SERVES 4

I N G R E D I E N T S

1 tbsp vegetable oil

2 garlic cloves, crushed

1 onion, chopped

3 celery sticks, sliced

1 apple, cored and chopped

1 tbsp medium-strength curry powder

1 tsp ground ginger

400 g/14 oz can chickpeas
   (garbanzo beans)

125 g/4½ oz dwarf green beans (thin
   beans), sliced

225 g/8 oz cauliflower, broken into florets

225 g/8 oz potatoes, cut into cubes

175 g/6 oz/2 cups sliced mushrooms

600 ml/1 pint/2½ cups vegetable stock

1 tbsp tomato purée (paste)

25 g/1 oz sultanas (golden raisins)

175 g/6 oz/scant 1 cup basmati rice

1 tbsp garam masala

M I N T   R A I T A

150 ml/¼ pint/⅔ cup natural
   (unsweetened) yogurt

1 tbsp chopped mint

1 Heat the oil in a large saucepan. Add the garlic, onion, celery and apple and fry over a medium heat, stirring frequently, for 3–4 minutes. Add the curry powder and ginger, and cook gently for 1 more minute.

2 Drain the chickpeas (garbanzo beans) and add to the onion mixture, together with the dwarf green beans (thin beans), cauliflower, potatoes, mushrooms, stock, tomato purée (paste) and sultanas (golden raisins). Bring to the boil, then reduce the heat. Cover and simmer for 35–40 minutes.

3 Meanwhile, make the raita. Mix the yogurt and mint together. Transfer to a small serving bowl, then cover and chill in the refrigerator.

4 Cook the rice in a large saucepan of boiling, lightly salted water for about 12 minutes, or until just tender. Drain, rinse with boiling water and drain again.

5 Just before serving, stir the garam masala into the curry. Divide between four warmed serving plates and serve with the rice. Garnish the raita with fresh mint and hand the bowl separately.

Coconut Vegetable Curry

A mildly spiced, but richly flavoured Indian-style dish full of different textures and flavours. Serve with naan bread to soak up the tasty sauce.

NUTRITIONAL INFORMATION

Calories	159	Sugars	.........8g
Protein	.........8g	Fat	...........6g
Carbohydrate	...19g	Saturates	.......1g

45 MINS   35 MINS

SERVES 6

I N G R E D I E N T S

1 large aubergine (eggplant),
   cut into 2.5 cm/1 inch cubes

2 tbsp salt

2 tbsp vegetable oil

2 garlic cloves, crushed

1 fresh green chilli,
   seeded and finely chopped

1 tsp grated root ginger

1 onion, finely chopped

2 tsp garam masala

8 cardamom pods

1 tsp ground turmeric

1 tbsp tomato purée (paste)

700 ml/1¼ pints/3 cups vegetable stock

1 tbsp lemon juice

225 g/8 oz potatoes, diced

225 g/8 oz small cauliflower florets

225 g/8 oz okra, trimmed

225 g/8 oz frozen peas

150 ml/¼ pint/⅔ cup coconut milk

salt and pepper

flaked coconut, to garnish

naan bread, to serve

1 Layer the aubergine (eggplant) in a bowl, sprinkling with salt as you go. Set aside for 30 minutes.

2 Rinse well under cold running water to remove all the salt. Drain and pat dry with kitchen paper (paper towels). Set aside.

3 Heat the oil in a large saucepan. Add the garlic, chilli, ginger, onion and spices and fry over a medium heat, stirring occasionally, for 4–5 minutes, until lightly browned.

4 Stir in the tomato purée (paste), stock, lemon juice, potatoes and cauliflower and mix well. Bring to the boil, lower the heat, cover and simmer for 15 minutes.

5 Stir in the aubergine (eggplant), okra, peas and coconut milk and season to taste with salt and pepper. Return to the boil and continue to simmer, uncovered, for a further 10 minutes, or until tender. Remove and discard the cardamom pods.

6 Pile on to a warmed serving platter, garnish with flaked coconut and serve immediately with naan bread.

Bread & Butter Savoury

Quick, simple, nutritious and a pleasure to eat – what more could you ask for an inexpensive midweek meal?

NUTRITIONAL INFORMATION

Calories 472	Sugars 7g
Protein 22g	Fat 33g
Carbohydrate ...25g	Saturates 20g

30 MINS   45 MINS

SERVES 4

INGREDIENTS

60 g/2 oz/¼ cup butter or margarine

1 bunch spring onions (scallions), sliced

6 slices of white or brown bread,
   crusts removed

175g/6 oz/1½ cups grated mature
   (sharp) Cheddar cheese

2 eggs

450 ml/16 fl oz/scant 2 cups milk

salt and pepper

flat leaf parsley sprigs, to garnish

1 Grease a 1.5 litre/2½ pint/1½ quart ovenproof dish with a little of the butter or margarine.

2 Melt the remaining butter or margarine in a small saucepan. Add the spring onions (scallions) and fry over a medium heat, stirring occasionally, until softened and golden.

3 Meanwhile, cut the bread into triangles and place half of them in the base of the dish. Cover with the spring onions (scallions) and top with half the grated cheese.

4 Beat together the eggs and milk and season to taste with salt and pepper. Layer the remaining triangles of bread in the dish and carefully pour over the milk mixture. Leave to soak for 15–20 minutes.

5 Sprinkle the remaining cheese over the soaked bread. Bake in a preheated oven, 190°C/375°F/Gas Mark 5, for 35–40 minutes, until puffed up and golden brown. Garnish with flat leaf parsley and serve immediately.

VARIATION

You can vary the vegetables used in this savoury bake, depending on what you have to hand. Shallots, mushrooms or tomatoes are all suitable.

White Nut Filo Parcels

These crisp, buttery parcels, filled with nuts and pesto, would make an interesting break with tradition for Sunday lunch.

NUTRITIONAL INFORMATION

Calories ....1100 Sugars 9g
Protein ....29g Fat 80g
Carbohydrate ...73g Saturates 15g

15 MINS   25 MINS

SERVES 4

INGREDIENTS

40 g/1½ oz/3 tbsp butter or margarine

1 large onion, finely chopped

275 g/9½ oz/2¼ cups mixed white nuts, such as pine nuts, unsalted cashew nuts, blanched almonds, unsalted peanuts, finely chopped

90 g/3 oz/1½ cups fresh white breadcrumbs

½ tsp ground mace

1 egg, beaten

1 egg yolk

3 tbsp pesto sauce

2 tbsp chopped basil

125 g/4½ oz/½ cup butter or margarine, melted

16 sheets filo pastry

salt and pepper

basil sprigs to garnish

TO SERVE

cranberry sauce

steamed vegetables

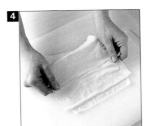

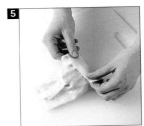

1 Melt the butter or margarine in a frying pan (skillet) and gently fry the onion for 2–3 minutes, until just softened but not browned.

2 Remove from the heat and stir in the nuts, two-thirds of the breadcrumbs, the mace and beaten egg. Season to taste with salt and pepper. Set aside.

3 Place the remaining breadcrumbs in a bowl and stir in the egg yolk, pesto sauce, basil, and 1 tablespoon of the melted butter or margarine. Mix well.

4 Brush 1 sheet of filo with melted butter or margarine. Fold in half and brush again. Repeat with a second sheet and lay it on top of the first one so that it forms a cross.

5 Put one-eighth of the nut mixture in the centre of the pastry. Top with one-eighth of the pesto mixture. Fold over the edges, brushing with more butter or margarine, to form a parcel. Brush the top with butter or margarine and transfer to a baking tray (cookie sheet). Make eight parcels in the same way and brush with the remaining butter or margarine.

6 Bake in a preheated oven at 220°C/425°F/Gas Mark 7 for 15–20 minutes, until golden. Transfer to serving plates, garnish with basil sprigs and serve with cranberry sauce and steamed vegetables.

Root Croustades

This colourful combination of grated root vegetables and mixed (bell) peppers would make a stunning dinner-party dish.

NUTRITIONAL INFORMATION

Calories 304   Sugars 17g
Protein . . . . .6g   Fat 19g
Carbohydrate . . .28g   Saturates 3g

2½ HOURS   1¼ HOURS

SERVES 4

I N G R E D I E N T S

1 orange (bell) pepper

1 red (bell) pepper

1 yellow (bell) pepper

3 tbsp olive oil

2 tbsp red wine vinegar

1 tsp French mustard

1 tsp clear honey

salt and pepper

flat leaf parsley sprigs, to garnish

green vegetables, to serve

C R O U S T A D E S

225 g/8 oz potatoes, coarsely grated

225 g/8 oz carrots, coarsely grated

350 g/12 oz celeriac (celery root),

    coarsely grated

1 garlic clove, crushed

1 tbsp lemon juice

25 g/1 oz/2 tbsp butter or

    margarine, melted

1 egg, beaten

1 tbsp vegetable oil

1 Place the (bell) peppers on a baking tray (cookie sheet) and bake in a preheated oven, 190°C/375°F/Gas Mark 5, for 35 minutes, turning after 20 minutes.

2 Cover with a tea towel (dish cloth) and leave to cool for 10 minutes.

3 Peel the skin from the cooked (bell) peppers; cut in half and discard the seeds. Thinly slice the flesh into strips and place in a shallow dish.

4 Put the oil, vinegar, mustard, honey and seasoning in a small screw-top jar and shake well to mix. Pour over the (bell) pepper strips, mix well and set aside to marinate for 2 hours.

5 To make the croustades, put the potatoes, carrots and celeriac (celery root) in a mixing bowl and toss in the garlic and lemon juice.

6 Mix in the melted butter or margarine and the egg. Season to taste with salt and pepper. Divide the mixture into 8 and pile on to 2 baking trays (cookie sheets) lined with baking parchment, forming each into a 10 cm/4 inch round. Brush with oil.

7 Bake in a preheated oven, 220°C/ 425°F/Gas Mark 7, for 30–35 minutes, until the croustades are crisp around the edges and golden. Carefully transfer to a warmed serving dish. Heat the (bell) peppers and the marinade for 2–3 minutes until warmed through. Spoon the (bell) peppers over the croustades, garnish with flat leaf parsley and serve immediately with green vegetables.

Mushroom & Nut Crumble

A filling, tasty dish that is ideal for a warming family supper. The crunchy topping is flavoured with three different types of nuts.

NUTRITIONAL INFORMATION

Calories 779   Sugars 5g
Protein ....16g   Fat 59g
Carbohydrate ...48g   Saturates 14g

 20 MINS   55 MINS

SERVES 4

I N G R E D I E N T S

350 g/12 oz/5 cups sliced open-
   cup mushrooms

350 g/12 oz/5 cups sliced chestnut
   (crimini) mushrooms, sliced

400 ml/14 fl oz/1¾ cups vegetable stock

60 g/2 oz/¼ cup butter or margarine

1 large onion, finely chopped

1 garlic clove, crushed

60 g/2 oz/½ cup plain (all-purpose) flour

4 tbsp double (heavy) cream

2 tbsp chopped parsley

salt and pepper

herbs, to garnish

C R U M B L E   T O P P I N G

90 g/3 oz/¾ cup medium oatmeal

90 g/3 oz/¾ cup wholemeal
   (whole wheat) flour

25 g/1 oz/¼ cup ground almonds

25 g/1 oz/¼ cup finely chopped walnuts

60 g/2 oz/½ cup finely chopped unsalted
   shelled pistachio nuts

1 tsp dried thyme

90 g/3 oz/⅓ cup butter or
   margarine, softened

1 tbsp fennel seeds

1 Put the mushrooms and stock in a large saucepan, bring to the boil, cover and simmer for 15 minutes, until tender. Drain, reserving the stock.

2 In another saucepan, melt the butter or margarine and fry the onion and garlic for 2–3 minutes, until just soft. Stir in the flour and cook for 1 minute.

3 Remove from the heat and gradually stir in the reserved mushroom stock. Return to the heat and cook, stirring, until thickened. Stir in the mushrooms, seasoning, cream and parsley and spoon into a shallow ovenproof dish.

4 To make the topping, in a bowl, mix together the oatmeal, flour, nuts, thyme and plenty of salt and pepper to taste.

5 Using a fork, mix in the butter or margarine until the topping resembles coarse breadcrumbs.

6 Sprinkle the topping mixture evenly over the mushrooms and then sprinkle with the fennel seeds. Bake in a preheated oven, at 190°C/375°F/Gas Mark 5, for about 25–30 minutes, or until the topping is golden and crisp. Garnish with fresh herbs and serve immediately.

Spinach Roulade

A delicious savoury roll, stuffed with mozzarella and broccoli. Serve as a main course or as an appetizer, in which case it would easily serve six.

NUTRITIONAL INFORMATION

Calories	287	Sugars	.........8g
Protein	........23g	Fat	..........12g
Carbohydrate	....8g	Saturates	.......6g

15 MINS

25 MINS

SERVES 4

INGREDIENTS

500 g/1 lb 2 oz small spinach leaves

2 tbsp water

4 eggs, separated

½ tsp ground nutmeg

salt and pepper

300 ml/½ pint/1¼ cups sugocasa,
   to serve

FILLING

175 g/6 oz small broccoli florets

25 g/1 oz/¼ cup freshly grated
   Parmesan cheese

175 g/6 oz/1½ cups grated
   mozzarella cheese

1 Wash the spinach and pack, still wet, into a large saucepan. Add the water. Cover with a tight-fitting lid and cook over a high heat for 4–5 minutes, until reduced and soft. Drain thoroughly, squeezing out excess water. Chop finely and pat dry.

2 Mix the spinach with the egg yolks, seasoning and nutmeg. Whisk the egg whites until very frothy but not too stiff, and fold into the spinach mixture.

3 Grease and line a 32 x 23 cm/ 13 x 9 inch Swiss roll tin (jelly roll pan). Spread the mixture in the tin (pan) and smooth the surface. Bake in a preheated oven, 220°C/425°F/Gas Mark 7, for about 12–15 minutes, until firm to the touch and golden.

4 Meanwhile, cook the broccoli florets in lightly salted boiling water for 4–5 minutes, until just tender. Drain and keep warm.

5 Sprinkle Parmesan on a sheet of baking parchment. Turn the base on to it and peel away the lining paper. Sprinkle with mozzarella and top with broccoli.

6 Hold one end of the paper and roll up the spinach base like a Swiss (jelly) roll. Heat the sugocasa and spoon on to warmed serving plates. Slice the roulade and place on top of the sugocasa.

Roast (Bell) Pepper Tart

This tastes truly delicious, the flavour of roasted vegetables being entirely different from that of boiled or fried.

NUTRITIONAL INFORMATION

Calories ....237 Sugars 3g
Protein ....6g Fat 15g
Carbohydrate ...20g Saturates 4g

🥔 25 MINS   🕐 40 MINS

SERVES 8

I N G R E D I E N T S

PASTRY

175 g/6 oz/1½ cups plain
   (all-purpose) flour

pinch of salt

75 g/2¾ oz/6 tbsp butter
   or margarine

2 tbsp green pitted olives,
   finely chopped

3 tbsp cold water

FILLING

1 red (bell) pepper

1 green (bell) pepper

1 yellow (bell) pepper

2 garlic cloves, crushed

2 tbsp olive oil

100 g/3½ oz/1 cup grated
   mozzarella cheese

2 eggs

150 ml/¼ pint/⅔ cup milk

1 tbsp chopped basil

salt and pepper

1 To make the pastry, sift the flour and salt into a bowl. Rub in the butter or margarine until the mixture resembles breadcrumbs. Add the olives and cold water, bringing the mixture together to form a dough.

2 Roll the dough out on a floured surface and use to line a 20 cm/8 inch loose-based flan tin (pan). Prick the base with a fork and leave to chill.

3 Cut all the (bell) peppers in half lengthways, seed and place them, skin side uppermost, on a baking tray (cookie sheet). Mix the garlic and oil and brush over the (bell) peppers. Cook in a preheated oven, 200°C/400°F/Gas Mark 6, for 20 minutes, or until beginning to char slightly. Let the (bell) peppers cool slightly and thinly slice. Arrange in the base of the pastry case, layering with the mozzarella.

4 Beat the egg and milk and add the basil. Season and pour over the (bell) peppers. Put the tart on a baking tray (cookie sheet) and return to the oven for 20 minutes, or until set. Serve hot or cold.

Cauliflower Bake

The red of the tomatoes is a great contrast to the cauliflower and herbs, making this dish appealing to both the eye and the palate.

NUTRITIONAL INFORMATION

Calories 305   Sugars 9g
Protein . . . . .15g   Fat 14g
Carbohydrate . . .31g   Saturates 6g

10 MINS   40 MINS

SERVES 4

I N G R E D I E N T S

500 g/1 lb 2 oz cauliflower, broken into

   florets

2 large potatoes, cubed

100 g/3½ oz cherry tomatoes

S A U C E

25 g/1 oz/2 tbsp butter or margarine

1 leek, sliced

1 garlic clove, crushed

25 g/1 oz/3 tbsp plain (all-purpose) flour

300 ml/½ pint/1¼ cups milk

75 g/2¾ oz/¾ cup mixed grated cheese,

   such as Cheddar, Parmesan

   and Gruyère (Swiss)

½ tsp paprika

2 tbsp chopped flat leaf parsley

salt and pepper

chopped parsley, to garnish

VARIATION

This dish could be made with broccoli instead of the cauliflower as an alternative.

1 Cook the cauliflower in a saucepan of boiling water for 10 minutes. Drain well and reserve. Meanwhile, cook the potatoes in a pan of boiling water for 10 minutes, drain and reserve.

2 To make the sauce, melt the butter or margarine in a saucepan and sauté the leek and garlic for 1 minute. Stir in the flour and cook, stirring constantly, for 1 minute. Remove the pan from the heat and gradually stir in the milk, 50 g/ 1¾ oz/½ cup of the cheese, the paprika and parsley. Return the pan to the heat and bring to the boil, stirring constantly. Season with salt and pepper to taste.

3 Spoon the cauliflower into a deep ovenproof dish. Add the cherry tomatoes and top with the potatoes. Pour the sauce over the potatoes and sprinkle on the remaining cheese.

4 Cook in a preheated oven, 180°C/ 350°F/Gas Mark 4, for 20 minutes, or until the vegetables are cooked through and the cheese is golden brown and bubbling. Garnish and serve immediately.

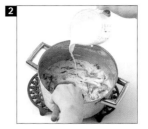  

Cauliflower & Broccoli Flan

This really is a tasty flan, the pastry case for which may be made in advance and frozen until required.

NUTRITIONAL INFORMATION

Calories 252   Sugars 3g
Protein ....7g   Fat 16g
Carbohydrate ...22g   Saturates 5g

15 MINS   50 MINS

SERVES 8

INGREDIENTS

PASTRY

175 g/6 oz/1½ cups plain (all-purpose) flour

pinch of salt

½ tsp paprika

1 tsp dried thyme

75 g/2¾ oz/6 tbsp margarine

3 tbsp water

FILLING

100 g/3½ oz cauliflower florets

100 g/3½ oz broccoli florets

1 onion, cut into eight

25 g/1 oz/2 tbsp butter or margarine

1 tbsp plain (all-purpose) flour

6 tbsp vegetable stock

125 ml/4 fl oz/½ cup milk

75 g/2¾ oz/¾ cup grated Cheddar cheese,

salt and pepper

paprika, to garnish

1 To make the pastry, sift the flour and salt into a bowl. Add the paprika and thyme and rub in the margarine. Stir in the water and bind to form a dough.

2 Roll out the pastry on a floured surface and use to line an 18 cm/7 inch loose-based flan tin (pan). Prick the base with a fork and line with baking parchment. Fill with baking beans and bake in a preheated oven, 190°C/375°F/ Gas Mark 5, for 15 minutes. Remove the parchment and beans and return the pastry case to the oven for 5 minutes.

3 To make the filling, cook the vegetables in a pan of lightly salted boiling water for 10–12 minutes, until tender. Drain and reserve.

4 Melt the butter in a pan. Add the flour and cook, stirring constantly, for 1 minute. Remove from the heat, stir in the stock and milk and return to the heat. Bring to the boil, stirring, and add 50 g/1¾ oz/½ cup of the cheese. Season to taste with salt and pepper.

5 Spoon the cauliflower, broccoli and onion into the pastry case. Pour over the sauce and sprinkle with the cheese. Return to the oven for 10 minutes, until the cheese is bubbling. Dust with paprika, garnish and serve.

Spicy Potato & Nut Terrine

This delicious baked terrine has a base of mashed potato which is flavoured with nuts, cheese, herbs and spices.

NUTRITIONAL INFORMATION

Calories	1100	Sugars	........13g
Protein	........34g	Fat	..........93g
Carbohydrate	...31g	Saturates	......22g

 15 MINS 1½ HOURS

SERVES 4

I N G R E D I E N T S

225 g/8 oz floury (mealy) potatoes, diced

225 g/8 oz pecan nuts

225 g/8 oz unsalted cashew nuts

1 onion, finely chopped

2 garlic cloves, crushed

125 g/4½ oz/1½ cups diced open-
    cap mushrooms

25 g/1 oz/2 tbsp butter

2 tbsp chopped mixed herbs

1 tsp paprika

1 tsp ground cumin

1 tsp ground coriander

4 eggs, beaten

125 g/4½ oz/½ cup full-fat soft cheese

60 g/2 oz/⅔ cup grated Parmesan cheese

salt and pepper

S A U C E

3 large tomatoes, peeled,
    seeded and chopped

2 tbsp tomato purée (paste)

75 ml/3 fl oz/⅓ cup red wine

1 tbsp red wine vinegar

pinch of caster (superfine) sugar

1 Lightly grease a 1 kg/2 lb loaf tin (pan) and line with baking parchment.

2 Cook the potatoes in a large pan of lightly salted boiling water for 10 minutes, or until cooked through. Drain and mash thoroughly.

3 Finely chop the pecan and cashew nuts or process in a food processor. Mix the nuts with the onion, garlic and mushrooms. Melt the butter in a frying pan (skillet) and cook the nut mixture for 5-7 minutes. Add the herbs and spices. Stir in the eggs, cheeses and potatoes and season to taste with salt and pepper.

4 Spoon the mixture into the prepared loaf tin (pan), pressing down firmly. Cook in a preheated oven, 190°C/375°F/Gas Mark 5, for 1 hour, or until set.

5 To make the sauce, mix the tomatoes, tomato purée (paste), wine, wine vinegar and sugar in a pan and bring to the boil, stirring. Cook for 10 minutes, or until the tomatoes have reduced. Press the sauce through a strainer or process in a food processor for 30 seconds. Turn the terrine out of the tin (pan) on to a serving plate and cut into slices. Serve with the tomato sauce.

Vegetable Roast Wellington

This is a vegetarian version of the classic 'Beef Wellington'. Served with sherry sauce and roast vegetables it is a tasty and impressive main dish.

20 MINS   45 MINS

SERVES 4

INGREDIENTS

450 g/1 lb can chickpeas
(garbanzo beans), drained

1 tsp yeast extract

150 g/5½ oz/1¼ cups chopped walnuts

150 g/5½ oz/1¼ cups fresh breadcrumbs

1 onion, finely chopped

100 g/3½ oz/1¼ cups mushrooms, sliced

50 g/1¾ oz/⅓ cup canned sweetcorn,
(corn) drained

2 garlic cloves, crushed

2 tbsp dry sherry

2 tbsp vegetable stock

1 tbsp chopped coriander (cilantro)

225 g/8 oz puff pastry

1 egg, beaten

2 tbsp milk

salt and pepper

SAUCE

1 tbsp vegetable oil

1 leek, thinly sliced

4 tbsp dry sherry

150 ml/¼ pint/⅔ cup vegetable stock

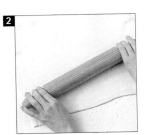

1 Process the chickpeas (garbanzo beans), yeast extract, nuts and breadcrumbs in a food processor for 30 seconds. In a frying pan (skillet), sauté the onion and mushrooms in their own juices for 3–4 minutes. Stir in the chickpea (garbanzo bean) mixture, corn and garlic. Add the sherry, stock, coriander (cilantro) and seasoning and bind the mixture together. Remove from the heat and allow to cool.

2 Roll out the pastry out on a floured surface to form a 35 x 30 cm/ 14 x12 inch rectangle. Shape the chickpea (garbanzo bean) mixture into a loaf shape and wrap the pastry around it, sealing the edges. Place seam side down on a dampened baking tray (cookie sheet) and score the top in a criss-cross pattern. Mix the egg and milk and brush over the pastry. Cook in a preheated oven, 200°C/ 400°F/Gas Mark 6, for 25–30 minutes.

3 Heat the oil for the sauce in a pan and sauté the leek for 5 minutes. Add the sherry and stock and bring to the boil. Simmer for 5 minutes and serve the sauce with the roast.

Chilli Tofu (Bean Curd)

A tasty Mexican-style dish with a melt-in-the-mouth combination of tofu (bean curd) and avocado served with a tangy tomato sauce.

NUTRITIONAL INFORMATION

Calories	806	Sugars	........20g
Protein	........37g	Fat	.........54g
Carbohydrate	...45g	Saturates	......19g

 30 MINS   35 MINS

SERVES 4

I N G R E D I E N T S

½ tsp chilli powder

1 tsp paprika

2 tbsp plain (all-purpose) flour

225 g/8 oz tofu (bean curd),
   cut into 1 cm/½ inch pieces

2 tbsp vegetable oil

1 onion, finely chopped

1 garlic clove, crushed

1 large red (bell) pepper, seeded and
   finely chopped

1 large ripe avocado

1 tbsp lime juice

4 tomatoes, peeled, seeded and chopped

125 g/4½ oz/1 cup grated Cheddar cheese

8 soft flour tortillas

150 ml/¼ pint/⅔ cup soured cream

salt and pepper

coriander (cilantro) sprigs
   to garnish

pickled green jalapeño chillies, to serve

S A U C E

850 ml/1½ pints/3¾ cups sugocasa

3 tbsp chopped parsley

3 tbsp chopped coriander (cilantro)

1 Mix the chilli powder, paprika, flour and salt and pepper on a plate and coat the tofu (bean curd) pieces.

2 Heat the oil in a frying pan (skillet) and gently fry the tofu (bean curd) for 3–4 minutes, until golden. Remove with a slotted spoon, drain on kitchen paper (paper towels) and set aside.

3 Add the onion, garlic and (bell) pepper to the oil and fry for 2–3 minutes, until just softened. Drain and set aside.

4 Halve the avocado, peel and remove the stone (pit). Slice lengthways, put in a bowl with the lime juice and toss to coat.

5 Add the tofu (bean curd) and onion mixture and gently stir in the tomatoes and half the cheese. Spoon one-eighth of the filling down the centre of each tortilla, top with soured cream and roll up. Arrange the tortillas in a shallow ovenproof dish in a single layer.

6 To make the sauce, mix together all the ingredients. Spoon the sauce over the tortillas, sprinkle with the remaining grated cheese and bake in a preheated oven, 190°C/375°F/Gas Mark 5, for 25 minutes, until golden and bubbling. Garnish with coriander (cilantro) sprigs and serve immediately with pickled jalapeño chillies.

Salads

A salad makes a refreshing accompaniment or side dish, but can also make a substantial main course meal. Salads are also a very good source of vitamins and minerals; always use the freshest possible ingredients for maximum flavour, texture and goodness. Salads are quick to 'rustle up' and good for times when you need to prepare a meal-

in-a-moment and have to use store-cupboard ingredients. A splash of culinary inspiration and you will find that you have prepared a fantastic salad that you had no idea was lurking in your kitchen! Experiment with new ingredients in order to add taste and interest to ordinary salad leaves. The only limit is your imagination!

Mexican Salad

This is a colourful salad with a Mexican theme, using beans, tomatoes and avocado. The chilli dressing adds a little kick.

NUTRITIONAL INFORMATION

Calories 307   Sugars 7g
Protein . . . . .5g   Fat 26g
Carbohydrate . . .13g   Saturates 5g

10–15 MINS   0 MINS

SERVES 4

INGREDIENTS

lollo rosso lettuce

2 ripe avocados

2 tsp lemon juice

4 medium tomatoes

1 onion

175 g/6 oz/2 cups mixed canned
    beans, drained

DRESSING

4 tbsp olive oil

drop of chilli oil

2 tbsp garlic wine vinegar

pinch of caster (superfine) sugar

pinch of chilli powder

1 tbsp chopped parsley

COOK'S TIP

The lemon juice is sprinkled on to the avocados to prevent discoloration when in contact with the air. For this reason the salad should be prepared, assembled and served quite quickly.

1 Line a large serving bowl with the lettuce leaves.

2 Using a sharp knife, cut the avocados in half and remove the stones (pits). Thinly slice the flesh and sprinkle with the lemon juice.

3 Thinly slice the tomatoes and onion and push the onion out into rings. Arrange the avocado, tomatoes and onion around the salad bowl, leaving a space in the centre.

4 Spoon the beans into the centre of the salad and whisk the dressing ingredients together. Pour the dressing over the salad and serve.

Moroccan Salad

Couscous is a type of semolina made from durum wheat. It is wonderful in salads, as it readily takes up the flavour of the dressing.

NUTRITIONAL INFORMATION

Calories 195   Sugars 15g
Protein ....8g   Fat 2g
Carbohydrate ...40g   Saturates 0.3g

30-35 MINS   0 MINS

SERVES 6

INGREDIENTS

175 g/6 oz/2 cups couscous

1 bunch spring onions (scallions),
    finely chopped

1 small green (bell) pepper, seeded
    and chopped

10 cm/4 inch piece of cucumber, chopped

175 g/6 oz can chickpeas (garbanzo
    beans), rinsed and drained

60 g/2 oz/⅔ cup sultanas (golden raisins)
    or raisins

2 oranges

salt and pepper

mint sprigs, to garnish

lettuce leaves, to serve

DRESSING

finely grated rind of 1 orange

1 tbsp chopped fresh mint

150 ml/¼ pint/⅔ cup natural yogurt

1 Put the couscous into a bowl and cover with boiling water. Leave it to soak for about 15 minutes to swell the grains, then stir gently with a fork to separate them.

2 Add the spring onions (scallions), green (bell) pepper, cucumber, chickpeas (garbanzo beans) and sultanas (golden raisins) or raisins to the couscous, stirring to combine. Season well with salt and pepper.

3 To make the dressing, place the orange rind, mint and yogurt in a bowl and mix together until well combined. Pour over the couscous mixture and stir to mix well.

4 Using a sharp serrated knife, remove the peel and pith from the oranges. Cut the flesh into segments, removing all the membrane.

5 Arrange the lettuce leaves on 4 serving plates. Divide the couscous mixture between the plates and arrange the orange segments on top. Garnish with sprigs of fresh mint and serve.

Salad with Yogurt Dressing

This is a very quick and refreshing salad, using a whole range of colourful ingredients which make it look as good as it tastes.

NUTRITIONAL INFORMATION

Calories 100	Sugars 8g
Protein 3g	Fat 6g
Carbohydrate 8g	Saturates 1g

 20 MINS   0 MINS

SERVES 4

INGREDIENTS

75 g/2¾ oz cucumber, cut into sticks

6 spring onions (scallions), halved

2 tomatoes, seeded and cut into eight

1 yellow (bell) pepper, cut into strips

2 celery sticks, cut into strips

4 radishes, quartered

75 g/2¾ oz/1 bunch rocket

1 tbsp chopped mint, to serve

DRESSING

2 tbsp lemon juice

1 garlic clove, crushed

150 ml/¼ pint/⅔ cup natural
   (unsweetened) yogurt

2 tbsp olive oil

salt and pepper

COOK'S TIP

Do not toss the dressing into the salad until just before serving, otherwise it will turn soggy.

1 Mix the cucumber, spring onions (scallions), tomatoes, (bell) pepper, celery, radishes and rocket together in a large serving bowl.

2 To make the dressing, stir the lemon juice, garlic, natural (unsweetened) yogurt and olive oil together. Season well with salt and pepper.

3 Spoon the dressing over the salad and toss to mix.

4 Sprinkle the salad with chopped mint and serve.

Mixed Bean Salad

You can use a mixture of any canned beans in this crunchy, very filling salad.

NUTRITIONAL INFORMATION

Calories 198   Sugars 6g
Protein ....10g   Fat 6g
Carbohydrate ...26g   Saturates 1g

  30 MINS   15-20 MINS

SERVES 8

I N G R E D I E N T S

400 g/14 oz can flageolet (small navy)
   beans, drained

400 g/14 oz can red kidney beans, drained

400 g/14 oz can butter beans, drained

1 small red onion, thinly sliced

175 g/6 oz dwarf green beans,

topped and tailed

1 red (bell) pepper, halved and deseeded

salt

D R E S S I N G

4 tbsp olive oil

2 tbsp sherry vinegar

2 tbsp lemon juice

1 tsp light muscovado sugar

1 tsp chilli sauce (optional)

1 Put the canned beans in a large mixing bowl. Add the sliced onion and mix together.

2 Cut the dwarf green beans in half and cook in lightly salted boiling water for about 8 minutes until just tender. Refresh under cold water and drain again. Add to the mixed beans and onions.

3 Place the (bell) pepper halves, cut side down, on a grill (broiler) rack and cook until the skin blackens and chars. Leave to cool slightly then pop them into a plastic bag for about 10 minutes. Peel away the skin from the (bell) peppers and discard. Roughly chop the (bell) pepper flesh and add it to the beans.

4 To make the dressing, place the oil, sherry vinegar, lemon juice, sugar and chilli sauce (if using) in a screw-top jar and shake vigorously.

5 Pour the dressing over the mixed bean salad and toss well. Leave to chill in the refrigerator until required.

VARIATION

Use any combination of beans in this salad. For a distinctive flavour, add 1 teaspoon of curry paste instead of the chilli sauce.

Middle Eastern Salad

This attractive-looking salad can be served with a couple of vegetable kebabs (kabobs) for a delicious light lunch or an informal supper.

NUTRITIONAL INFORMATION

Calories ....163 Sugars 12g
Protein ....8g Fat 3g
Carbohydrate ...27g Saturates 0.4g

15 MINS   0 MINS

SERVES 4

INGREDIENTS

400 g/14 oz can chickpeas
   (garbanzo beans)

4 carrots

1 bunch spring onions (scallions)

1 medium cucumber

½ tsp salt

½ tsp pepper

3 tbsp lemon juice

1 red (bell) pepper, sliced

1 Drain the chickpeas (garbanzo beans) and place them in a large salad bowl.

2 Using a sharp knife, thinly slice the carrots. Cut the spring onions (scallions) into small pieces. Thickly slice the cucumber and then cut the slices into quarters.

3 Add the carrot slices, spring onions (scallions) and cucumber to the chickpeas (garbanzo beans) and mix.

4 Season to taste with the salt and pepper and sprinkle with the lemon juice. Toss the salad ingredients together gently, using 2 serving spoons.

5 Using a sharp knife, thinly slice the red (bell) pepper. Arrange the slices of

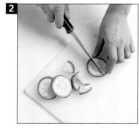

red (bell) pepper decoratively on top of the chickpea (garbanzo bean) salad. Serve the salad immediately or chill in the refrigerator and serve when required.

VARIATION

This salad would also be delicious made with *ful medames*. If they are not available canned, use 150g/5½ oz/1 cup dried, soaked for 5 hours and then simmered for 2½ hours. Another alternative would be canned gunga beans.

Sweet Potato & Nut Salad

Pecan nuts with their slightly bitter flavour are mixed with sweet potatoes to make a sweet and sour salad with an interesting texture.

NUTRITIONAL INFORMATION

Calories	330	Sugars	........5g
Protein	........4g	Fat	.........20g
Carbohydrate	...36g	Saturates	.......2g

  25 MINS   10 MINS

SERVES 4

INGREDIENTS

500 g/1 lb 2 oz sweet potatoes, diced

2 celery sticks, sliced

125 g/4½ oz celeriac (celery root), grated

2 spring onions (scallions), sliced

50 g/1¾ oz/½ cup pecan nuts, chopped

2 heads chicory (endive), separated

1 tsp lemon juice

thyme sprigs, to garnish

DRESSING

4 tbsp vegetable oil

1 tbsp garlic wine vinegar

1 tsp soft light brown sugar

2 tsp chopped thyme

1 Cook the sweet potatoes in a large saucepan of boiling water for 5 minutes, until tender. Drain thoroughly and set aside to cool.

2 When cooled, stir in the celery, celeriac (celery root), spring onions (scallions) and pecan nuts.

3 Line a salad plate with the chicory (endive) leaves and sprinkle with lemon juice.

4 Spoon the sweet potato mixture into the centre of the leaves.

5 In a small bowl, whisk the dressing ingredients together.

6 Pour the dressing over the salad and serve at once, garnished with fresh thyme sprigs.

COOK'S TIP

Sweet potatoes do not store as well as ordinary potatoes. It is best to store them in a cool, dark place (not the refrigerator) and use within 1 week of purchase.

Gado Gado

This is a well-known and very popular Indonesian salad of mixed vegetables with a peanut dressing.

NUTRITIONAL INFORMATION

Calories 392   Sugars 8g
Protein ....9g   Fat 35g
Carbohydrate ....11g Saturates 5g

 10 MINS   25 MINS

SERVES 4

INGREDIENTS

100 g/3½ oz/1 cup shredded
    white cabbage

100 g/3½ oz French (green) beans,
    cut into three

100 g/3½ oz carrots, cut into matchsticks

100 g/3½ oz cauliflower florets

100 g/3½ oz beansprouts

DRESSING

100 ml/3½ fl oz/½ cup vegetable oil

100 g/3½ oz/1 cup unsalted peanuts

2 garlic cloves, crushed

1 small onion, finely chopped

½ tsp chilli powder

½ tsp light brown sugar

425 ml/¾ pint/2 cups water

juice of ½ lemon

salt

sliced spring onions (scallions),
    to garnish

1 Cook the vegetables separately in a saucepan of salted boiling water for 4–5 minutes, drain well and chill.

2 To make the dressing, heat the oil in a frying pan (skillet) and fry the peanuts, tossing frequently, for 3–4 minutes.

3 Remove from the pan with a slotted spoon and drain on absorbent kitchen paper (paper towels). Process the peanuts in a food processor or crush with a rolling pin until a fine mixture is formed.

4 Pour all but 1 tablespoon of the oil from the pan and fry the garlic and onion for 1 minute. Add the chilli powder, sugar, a pinch of salt and the water and bring to the boil.

5 Stir in the peanuts. Reduce the heat and simmer for 4–5 minutes. until the sauce thickens. Add the lemon juice and set aside to cool.

6 Arrange the vegetables in a serving dish and spoon the peanut dressing into the centre. Garnish and serve.

Three-Bean Salad

Fresh dwarf (thin) beans are combined with soya beans and red kidney beans in a chive and tomato dressing to make a tasty salad.

NUTRITIONAL INFORMATION

Calories 276   Sugars 7g
Protein ....18g   Fat 15g
Carbohydrate ...18g   Saturates 4g

15 MINS   10 MINS

SERVES 6

I N G R E D I E N T S

3 tbsp olive oil

1 tbsp lemon juice

1 tbsp tomato purée (paste)

1 tbsp light malt vinegar

1 tbsp chopped chives

175 g/6 oz dwarf (thin) beans

400 g/14 oz can soya beans,
    rinsed and drained

400 g/14 oz can red kidney beans, rinsed
    and drained

2 tomatoes, chopped

4 spring onions (scallions), chopped

125 g/4½ oz feta cheese, cut into cubes

salt and pepper

mixed salad leaves (greens), to serve

chopped chives, to garnish

1 Put the olive oil, lemon juice, tomato purée (paste), light malt vinegar and chopped chives into a large bowl and whisk together well until thoroughly combined. Set aside.

2 Cook the dwarf (thin) beans in boiling, lightly salted water for 4–5 minutes, until just cooked. Drain, refresh under cold running water and drain again. Pat dry with kitchen paper (paper towels).

3 Add the dwarf (thin) beans, soya beans and red kidney beans to the dressing, stirring to mix.

4 Add the tomatoes, spring onions (scallions) and feta cheese to the bean mixture, tossing gently to coat in the dressing. Season well with salt and pepper.

5 Arrange the mixed salad leaves (greens) on 6 serving plates. Pile the bean salad on to the plates and garnish with chopped chives.

Warm Goat's Cheese Salad

This delicious salad combines soft goat's cheese with walnut halves, served on a bed of mixed salad leaves (greens).

NUTRITIONAL INFORMATION

Calories	408	Sugars 8g
Protein	.........9g	Fat 38g
Carbohydrate	....8g	Saturates 8g

5 MINS   5 MINS

SERVES 4

INGREDIENTS

90 g/3 oz/¾ cup walnut halves

mixed salad leaves (greens)

125 g/4½ oz soft goat's cheese

snipped chives, to garnish

DRESSING

6 tbsp walnut oil

3 tbsp white wine vinegar

1 tbsp clear honey

1 tsp Dijon mustard

pinch of ground ginger

salt and pepper

VARIATION

You could also use a ewe's milk cheese, such as feta, in this recipe for a sharper flavour.

1 To make the dressing, whisk together the walnut oil, wine vinegar, honey, mustard and ginger in a small saucepan. Season to taste with salt and pepper.

2 Heat the dressing gently, stirring occasionally, until warm. Add the walnut halves and continue to heat for 3–4 minutes.

3 Arrange the salad leaves (greens) on 4 serving plates and place spoonfuls of goat's cheese on top. Lift the walnut halves from the dressing with a slotted spoon, and scatter them over the salads.

4 Transfer the warm dressing to a small jug. Sprinkle chives over the salads and serve with the dressing.

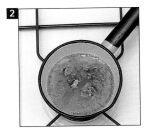

Red Cabbage & Pear Salad

Red cabbage is much underused – it is a colourful and tasty ingredient which is perfect with fruits, such as pears and apples.

NUTRITIONAL INFORMATION

Calories ....143 Sugars 14g
Protein ....2g Fat 9g
Carbohydrate ...15g Saturates 1g

 15 MINS   0 MINS

SERVES 4

INGREDIENTS

350 g/12 oz/4 cups finely shredded
    red cabbage

2 Conference pears, cored and thinly sliced

4 spring onions (scallions), sliced

1 carrot, grated

chives, to garnish

lollo biondo leaves, to serve

DRESSING

4 tbsp pear juice

1 tsp wholegrain mustard

3 tbsp olive oil

1 tbsp garlic wine vinegar

1 tbsp chopped chives

salt and pepper

1 Put the cabbage, pears and spring onions (scallions) in a bowl and mix together well.

2 Line a serving dish with lettuce leaves and spoon the cabbage and pear mixture into the centre.

3 Sprinkle the carrot into the centre of the cabbage to form a domed pile.

4 To make the dressing, mix together the pear juice, wholegrain mustard, olive oil, garlic wine vinegar and chives. Season to taste with salt and pepper.

5 Pour the dressing over the salad, garnish and serve immediately.

COOK'S TIP
Mix the salad just before serving to prevent the colour from the red cabbage bleeding into the other ingredients.

Potato & Radish Salad

The radishes and the herb and mustard dressing give this colourful salad a mild mustard flavour which complements the potatoes perfectly.

NUTRITIONAL INFORMATION

Calories ....140 Sugars 3g
Protein ....3g Fat 6g
Carbohydrate ...20g Saturates 1g

50 MINS   20 MINS

SERVES 4

INGREDIENTS

500 g/1 lb 2 oz new potatoes, scrubbed
  and halved

½ cucumber, thinly sliced

2 tsp salt

1 bunch radishes, thinly sliced

DRESSING

1 tbsp Dijon mustard

2 tbsp olive oil

1 tbsp white wine vinegar

2 tbsp mixed chopped herbs

1 Cook the potatoes in a saucepan of boiling water for 10–15 minutes, or until tender. Drain and set aside to cool.

2 Meanwhile, spread out the cucumber slices on a plate and sprinkle with the salt. Leave to stand for 30 minutes, then rinse under cold running water and pat dry with kitchen paper (paper towels).

3 Arrange the cucumber and radish slices on a serving plate in a decorative pattern and pile the cooked potatoes in the centre of the slices.

4 In a small bowl, mix all the dressing ingredients together, whisking until thoroughly combined. Pour the dressing over the salad, tossing well to coat all of the ingredients. Chill in the refrigerator before serving.

COOK'S TIP

The cucumber adds not only colour, but also a real freshness to the salad. It is salted and left to stand to remove the excess water, which would make the salad soggy. Wash the cucumber well to remove all of the salt, before adding to the salad.

Three-Way Potato Salad

Small new potatoes, served warm in a delicious dressing. The nutritional information is for the potato salad with the curry dressing only.

NUTRITIONAL INFORMATION

Calories 310	Sugars 12g
Protein 6g	Fat 19g
Carbohydrate . . .31g	Saturates 4g

 15–20 MINS   20 MINS

SERVES 4

INGREDIENTS

500 g/1 lb 2 oz new potatoes (for each
   dressing)

herbs, to garnish

LIGHT CURRY DRESSING

1 tbsp vegetable oil

1 tbsp medium curry paste

1 small onion, chopped

1 tbsp mango chutney, chopped

6 tbsp natural (unsweetened) yogurt

3 tbsp single (light) cream

2 tbsp mayonnaise

salt and pepper

1 tbsp single (light) cream, to garnish

VINAIGRETTE DRESSING

6 tbsp hazelnut oil

3 tbsp cider vinegar

1 tsp wholegrain mustard

1 tsp caster (superfine) sugar

few basil leaves, torn

PARSLEY CREAM

150 ml/¼ pint/⅔ cup soured cream

3 tbsp light mayonnaise

4 spring onions (scallions), finely chopped

1 tbsp chopped fresh parsley

1 To make the Light Curry Dressing, heat the vegetable oil in a saucepan, add the curry paste and onion and fry, stirring frequently, until the onion is soft. Remove from the heat and set aside to cool slightly.

2 Mix together the mango chutney, yogurt, cream and mayonnaise. Add the curry mixture and blend together. Season with salt and pepper.

3 To make the Vinaigrette Dressing, whisk the oil, vinegar, mustard, sugar and basil together in a small jug or bowl. Season with salt and pepper.

4 To make the Parsley Cream, combine the mayonnaise, soured cream, spring onions (scallions) and parsley, mixing well. Season with salt and pepper.

5 Cook the potatoes in lightly salted boiling water until just tender. Drain well and set aside to cool for 5 minutes, then add the chosen dressing, tossing to coat. Serve, garnished with fresh herbs, spooning a little single (light) cream on to the potatoes if you have used the curry dressing.

Mexican Potato Salad

The flavours of Mexico are echoed in this dish where potato slices are topped with tomatoes and chillies, and served with guacamole.

NUTRITIONAL INFORMATION

Calories	260	Sugars	.........6g
Protein	.........6g	Fat	...........9g
Carbohydrate	...41g	Saturates	.......2g

  20 MINS 20 MINS

SERVES 4

I N G R E D I E N T S

4 large waxy potatoes, sliced

1 ripe avocado

1 tsp olive oil

1 tsp lemon juice

1 garlic clove, crushed

1 onion, chopped

2 large tomatoes, sliced

1 green chilli, chopped

1 yellow (bell) pepper, seeded and sliced

2 tbsp chopped coriander (cilantro)

salt and pepper

lemon wedges, to garnish

1 Cook the potato slices in a saucepan of boiling water for 10–15 minutes, or until tender. Drain and set aside to cool.

2 Meanwhile, cut the avocado in half and remove the stone (pit). Mash the avocado flesh with a fork (you could also scoop the avocado flesh from the 2 halves using a spoon and then mash it).

3 Add the olive oil, lemon juice, garlic and chopped onion to the avocado flesh and stir to mix. Cover the bowl with clear film (plastic wrap), to minimize discolouration, and set aside.

4 Mix the tomatoes, chilli and yellow (bell) pepper together and transfer to a salad bowl with the potato slices.

5 Arrange the avocado mixture on top of the salad and sprinkle with the coriander (cilantro). Season to taste with salt and pepper and serve garnished with lemon wedges.

VARIATION

You can omit the green chilli from this salad if you do not like hot dishes.

Potato & Banana Salad

This hot fruity salad combines sweet potato and fried bananas with colourful mixed (bell) peppers, tossed in a honey-based dressing.

NUTRITIONAL INFORMATION

Calories 424   Sugars 29g
Protein . . . . .5g   Fat 17g
Carbohydrate . . .68g   Saturates 8g

15 MINS   20 MINS

SERVES 4

I N G R E D I E N T S

500 g/1 lb 2 oz sweet potatoes, diced

50 g/1¾ oz/4 tbsp butter

1 tbsp lemon juice

1 garlic clove, crushed

1 red (bell) pepper, seeded and diced

1 green (bell) pepper, seeded and diced

2 bananas, thickly sliced

2 thick slices white bread, crusts
   removed, diced

salt and pepper

D R E S S I N G

2 tbsp clear honey

2 tbsp chopped chives

2 tbsp lemon juice

2 tbsp olive oil

1 Cook the sweet potatoes in a saucepan of boiling water for 10–15 minutes, until tender. Drain thoroughly and reserve.

2 Meanwhile, melt the butter in a frying pan (skillet). Add the lemon juice, garlic and (bell) peppers and cook, stirring constantly for 3 minutes.

3 Add the banana slices to the pan and cook for 1 minute. Remove the bananas from the pan with a slotted spoon and stir into the potatoes.

4 Add the bread cubes to the frying pan (skillet) and cook, stirring frequently, for 2 minutes, until they are golden brown on all sides.

5 Mix the dressing ingredients together in a small saucepan and heat until the honey is runny.

6 Spoon the potato mixture into a serving dish and season to taste with salt and pepper. Pour the dressing over the potatoes and sprinkle the croûtons over the top. Serve immediately.

COOK'S TIP

Use firm, slightly underripe bananas in this recipe as they won't turn soft and mushy when they are fried.

Potato, Bean & Apple Salad

Use any mixture of beans you have to hand in this recipe, but the wider the variety, the more colourful the salad.

NUTRITIONAL INFORMATION

Calories 183	Sugars 8g	
Protein 6g	Fat 7g	
Carbohydrate ...26g	Saturates 1g	

 20 MINS 20 MINS

SERVES 4

INGREDIENTS

225 g/8 oz new potatoes, scrubbed
   and quartered

225 g/8 oz mixed canned beans, such as
   red kidney beans, flageolet and borlotti
   beans, drained and rinsed

1 red eating apple, diced and tossed
   in 1 tbsp lemon juice

1 yellow (bell) pepper, seeded and diced

1 shallot, sliced

½ fennel bulb, sliced

oak leaf lettuce leaves

DRESSING

1 tbsp red wine vinegar

2 tbsp olive oil

½ tbsp American mustard

1 garlic clove, crushed

2 tsp chopped fresh thyme

VARIATION

Use Dijon or wholegrain mustard in place of American mustard for a different flavour.

1 Cook the quartered potatoes in a saucepan of boiling water for 15 minutes, until tender. Drain and transfer to a mixing bowl.

2 Add the mixed beans to the potatoes, together with the apple, (bell) pepper, shallots and fennel. Mix well, taking care not to break up the cooked potatoes.

3 To make the dressing, whisk all the dressing ingredients together until thoroughly combined, then pour it over the potato salad.

4 Line a serving plate or salad bowl with the oak leaf lettuce leaves and spoon the potato mixture into the centre. Serve immediately.

Garden Salad

This chunky salad includes tiny new potatoes tossed in a minty dressing, and has a mustard dip for dunking.

NUTRITIONAL INFORMATION

Calories 227   Sugars 6g
Protein ....4g   Fat 17g
Carbohydrate ...16g   Saturates 4g

   15-20 MINS 20 MINS

SERVES 8

I N G R E D I E N T S

500 g/1 lb 2 oz tiny new or salad potatoes

225 g/8 oz broccoli florets

125 g/4½ oz sugar snap peas

2 large carrots

4 celery sticks

1 yellow or orange (bell) pepper, seeded

1 bunch spring onions (scallions)

1 head chicory (endive)

D R E S S I N G

3 tbsp olive oil

1 tbsp white wine vinegar

1 tsp Dijon mustard

2 tbsp chopped mint

M U S T A R D   D I P

6 tbsp soured cream

3 tbsp thick mayonnaise

2 tsp balsamic vinegar

1½ tsp coarse-grain mustard

½ tsp creamed horseradish

pinch of brown sugar

salt and pepper

1 Cook the potatoes in boiling salted water for about 10 minutes, until just tender. While they cook, combine the dressing ingredients.

2 Drain the potatoes thoroughly, add to the dressing while hot, toss well and set aside until cold, giving them an occasional stir.

3 To make the dip, combine the soured cream, mayonnaise, vinegar, mustard, horseradish and sugar and season to taste with salt and pepper. Transfer to a small serving bowl, cover and refrigerate until ready to serve.

4 Cut the broccoli into bite-sized florets and blanch for 2 minutes in boiling water. Drain and toss immediately in cold water; when cold, drain thoroughly.

5 Blanch the sugar snap peas in boiling water for 1 minute. Drain, rinse in cold water and drain again.

6 Cut the carrots and celery into matchsticks about 6 x 1 cm/ 2½ x ½ inches. Slice the (bell) pepper or cut it into small cubes. Cut off some of the green parts of the spring onions (scallions) and separate the chicory (endive) leaves.

7 Arrange the vegetables attractively in a fairly shallow bowl with the potatoes piled up in the centre. Serve accompanied with the mustard dip.

Marinated Vegetable Salad

Lightly steamed vegetables taste superb served slightly warm in a marinade of olive oil, white wine, vinegar and fresh herbs.

NUTRITIONAL INFORMATION

Calories 114	Sugars 4g	
Protein 3g	Fat 9g	
Carbohydrate 5g	Saturates 1g	

🍲 10 MINS 🕐 10 MINS

SERVES 6

I N G R E D I E N T S

175 g/6 oz baby carrots

2 celery hearts, cut into 4 pieces

125g/4½ oz sugar snap peas or mangetout (snow peas)

1 fennel bulb, sliced

175 g/6 oz small asparagus spears

1½ tbsp sunflower seeds

dill sprigs, to garnish

D R E S S I N G

4 tbsp olive oil

4 tbsp dry white wine

2 tbsp white wine vinegar

1 tbsp chopped dill

1 tbsp chopped parsley

salt and pepper

1 Put the carrots, celery, sugar snap peas or mangetout (snow peas), fennel and asparagus into a steamer and cook over gently boiling water until just tender. It is important that they retain a little 'bite'.

2 Meanwhile, make the dressing. Mix together the olive oil, wine, vinegar and chopped herbs, whisking until thoroughly combined. Season to taste with salt and pepper.

3 When the vegetables are cooked, transfer them to a serving dish and pour over the dressing at once. The hot vegetables will absorb the flavour of the dressing as they cool.

4 Spread out the sunflower seeds on a baking tray (cookie sheet) and toast them under a preheated grill (broiler) for 3-4 minutes or until lightly browned. Sprinkle the toasted sunflower seeds over the vegetables.

5 Serve the salad while the vegetables are still slightly warm, garnished with sprigs of fresh dill.

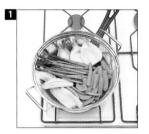
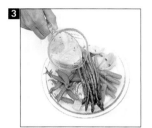

Melon & Strawberry Salad

This refreshing fruit-based salad is perfect for a hot summer's day and would go well with a barbecued (grilled) food.

NUTRITIONAL INFORMATION

Calories	112	Sugars	22g
Protein	5g	Fat	1g
Carbohydrate	22g	Saturates	0.3g

 15 MINS   0 MINS

SERVES 4

INGREDIENTS

½ iceberg lettuce, shredded

1 small honeydew melon

225 g/8 oz/1½ cups sliced strawberries

5 cm/2 inch piece of cucumber, thinly sliced

mint sprigs to garnish

DRESSING

200 g/7 fl oz/scant 1 cup natural (unsweetened) yogurt

5 cm/2 inch piece of cucumber, peeled

a few mint leaves

½ tsp finely grated lime or lemon rind

pinch of caster (superfine) sugar

3–4 ice cubes

1 Arrange the shredded lettuce on 4 serving plates.

VARIATION

Omit the ice cubes in the dressing if you prefer, but make sure that the ingredients are well-chilled. This will ensure that the finished dressing is really cool.

2 Cut the melon lengthways into quarters. Scoop out the seeds and cut through the flesh down to the skin at 2.5 cm/1 inch intervals. Cut the melon close to the skin and detach the flesh.

3 Place the chunks of melon on the beds of lettuce with the strawberries and cucumber slices.

4 To make the dressing, put the yogurt, cucumber, mint leaves, lime or lemon rind, caster (superfine) sugar and ice cubes into a blender or food processor. Blend together for about 15 seconds, until smooth. Alternatively, chop the cucumber and mint finely, crush the ice cubes and combine with the other ingredients.

5 Serve the salad with a little dressing poured over it. Garnish with sprigs of fresh mint.

Melon & Mango Salad

A little freshly grated root ginger mixed with creamy yogurt and clear honey makes a perfect dressing for this refreshing melon salad.

NUTRITIONAL INFORMATION

Calories 189   Sugars 30g
Protein . . . . .5g   Fat 7g
Carbohydrate . . .30g   Saturates 1g

     15-20 MINS   0 MINS

SERVES 4

I N G R E D I E N T S

1 cantaloupe melon

60 g/2 oz/½ cup black grapes, halved
   and seeded

60 g/2 oz/½ cup seedless green grapes

1 large mango

1 bunch of watercress

iceberg lettuce leaves, shredded

2 tbsp olive oil

1 tbsp cider vinegar

1 passion fruit

salt and pepper

D R E S S I N G

150 ml/¼ pint/¾ cup natural (unsweetened)
   thick yogurt

1 tbsp clear honey

1 tsp grated root ginger

COOK'S TIP

Grated root ginger gives a
marvellous flavour to this
recipe, but if you can't get fresh
ginger, substitute ½ teaspoon of
ground ginger instead.

1 First, make the dressing for the melon. Mix together the yogurt, honey and ginger in a small bowl, stirring to combine.

2 Halve the melon and scoop out the seeds. Slice, peel and cut into chunks. Mix with the grapes.

3 Slice the mango on each side of its large flat stone (pit). On each mango half, slash the flesh into a criss-cross pattern down to, but not through the skin. Push the skin from underneath to turn the mango halves inside out. Now remove the flesh and add to the melon mixture.

4 Arrange the watercress and lettuce on 4 serving plates. Make the dressing for the salad leaves (greens). Whisk together the olive oil and cider vinegar and season to taste with salt and pepper. Drizzle the dressing over the watercress and lettuce.

5 Divide the melon mixture equally between the 4 plates and spoon over the yogurt dressing. Scoop the seeds out of the passion fruit and sprinkle them over the salads. Serve immediately.

Grapefruit & Coconut Salad

This salad is quite deceptive – it is, in fact, surprisingly filling, even though it looks very light.

NUTRITIONAL INFORMATION

Calories 201	Sugars 13g	
Protein 3g	Fat 15g	
Carbohydrate . . .14g	Saturates 9g	

 10 MINS   10 MINS

SERVES 4

I N G R E D I E N T S

125 g/4½ oz/1 cup grated coconut

2 tsp light soy sauce

2 tbsp lime juice

2 tbsp water

2 tsp sunflower oil

1 garlic clove, halved

1 onion, finely chopped

2 large ruby grapefruits, peeled
   and segmented

90 g/3 oz/1½ cups alfalfa sprouts

1 Toast the coconut in a dry frying pan (skillet) over a low heat, stirring constantly, for about 3 minutes, or until golden brown. Transfer the toasted coconut to a bowl.

2 Add the light soy sauce, lime juice and water to the toasted coconut and mix together well.

3 Heat the oil in a saucepan and fry the garlic and onion until soft. Stir the onion into the coconut mixture. Remove and discard the garlic.

4 Divide the grapefruit segments between 4 plates. Sprinkle each with a quarter of the alfalfa sprouts and spoon over a quarter of the coconut mixture.

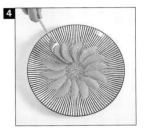

COOK'S TIP

Alfalfa sprouts can be bought in trays or packets from most supermarkets, but you can easily grow your own, if you like to have a constant and cheap supply.

Alfalfa & Spinach Salad

This is a really refreshing salad that must be assembled just before serving to prevent everything being coloured by the beetroot (beet).

NUTRITIONAL INFORMATION

Calories 139   Sugars 7g
Protein ....2g   Fat 11g
Carbohydrate ....8g   Saturates 2g

 10 MINS   0 MINS

SERVES 4

I N G R E D I E N T S

100 g/3½ oz baby spinach

75 g/2¾ oz/1⅓ cups alfalfa sprouts

2 celery sticks, sliced

4 cooked beetroot, cut into eight

D R E S S I N G

4 tbsp olive oil

4½ tsp garlic wine vinegar

1 garlic clove, crushed

2 tsp clear honey

1 tbsp chopped chives

1 Place the spinach and alfalfa sprouts in a large bowl and mix together.

2 Add the celery to the bowl and mix together well.

3 Toss in the beetroot and mix until well combined.

4 To make the dressing, mix the oil, wine vinegar, garlic, honey and chopped chives.

5 Pour the dressing over the salad, toss well and serve immediately.

VARIATION

Add the segments of 1 large orange to the salad to make it even more colourful and refreshing. Replace the garlic wine vinegar with a different flavoured oil such as chilli or herb, if you prefer.

Green Vegetable Salad

This salad uses lots of green-coloured ingredients which look and taste wonderful with the minty yogurt dressing.

NUTRITIONAL INFORMATION

Calories 50	Sugars 6g	
Protein 4g	Fat 1g	
Carbohydrate 6g	Saturates 0.4g	

 10-15 MINS   10 MINS

SERVES 4

INGREDIENTS

2 courgettes (zucchini), cut into sticks

100 g/3½ oz French (green) beans, cut into three

1 green (bell) pepper, seeded and cut into strips

2 celery sticks, sliced

1 bunch watercress

DRESSING

200 ml/7 fl oz/¾ cup natural (unsweetened) yogurt

1 garlic clove, crushed

2 tbsp chopped mint

pepper

COOK'S TIP

The salad must be served as soon as the yogurt dressing has been added – the dressing will start to separate if kept for any length of time.

1 Cook the courgettes (zucchini) and French (green) beans in a saucepan of salted boiling water for 7–8 minutes. Drain and set aside to cool completely.

2 Mix the courgettes (zucchini) and French (green) beans with the (bell) pepper, celery and watercress in a large serving bowl.

3 To make the dressing, mix together the natural (unsweetened) yogurt, garlic and chopped mint in a bowl. Season with pepper to taste.

4 Spoon the dressing on to the salad and serve immediately.

Green & White Salad

This potato, rocket (arugula) and apple salad is flavoured with creamy, salty goat's cheese – perfect with salad leaves (greens).

NUTRITIONAL INFORMATION

Calories 282	Sugars 10g	
Protein 8g	Fat 17g	
Carbohydrate ...26g	Saturates 5g	

 15 MINS 20 MINS

SERVES 4

INGREDIENTS

2 large potatoes, unpeeled and sliced

2 green eating apples, diced

1 tsp lemon juice

25 g/1 oz/¼ cup walnut pieces

125 g/4½ oz goat's cheese, cubed

150 g/5½ oz/2–3 bunches rocket
    (arugula) leaves

salt and pepper

DRESSING

2 tbsp olive oil

1 tbsp red wine vinegar

1 tsp clear honey

1 tsp fennel seeds

COOK'S TIP

Serve this salad immediately to prevent the apple from discolouring. Alternatively, prepare all of the other ingredients in advance and add the apple at the last minute.

1 Cook the potatoes in a pan of boiling water for 15 minutes, until tender. Drain and set aside to cool. Transfer the cooled potatoes to a serving bowl.

2 Toss the diced apples in the lemon juice, drain and stir them into the cold potatoes.

3 Add the walnut pieces, cheese cubes and rocket (arugula) leaves, then toss the salad to mix.

4 In a small bowl, whisk the dressing ingredients together until well combined and pour the dressing over the salad. Serve immediately.

Multicoloured Salad

The beetroot (beet) adds a rich colour to this dish, tinting the potato an appealing pink. Mixed with cucumber it is a really vibrant salad.

NUTRITIONAL INFORMATION

Calories 174   Sugars 8g
Protein ....4g   Fat 6g
Carbohydrate ...27g   Saturates 1g

 15–20 MINS   20 MINS

SERVES 4

INGREDIENTS

500 g/1 lb 2 oz waxy potatoes, diced

4 small cooked beetroot
    (beets), sliced

½ small cucumber, thinly sliced

2 large dill pickles, sliced

1 red onion, halved and sliced

dill sprigs, to garnish

DRESSING

1 garlic clove, crushed

2 tbsp olive oil

2 tbsp red wine vinegar

2 tbsp chopped fresh dill

salt and pepper

1 Cook the diced potatoes in a saucepan of boiling water for about 15 minutes, or until just tender. Drain and set aside to cool.

2 When cool, mix the potato and beetroot (beets) together in a bowl and set aside.

3 To make the dressing, whisk together the garlic, olive oil, vinegar and dill and season to taste with salt and pepper.

4 When ready to serve, line a large serving platter with the slices of cucumber, dill pickles and red onion. Spoon the potato and beetroot (beet) mixture into the centre of the platter.

5 Pour the dressing over the salad and serve immediately, garnished with fresh dill sprigs.

VARIATION

Line the salad platter with 2 heads of chicory (endive), separated into leaves, and arrange the cucumber, dill pickle and red onion slices on top of the leaves.

Carrot & Nut Coleslaw

This simple salad has a dressing made from poppy seeds pan-fried in sesame oil to bring out their flavour and aroma.

NUTRITIONAL INFORMATION

Calories ....220 Sugars 7g
Protein ....4g Fat 19g
Carbohydrate ...10g Saturates 3g

 15 MINS   5–10 MINS

SERVES 4

I N G R E D I E N T S

1 large carrot, grated

1 small onion, finely chopped

2 celery sticks, chopped

¼ small hard white cabbage, shredded

1 tbsp chopped parsley

4 tbsp sesame oil

½ tsp poppy seeds

60 g/2 oz/½ cup cashew nuts

2 tbsp white wine vinegar or cider vinegar

salt and pepper

parsley sprigs, to garnish

1 In a large salad bowl, mix together the carrot, onion, celery and cabbage. Stir in the chopped parsley and season to taste with salt and pepper.

2 Heat the sesame oil in a saucepan with a lid. Add the poppy seeds and cover the pan. Cook over a medium-high heat until the seeds start to make a popping sound. Remove from the heat and set aside to cool.

3 Spread out the cashew nuts on a baking tray (cookie sheet). Place them under a medium-hot grill (broiler) and toast until lightly browned, being careful not to burn them. Leave to cool.

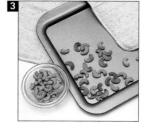

4 Add the vinegar to the oil and poppy seeds, then pour the dressing over the carrot mixture. Add the cooled cashew nuts. Toss together to coat well.

5 Garnish the salad with sprigs of fresh parsley and serve immediately.

Hot Salad

This quickly-made dish is ideal for a cold winter's night. Serve with crusty bread, freshly made rolls or garlic bread.

NUTRITIONAL INFORMATION

Calories	154	Sugars 13g
Protein	.........4g	Fat 9g
Carbohydrate	...14g	Saturates 6g

 10 MINS   10 MINS

SERVES 4

I N G R E D I E N T S

½ medium-sized cauliflower

1 green (bell) pepper

1 red (bell) pepper

½ cucumber

4 carrots

2 tbsp butter

salt and pepper

crusty bread, rolls or garlic bread,

to serve

DRESSING

3 tbsp olive oil

1 tbsp white wine vinegar

1 tbsp light soy sauce

1 tsp caster (superfine) sugar

salt and pepper

1 Cut the cauliflower into small florets, using a sharp knife. Seed the (bell) peppers and cut the flesh into thin slices. Cut the cucumber into thin slices. Thinly slice the carrots lengthways.

2 Melt the butter in a large heavy-based saucepan. Add the cauliflower florets, (bell) peppers, cucumber and carrots and fry over a medium heat, stirring constantly, for 5-7 minutes, until tender, but still firm to the bite. Season with salt and pepper.

Lower the heat, cover with a lid, and simmer for 3 minutes.

3 Meanwhile, make the dressing. Whisk together all the ingredients until thoroughly combined.

4 Transfer the vegetables to a serving dish, pour over the dressing, toss to mix well and serve immediately.

VARIATION
You can replace the vegetables in this recipe with those of your choice, such as broccoli, spring onions (scallions) and courgettes (zucchini).

Index